INSPIRED WISDOM FOR PROGRESSIVE LIVING

An Improved Perception
for an Impressive Living
Devotional Journal 2016

Pastor
Stephen Kyeyune

authorHOUSE®

AuthorHouse™
1663 Liberty Drive
Bloomington, IN 47403
www.authorhouse.com
Phone: 1 (800) 839-8640

Scripture taken from the New King James Version®. Copyright © 1982 by Thomas Nelson. Used by permission. All rights reserved.

Published by AuthorHouse 05/12/2017

ISBN: 978-1-5246-9104-2 (sc)
ISBN: 978-1-5246-9103-5 (e)

Library of Congress Control Number: 2017907230

Print information available on the last page.

Any people depicted in stock imagery provided by Thinkstock are models, and such images are being used for illustrative purposes only. Certain stock imagery © Thinkstock.

This book is printed on acid-free paper.

Contents

From my Desk 1

January for Prosperity 13
    How to Succeed...17
    Tips to effective leadership................................ 34

February – Romance.. 54
    End of February for Spiritual Growth.................. 59

March - Apologetic 90
    End of April - Temptation 141

April – Resurrection...158

May - Memorial 164
    Remembering those who passed on to eternity 170

June – Celebration of Family............................173
    Communication 176
    Mother's Day..197
    Father's Day.. 202
    Life after Divorce.. 207

July: Our Liberty in Christ 210

July: Political Liberty.. 233
    Post-election postings 261
    Reviewing the Triumph of Trump......................... 265

August – Evangelism 272

September – Labor Day 292

October – Halloween 294

November for Praying 296
    End of November for Thanksgiving 321

December – Birth of Christ 325
    End of December – Return of our Lord 331
    Wisdom 336
    The Proverbs 350
    Humor 366

From my Desk

Internet has become our primary source where we go in search for current news, entertainment, shopping, and connecting with friends. We are obsessed with publishing blog posts and clicking on multiple websites for valuable information, jumping from site to site, tweet to tweet, breaking news story to hottest take. Internet service is a sizable means of communication with unlimited resources to connect the world and to spur competition.

The social media has given us access to each other and to ideas. Internet avails us opportunities to thrive. In America, we have the most creative, diverse, innovative culture and open society - in a world where the ability to imagine and generate new ideas with speed and to implement them through global collaboration is the most important competitive advantage.

Internet has become the central nervous system connecting the people from different parts of the world. Given the fact, it is believed that more than a third of all people around the world live in countries without internet freedom, as governments move in to swat the same freedom in the name of political tranquility.

To all my friends on Facebook. I am proud to have you as friends. I value each one of you. You have been of great encouragement to me. "The spirited horse, which will try to win the race of its own accord, will run even faster if encouraged."

We are not friends by coincidence but by divine appointment. As the saying goes, "We do not meet people by accident. They are meant to cross our path for a reason." Certainly, the indisputable fact is that we are sons and daughters of the Immortal kind, possessors of an incorruptible life.

As we are entering and navigating 2017, Cheers to all of you my friends, thanks for being part of my world. Indeed, friends are the best medicine. God designed life in such manner that we compliment & support each other, and we shall be that way. We may never meet but our friendship will stay as long as the relationship lives. Friendship is not easily won over by a click or a plea. It is a slow process involving building up the proper understanding of the heart and the mind and hence trust. The grace of God will build a solid bridge between your heart and mine. Yes, there will be mountains to climb, but godly love never fails because it covers a multitude of mistakes. One advantage of any relationship is that, when you fall out with the people you are committed to, love keeps you together until you fall in love again.

Social media has turned up to be a resource for expanding our circle of friends and sharing thoughts and ideas. You have involved me in your circles of friendship to learn. I look forward to learn more about you, your families and friends as we pursue to restoring the American dream of life, liberty, and the pursuit of happiness.

It is amazing how one simple click of a mouth or visit to a home page can change your mood or perspective on things. Cell phones are mobile mini computers carried in our pockets wherever we go, ready to chat. Already there are more mobile phones than computers connected to the internet. Smartphones are generally cheaper than computers. With their primary role as communication devices, they are often more useful. The Smartphone of today will be the standard phone a few years from now.

Social media has become a lynchpin of the distribution of news and information around the world. Teaching now on making social media is simple. This statistic shows a timeline with the worldwide number of monthly active Facebook users from 2008 to 2016. As of the third quarter of 2016, Facebook had 1.79 billion monthly active users. This statistic shows a timeline with the amount of monthly active Twitter users worldwide. As of the third quarter of 2016, the microblogging service averaged at 317 million monthly active users. At the beginning of 2015, Twitter had surpassed 302 MAU per quarter.

Facebook CEO Mark Zuckerberg lives up to his role as "the world's most powerful editor". Facebook has been effective in providing current news. Facebook's popularity means that its algorithms can exert enormous power over public opinion. People feel free to post any story on their home pages without fear of any repercussion. Internet service provider disclaims any responsibility for the material posted. They assert the right of freedom of expression of a party who has chosen to remain anonymous. Except that recently, there has been a tendency of blocking and shutting down people who post anti-liberal news. For example some people were harassed for posting the international news concerning a Muslim who raped the German girl. Also, some were harassed for posting the story concerning a Muslim with the machete who hacked the Christians. It was a red flag, because it appeared as if Facebook has joined the media witch-hunt for Christian's with biblical views, but not Muslims or other thug groups like BLM.

In a major victory for traditional phone companies, the European Commission, the executive arm of the 28-nation bloc, recently recommended tighter privacy and security for services like Facebook-owned message service WhatsApp and Microsoft's video phone portal Skype.

Speaking in Rome, Zuckerberg addressed the question of Facebook's role in the news media and appeared to downplay his editorial responsibilities. "We are a tech company, not a media company," he said. "The world needs news companies, but also technology platforms, like what we do, and we take our role in this very seriously."

Facebook is a place where you go in search of inspiring, entertaining and humorous quotations. We all have an insatiable need to be motivated and entertained. I am in particular moved by the posted sage words or humorous anecdotes.

3

Facebook is a place where lovers show the world their romance. Taking into consideration of the posted photos, it seems that all couples on Facebook are romantic. If you love your spouse show them that you do in reality. Posting the pictures of you and your spouse is not enough. They say a picture is worth a thousand words but sometimes a picture is worth a thousand lies.

The intentions of postings a photo on your wall speak volume. I am in particular aggravated by some of you who have developed a habit of posting the photos of disabled children and corpses. I think the disabled and the deceased people deserve privacy too. To make the matter worse, often, the culprits request everybody to type in "Amen". The word "Amen" means "so it be". "I don't see how this word depicts a gesture of compassion! Where is the empathy? Where is the compassion and humanity? What is wrong with some people? It's so sad to see how selfish and rude the society has become! I am sorry if I stepped on your toe, but it is hard for me to look the other side and act as if I am not bothered. Be a voice for the voiceless by passing on this message to your friend."

"Social media is the ultimate equalizer. It gives a voice and a platform to anyone willing to." As for the believers, FB presents to us a golden opportunity to minister and to be ministered to. Therefore if you are on FB just to talk trivial chitchat, then you are wasting your time. It means you don't know what it is to be a follower of Christ or witness for Christ. "If Christ is not everything to you, please get back into the world and forget following Him. He demands 100% from you, because He gave Himself 100% for you."

I want to emphasize the need to put our faith into actions. If you want to be promoted to a higher level, you won't get it by liking, sharing, or typing 'Amen' on any picture posted on a Facebook account. You can only get it by getting down on your knees every morning, say a prayer then go and hustle. I like Gashumba's posting "If you need a miracle in your life, associate with positive people, associate with those who have a future they are pursuing, don't listen to negative forces, don't engage yourself with idle talks. Don't hate, but emulate. If prayers alone were to change the world, Africa would be like Europe"

Many young folks are obsessed and addicted to social media. Idleness is the enemy of success. John Stonestreet suggests that we can unplug our computers and save time for other things. He uses the example of Jesus. Jesus lived in a time that was, compared to ours, a still-life painting. And yet even then, he felt the need to regularly withdraw from the noise and distractions of his times. I doubt that any of us, starting with me, could last five minutes in the quietness of first-century Palestine. "Modern telecommunications technology is not "morally neutral." It comes with a definition of what it means to be human that's at root inhumane. The question is: how badly do we want to be human? And will we unplug to pursue it?"

I want to emphasize the need of education. If you say yes to education, whether through educating your children or yourself, or by marrying an educated woman, you have said yes to change, not status quo. Unfortunately, the youth generation of today is slowly losing interest in education, partly because of the skyrocket rate of unemployment among the elites. Please focus on career generating education and activities.

Generally speaking, social media has become an effective tool for soothing the hurting souls. On the negative side, it is another way of rehearsing pain and evil because once you share your story, it is likely to be re-shared and posted forever by even people with ill intentions of bashing you.

There are many touching stories posted on FB. Most of them are appealing for sympathy. Social media is the place where you can easily pick up a fight in the twinkling of an eye. The internet has turned into both a circus and battleground. Internet is a place where everything can be manipulated by a click of a mouth button: "Popularity is rigged and can be bought. Censorship is in full effect. Popular opinion is fabricated, and the perception of a viewpoint's popularity is typically orchestrated and manipulated by legions of paid trolls." Never take the posted stories at face value. Before you judge somebody based on the posted information, look for a hidden reason or ulterior motives. Are they lying? Is this a trick?

Some of the offended people post their stories in search for help. Just because you are offended, it does not mean you are right. Some of us are trained counselors but with limited information provided and one-sided story, without getting acquainted with the story of the other party involved in the conflict, it is not easy to provide an appropriate counseling. The reality is that there are many heartbroken people out there. You will never know exactly what another person is going through or what their whole story is. Some are badly hurt and are mean. When people start to belittle you or judge you, keep your head up and walk away. Never get low to their level, just know that they are wounded.

Every person has rough times. Sometimes when you explore the world (within you), you are most likely to hit concrete walls and dead ends. The good news is that there is an exit. Refuse to drown. Catch the trade winds in your sails and sail to the safe harbor. I want to pause and ask, "When you are in trouble late at night, whom do you call?" Most probably you dial 911 to notify the law enforcement officers. Likewise, when you are searching for information, you are most likely to go to Google. My advice to you is that before you Google it, turn it to God in prayers.

There is one truth and one belief recommended by the Scriptures. Other beliefs may block you from understanding or believing the only truth (higher truth from above). Acknowledging the truth protects you from falsehood because it blocks you from believing the contradictory messages. In this world, God must be the author, editor and finisher of your story of the life.

Philosophy is the study of the fundamental nature of knowledge, reality, and existence, especially when considered as an academic discipline. It is the man's endless research of his own existence, depending on purely human wisdom and capabilities. Each research is built on another man's foundation. Unlike philosophy, the revelation is God coming from heaven, reaching out to man down on the earth, showing us the purpose of our existence. The scriptures reveal God's plan for the fallen man. Read the Bible regularly. This book is not a substitute for the Bible. I like what C H Spurgeon said: "Visit my good books but live in the Bible".

I neither write for money nor for fame but to glorify God. "The important thing is not if you receive a five star or a one star review, or even if you receive an accolade for what you wrote. The important thing is that you honored God with your writing, and that you wrote what He wanted you to write, in His time..." ~ Alison Chenoweth

I am a teacher by calling. Writing magnifies my teachings. I enjoy doing it. To me, teaching is a hydrant in the yard and writing is a faucet upstairs in the house. Opening the first takes pressure off the second. "A writer never has a vacation. For a writer life consists of either writing or thinking about writing." — Eugene Ionesco

My concern is not who will buy my book but if you will read my book. You don't cook what people won't eat. Likewise, it is useless to write when nobody is ready to read what you are writing. It is imperative to add some ingredients like humor in order to appeal to the appetite of the readers. "A novelist writes a novel, and people read it. But reading is a solitary act. While it may elicit a varied and personal response, the communal nature of the audience is like having five hundred people read your novel and respond to it at the same time. I find that thrilling."

I am calling out to people who are bookworms, book lovers, and bibliophiles from all walks of life to add me in the circles of their friends. This is one way of promoting the fading culture of reading. Learning never ends. Any fool can know but only the wise acquires knowledge with prior intention of understanding. I like this statement: "Let us tenderly and kindly cherish therefore, the means of knowledge. Let us dare to read, think, speak, and write." — John Adams

We have a tendency to promote language and logic skills as true intelligence but treat reading nothing more than interesting pastimes. Yet, intellectuals, due to increased brain activities, sleep less hours at night while reading. "A person who won't read has no advantage over one who can't read."

Throughout history prominent researchers and aristocrats were men and women who were actively involved in intensive reading. No wonder libraries are the shrines of all past dignitaries as icons of wisdom, and without delusion or imposture, are preserved.

Writing goes hand in hand with reading because if you don't have the time to read, you won't have the time (or the tools) to write. The culture of ignorance is staggering simply because most people ignore the necessity of reading. It is like most people clamor for ignorance than knowledge! "Either write something worth reading or do something worthy writing."

Recent survey carried out in Uganda indicated that 80% of the teachers won't read. If the teacher has difficulties in a certain subject, they will not be able to teach it. If teachers lack something, it will be transferred to pupils.

One of the disadvantages of Internet is that it has contributed to the laziness of thinking by promoting copying. The culture of Copy & Paste is akin to spoon feeding. "Spoon feeding in the long run teaches us nothing but the shape of the spoon." Edward de Bono blames it on modern technology. There's a danger in the internet and social media. The notion that information is enough, that more and more information is enough, that you don't have to think, you just have to get more information - gets very dangerous.

Somebody said that a room without books is like a body without a soul. Pick a book whenever you can. Make it a habit to read. If necessary stay late at night or wake up early to read. Don't be afraid to be called a book worm or to be scorned that you married to the books.

Everyone has a story to tell. Every great writer began as a lesser writer. Create a world of your own and your readers will be proud to live in it. There is no such a thing as perfect writing. Never despise the little you can offer because small beginning can erupt in great ending. Writing improves by exercising. "Exercise the writing muscle every day, even if it is only a letter, notes, a title list, a character sketch, a journal entry. Writers are like dancers, like athletes. Without that exercise, the muscles seize up." — Jane Yolen

Don't be afraid to write. Your story might be the key that unlocks someone's prison. Don't hesitate to share it. According to Voltaire, "Writing is the painting of the voice." Social media allows us to briefly write our stories. Start by gleaning your childhood and juvenile memoirs. The person in life that you will always be with the most is yourself. When you write your own story you are privileged to be your own biggest critic; before anyone else criticize you, you have already criticized yourself reasonably! Write without fear of being judged. "Remember, people will either love what your write or they won't; the important thing is, you wrote it!"

The benefits of writing your own story outweigh the dangers, in particular, your privacy. If you don't write in your space, somebody will do it. Protect the time and space in which you write, and keep away the malicious writers by marking your territory with your pen. "Until the lions learn how to write, every story will glorify the hunter" ~ African proverb.

Everything you have experienced in this life is a story to tell. Remember that you can lose your past by forgetting it but you can never lose your future because you can lose only the things you already own! "Writers don't forget the past; they turn it into raw material." — Joyce Rachelle

You can benefit from your story. Self-education is, I firmly believe, the only kind of education there is. The path of the righteous grows brighter and brighter. Never be afraid to testify to the world. Write your testimony and post it without fear. Somebody can benefit from your story.

Today, fiction books sell like hot cakes. Fiction stories are good but challenging too. As Eric Metaxas says, "It is possible to write an interesting story out of logic but yet not inspiring. But most importantly, simply telling someone something rarely convinces them of anything. Facts, statistics, moral assertions: They speak to the head, not to the heart." There's a rule that good writers and debaters try to observe, and you may have heard it before: Show, don't tell. In other words, don't lecture your readers to make a point. Show them what you're talking about. Tell a story. Provide illustrations. Aim at the heart.

Facebook is a place where you find heartfelt stories. I like that 'once upon a time' quality, where the telling of a tale has an elevated sense of story. "You & I who still enjoy fairy tales have less reason to wish actual childhood back. We have kept its pleasures & added grown-up ones as well" ~ C.S. Lewis

The most interesting stories are the ones that are written from the point of weakness as opposed to strength. As a precaution, please be discerning when sharing matters concerning your private lives. Try to keep sensitive matters to yourself. At times sharing your problem simply magnifies it. Some people say that Facebook causes too much drama. The truth is you cause your own drama by posting the sensitive issues on Facebook.

Facebook is a place where you find both the true and false stories. Fake or hoax stories are rampant due to Facebook's inability (or refusal) to address the problem. Fake news is not a problem unique to Facebook, but Facebook's enormous audience, and the mechanisms of distribution on which the site relies — i.e., the emotionally charged activity of sharing, and the show-me-more-like-this feedback loop of the news feed algorithm — makes it the only site to support a genuinely lucrative market in which shady publishers arbitrage traffic by enticing people off of Facebook and onto ad-festooned websites, using stories that are alternately made up, incorrect, exaggerated beyond all relationship to truth, or all three.

Social media has put a new face and changed the direction of campaigning in the races of political offices. Facebook was Trump's main means of communication. Mr. Trump said that he is proud of how he has used social media to create his own version of events and communicate it to his followers. He suggested in the "60 Minutes" interview that he is reluctant to surrender that platform when he takes the oath of office in January. "I'm not saying I love it, but it does get the word out," Mr. Trump said of Twitter during the interview, adding that his millions of followers on various social media sites had given him "such power" that it helped him win the election.

Liberal media is turning on Facebook, publishing a flurry of posts that claim, despite Facebook's best efforts to filter out "false news", some "false news" still managed to get through onto people's feed and this lost the election for Hillary. "The "Facebook is to blame" narrative is part of a new analysis by Pew Research Centre which says more than 44% of Americans consulted Facebook to get information throughout the campaign cycle, which was replete with highly offensive, controversial and fake news about the Democratic candidate."

Facebook is a place where you can get your ideas approved in the shortest time possible. You can deservingly or undeservingly get a thousand "Likes" at the mere click of the mouth, even from the people who don't agree with you. It is true that people on Facebook often approve what they have not read and criticize what they haven't thought of first. It is embarrassing to prematurely comment on a posting before analyzing it.

The comments of friends are staggering, and at times challenging. Sometimes the exchange of comments escalates into non-verbal fighting of words. I want to say that we (believers) are supposed to fight on our knees as opposed on the Internet. The best way to earn a "Like" and a positive comment without criticism is sharing the scriptures. I write on my wall without fear of criticism. "I would rather be attacked than unnoticed. For the worst thing you can do to an author is to be silent as to his works" - Samuel Johnson

I want to take this opportunity to thank my friends for your edifying messages. The wording of your posted messages is staggering. As one writer said that "Poetry is when an emotion has found its thought and the thought has found words" We are here to glorify God in everything we do. If we are upright in our speech and seek to bless others with our words, then we reveal that we are in Christ, and we are laying up treasure in heaven. Much more, what we say does not merit our righteous standing before God if our words are not backed up by our sincere trusting in God. Let our words be the manifestation of the trusting heart.

My favorite moment is answering your questions. The social media provides a platform for us to ask and find biblical answers to the questions we have about God, Jesus, ourselves, and the big questions of life. I like to give an answer to every question in-boxed to me. If I don't, it is because I can't. My daily prayer is for God to increase His enlightenment so that I can see as He sees with my spiritual eyes.

I am not bothered by tough questions because they encourage me to do more studying and researches. "In learning you will teach, and in teaching you will learn." As a teacher myself, it saddens me to think that Christians don't know that it's perfectly okay to ask hard questions. In fact, it's critical! What's more, the Church should be the best place to ask those questions. I am not a genius with ready answers to all kinds of questions except those answers given in the Scriptures. I have responsibility to search the Scriptures and rightly divide the Word in order to say what God intended to say in the Scriptures.

Praying is the world's greatest wireless connection. I like to pray and to intercede for others. I am humbled by multiple prayers requests posted on your walls. The world is full of people hurting in a variety of ways but all of us speak the same language of prayer. People, who pray together, stay together. As the early Church was, so we will continue to be in one accord. It means mouth to mouth confession, and heart to heart believing. Same confession and same believing are possible when God is our source: From His heart to our hearts.

I want to end by addressing the issue of hackers. They don't have to guess your password. They use software to extract it from your devices or account. These are real people but the example of which we don't want be.

January for Prosperity

2017 is knocking at the door. The New Year comes with new opportunities. Watch out for them, be sober, be vigilant; swiftly take advantage of them, they can bring renewal into your entire life. "We all get one shot at life to make something of our existence. What we do with that one shot every single day that we wake up alive matters." Step out of your comfort zone. Comfort zones never change the world. World changers are passionate for real change and are ready to change when change comes.

****

Somebody asked that "Isn't the change of years a mere change of the numbers on our calendars without any significant change?" I believe that life is a transition process in proportional to the shifting of time. God's favor towards mankind has been shifting depending on the different dispensations. In practical reality, every moment lived will never be lived again, and cannot be unlived. What makes the year new is your attitude. You can progressively change your status by changing your attitude, regardless of the time change. Your attitude is your response and reactions towards the circumstances surrounding you. Your attitude is influenced by your character. Your character is defined by whom you worship. As we are rolling a red carpet for the New Year, choose to act instead of reacting. Don't wait for what 2017 has to offer, you have to take what you desire from 2017 right now. The opportunities of the New Year are not mysterious. You learn from the past in order to be current with the future. Instead of making concurrent resolutions for a prosperous future, swing into action now. Make a decision never to waste none of your present time. The key to success is the same for 2016 and 2017 - It unlocks all seasons, and it is already in your hand. Nobody will open the door for you except yourself!

****

The past year is almost history but the past experience is real. I don't wish that the old year could have dragged on a little longer, partly because of the past experiences. Also, I don't want to cry for the already spilled milk. You can use the past experience, even the negatives of life, to move on into a bright future. If you are a believer, you are a credible witness of Christ. We are the dwelling place of God (temple) because the Spirit of God took residence in us. In the Old Testament, God built the sanctuary from inside to outside. The Tabernacle was an ugly structure from outside. It consisted of a tent-like structure (the tabernacle proper) covered by rug-like coverings for a roof. But its beauty was inside. The innermost holy place (holy of hollies) made it a sanctuary. The moral lesson is that the beauty within us should never be overwhelmed by the ugliness from outside. Don't allow the ugly experiences of 2016 to dictate your future. Focus on the beauty treasured within you. Use your past as your school master. You might as well forget the past experiences but not the lessons from them. Here is a tip: "Pain makes you stronger, tears make you braver, and heartbreaks make you wiser, so thank your past for a better future."

****

Whether it be in relationship or witnessing, we are going to overcome as a unit of one. Your adversary fears the power of unity. "Coming together is a beginning; keeping together is progress; working together is the success." It is imperative that each of us take on the responsibility in shifting our own behaviors, so that we may trigger the required results. At times solitude is good but God's perfect plan for you is to engage other people, not all people but those positioned to incline to your calling. Don't be afraid; sometimes vulnerability is our greatest weapon.

****

Luke 12:16-20 - "The ground of a certain rich man yielded an abundant harvest. He thought to himself, 'What shall I do? I have no place to store my crops.' "Then he said, 'This is what I'll do. I will tear down my barns and build bigger ones, and there I will store my surplus grain. And I'll say to myself, "You have plenty of grain laid up for many years. Take life easy; eat, drink and be merry."' "But God said to him, 'You fool! This very night your life will be demanded from you. Then who will get what you have prepared for yourself? Logically, this rich man did the right things - He planned, multiplied and saved. But he is called a fool because he ignored the absolute authority of God. The word fool in this context means immoral. This New Year, decide to put God at the center of your plans so that He may fight for you. Jehovah-Nissi means the Lord is my Banner. Nissi means Banner, and it is usually hoisted on a great victory (Exodus 17:15). Whenever there is death and grieving affecting the entire nation, the banners (flags) of our earthly rulers are lowered half-mast because victory has been swallowed in death. But the banner of our Lord Jehovah is always hoisted high; it is never lowered. The reason is because in Him there is no shadow of death. Death is everywhere around us but death is not to be feared by the wise whose rock is Christ. Life without Christ is a state of languor without hope. Have a prosperous year full of hope.

****

We are slamming a door behind 2016, and welcoming the New Year. It is imperative that you move through this transition with precise discernment. Make yourself available to the God of tomorrow. "Be ready to go with the flow of My Spirit and I will take you to the spiritual heights that you could have only dreamed of until now."

****

Enter the New Year with open minds. The open world begins with an open mind. You can learn what you don't know, and you can unlearn what you learned. Knowledge can be perception or deception, depending on the tree from which you eat: the tree of Life or the tree of knowledge of good and evil. A person who makes a great impact in this world is the one whose minds are in the afterworld. You can't study God but you can definitely know His plan for humanity by immersing yourself in the Scriptures. The advantage of reading your Bible is that you can use other scriptures to interpret your scripture.

****

2017 is a year reckoned for resetting. "There are areas of your life that lack control, and you need to get back to a place of optimum safety and security----spiritually and physically. Find yourself on solid ground by setting your will under the will of God. Pray that God may use your life-experience to impact the lives of others (those around you). The Bible say that "Even a child is known by his deeds, whether what he does is pure and right" (Proverbs 20:11).

****

2016 is history but not our problems. Yes, we had some achievements but 'achievement' is not the ultimate success. You were put on this universe to live out your purpose, and to do it courageously. Begin by changing your perception. When you change your perceptions, you have the effect of changing everything. Your perception is ever changing, and you will keep on backing up in blind spots until you find Christ. Remember that our perfection is beyond our humanity; it is in Christ. "Without Jesus, we are all in the gutter and doomed. Our own perception could either be our path to obliteration or an invisible cage that bottles us up." Mankind is closed up, till he sees all things through the light of Christ. Any point outside Christ is a blind spot. Acknowledging this fact enables us to take the first step toward change.

****

Message for the New Year: "God has already arranged for the comeback of every setback, a vindication for every wrong, a new beginning for every disappointment. We can make our plans, but the Lord determines our steps. We may throw the dice, but the Lord determines how they fall." - Sam Kyeyune

****

"A new year is like a blank book. The pen is in your hands. It is your chance to write a beautiful story for yourself. Happy New Year!" ~ Joy Elizabeth Ventura

****

Psalm 90:12 - "So teach us to number our days, that we may apply our hearts unto wisdom." It is a calling to pause in our pursuit of happiness. Most of us are crazy-busy figuring out how to survive at the expense of the integrity of our lives. We are trapped in this life, and craving transcendence is reduced to an illusion. The predicament is searching for fulfillment in wrong places. "Money is numbers, and numbers never end. If it takes money to be happy, your search for happiness will never end". We live in denial that time is slipping out of our hands and none of us is in control of it. Faith is embracing the unlimitedness of time. Fulfilled joy is being like-minded as Christ.

****

Ecclesiastes 3:10-11 – "I have seen the God-given task with which the sons of men are to be occupied. 11 He has made everything beautiful in its time. Also He has put eternity in their hearts, except that no one can find out the work that God does from beginning to end."

How to Succeed

When we do business with people, we need money. When we do business with God, we need faith. Faith is the currency in the Kingdom of God ~ Reinhard Bonnke

****

"Money is numbers, and numbers never end. If it takes money to be happy, your search for happiness will never end" ~ Robert Marley

****

If God unveiled to you the magnitude of the blessings coming your way, you would appreciate the magnitude of the trials and battles you are fighting currently.

****

There are a variety of ways in which our brains are fundamentally wired, and they shape how we think and function, right down to our careers and strategies. All of us are gifted to do something. God did not create a useless person. It is not a matter of whether you are gifted but how you are gifted. Don't just do something just because it's a trendy idea and will make you a lot of money. Do something that you are gifted to do. I mean something that you are passionate about and really believe in, and it will carry you through. God gifted you to be everything you have ever dreamed to be. Your gift is not beyond you, it is deep at the center of your being, requiring to be exploited. "Take charge of your life! The tides do not command the ship. The sailor does." Remember that idleness is a risky venture, because it justifies incompetence. You can do better than staying home hunting the squirrels and killing the snakes in the village!

****

Lend your ear to the optimists as opposed to the pessimists. Be careful of what enters into your ears. Our brains make long-term decisions depending on the majorly of what we hear from the people around us. If you listen to negativities, you are most likely to act & behave negatively. Avoid idle people who can't manage their own lives but who always seem to have answers for other people's problems. Such are vision slayers! Surround yourself with the dreamers and the doers, the believers and the thinkers; but most probably surround yourself with those who see greatness within you even when you cannot see it yourself. Keep the all-time complainers out of your circles. "You were created to be a developer, not a destroyer, an achiever not a loser, a runner not a crawler." Tell those who say it's impossible that it might be impossible to them but not to you because you can do all things through Christ that strengthen you (Philippians 4:13).

****

Focusing on ideas is a recipe of the thoughtful dialogue and open-minded conversation. It is your right to have a strong opinion of certain principles, to speak your mind, and to be what some call 'opinionated. However, ideas may be valid but they are not equally true. Also, all good ideas are not godly. Good ideas should not just be good but they must stand the test of time. Given the fact, we are relational beings. We must accommodate those who don't agree with us, without compromising our values. We are called to love all people including those who won't love us back. But be selective and discerning to ensure that your closest companions are of material help. "If you want to become a great sportsman, what business do you have hanging around brick-layers? If you hang around nine lazy people, you will most likely become the tenth!"

****

Your whole life in the past year has been an assignment given to you. That includes things that excited you and things that oppressed you. It is the testimony of the real people that experienced real tragedies that people are waiting to hear. Quit grumbling and whining and cast your nets into the deep for a greater catch in the coming year.

****

"A dream written down with a date becomes a goal. A goal broken down into steps becomes a plan. A plan backed by action makes your dream come true".

****

Thoughts begin to radically change when we grasp the realization we are God's beloved ones and His desire is our welfare.

****

Without dreams we reach nothing. Without love we feel nothing. And without God we are nothing.

****

When giving up is no longer an option. You have no other choice but to Overcome.

****

There are three words that are irreversible: Time, opportunities and words spoken.

****

Opportunities come in different shapes, at times they are less than what you anticipate. Never let such opportunities pass you. With the help of God, you can turn an anthill into a mountain.

****

Success is not a destiny but a journey involving checks, balancing, and stoppages, but keep on moving forward in the right direction, you will cross over to the other end. Remember that difficult roads often lead to beautiful destinations.

****

"Destiny is not a matter of chance; it is a matter of choice. It is not a thing to be waited for; it is a thing to be achieved" ~ William Jennings Bryan

****

Never give up because all your struggles, hardships, delays, and failures are working towards your future greatness. To fail does not mean that you are a failure. "Failure is not failing until you quit". Trophies are awarded to finishers.
****

"Always remember that striving and struggle precede success, even in the dictionary" ~ Sarah Ban Breathnach

****

"If you have a hundred reasons to give up, I have one reason to hold on my life. Jesus is the reason!"

****

When things don't go according to your plan it doesn't mean that things are not going according to God's plan. God often uses our deepest pain as the launching pad to our greatest calling.

****

God did not make a useless person. If you bad in one thing, it doesn't mean you are not good in other things. Use your weakness as an asset by focusing on your strength. Keep on practicing. As awesome as it would be, no one has ever become great at something without practice. Whether it be in sports, video games, or just in general.

****

Matthew 6:11 - "Give us today our daily bread." God grants to us the grace of one day at time. When we focus on the God of tomorrow, we are not worried about tomorrow. We don't live in the past and the future but in the present.

****

Psalm 23:4 – "Even though I walk through the darkest valley, I will fear no evil, for you are with me". We don't walk in the valleys to stay but to cross over to the other end. Tomorrow it will be day and the sun shall shine over you.

****

Exodus 14:21-22 – "Then Moses stretched out his hand over the sea; and the LORD swept the sea back by a strong east wind all night and turned the sea into dry land, so the waters were divided. The sons of Israel went through the midst of the sea on the dry land, and the waters were like a wall to them on their right hand and on their left." God did not take away the Red Sea but He parted the sea so that the Israelites could cross over. God might not take away your problems but He will make a way for you to go through them victoriously.

****

Survival is not mandatory but it is necessary. It is called fighting for survival because there is always something to fight for and to fight against. Logically, there cannot be a fight without the existence of the adversity. An easy life is not necessarily the best life. To survive is to find some meaning in the suffering. A man is what he makes himself to be. In spite of the adversity and the bitter moments, when we endure and persevere, again we rise!

****

It is estimated that there are 360 joints in the human body. It is not a coincidence that 20 joints are found in the ear, this being the most active organ. Joints are designed for flexibility, stretching, and movements. This is typically the nature of our life experiences. Life is a process of becoming, a progress, and not a station. The good life is not a state of being. It is a direction, not a destination. Keep on moving in spite of the negatives of life. Mistakes are an essential portion of life if we can learn from them. Experience is a good teacher. The spectacles of experience involve our past (positives and negatives of life). It is through them that we can see clearly not to error another time.

****

Making a decision and following through it are two different things, yet equally important. Consult God in prayers before making an important life-changing decision. Then consult Him in order to follow through it.

Inspired wisdom and skills are essential in the process of decision making. Take every opportunity extended to you to talk to God in order to ensure that you are in the perfect will of God, and in order to overcome the evil times. The Bible says that "Be very careful, then, how you live—not as unwise but as wise, making the most of every opportunity, because the days are evil. Therefore do not be foolish, but understand what the Lord's will is (Ephesians 5:15-18).

****

"Rain drops are in the storm for your benefit; they are not the causes of the storm but the reason for the storm". My prayer is: "Dear God thank you for my storms. The rain was needed for my faith to grow"

****

"Knowledge is like an endless resource; a well of water that satisfies the innate thirst of the growing human soul. Therefore never stop learning... because the day you do, you will also stop maturing."

****

Never live in accordance to the norms of the society. According to Tim Kreutter, many people never question their way of living. They don't ask the bigger questions as to why they are living or what they are seeking – nor, why they never seem to find much fulfillment in what they are doing. By avoiding all self-reflection, we operate like robots following the programming of our birth culture and immediate environment. Only true self-examination leads toward growth and creating a meaningful life.

****

"You deserve to be successful and wealthy. You have something special, you have greatness within you. That's my story and I'm sticking to it." - Les Brown

****

Success is how high you bounce when you hit the Bottom.

****

The greatest pleasure in life is doing what people say you cannot do!

****

Success comes dressed in unpredicted ways, disguising as failure. Sometimes when you think you are losing, you are winning!

****

Your worth does not depend on someone's inability to see your worth.

****

Work as if everything depends on you, and pray as if everything depends on God.

****

You have to do what is right in the possible, so that God can do what's needed in the impossible - Pastor Don Allen

****

Dream big time. A dream is a vision waiting for manifestation. Some people can't stand the fact that you dream bigger than they do. So their job is to try and discourage you by tearing you down."Reality will cripple you but your dreams will push you towards your destiny" P. Keyz

****

Colossians 3:23 - "And whatsoever ye do, do it heartily, as to the Lord, and not unto men". Find your worth in Christ, not people or things of this world. When your objective is to please God as opposed to men, you will never be offended by the reactions of the people.

****

You don't fail overnight. Instead, failure is a few errors in judgment, repeated every day. The real challenge is not to rectify your mistakes but the attitude of the people surrounding you. People are going to put you to a close scrutiny to justify their inadequacies. The fact is that there is no man so good that if he places all his actions and thoughts under the scrutiny of the laws, he would not deserve hanging ten times in his life. "Love has no errors, for all errors are the want for love" ~ William Law

****

Most Good people never know their value in the eyes of others. A people who value their privileges more than their principles... should lose both..... For to give real service, one must give something that can't be valued or measured by money, that is sincerity and integrity.

****

It is possible to be comfortable and yet miserable, and it is possible to be uncomfortable and yet joyful. The worst place to be is in your little comfort zone. The best place to be is in the secret place of the Lord. Step out of your comfort zone by stepping deep into the calling of God. Yes, there might be some pain involved but certainly you will reach into the Promised Land.

****

Greed is discontentment. It is craving for material things that cannot be satisfied. It is the wondering of the heart in the abbsy without a possibility of settling at the intended destiny.

****

Life is like a race between a cat & a rat. Mostly a rat wins because a cat runs for food but a rat runs for life. Remember "PURPOSE is more important than NEED" ~ Ssenyonjo Enock

****

It's not important to hold all the good cards in life, but it's important how well you play with the cards you hold.

****

The trials of life are not there to stop you but to facilitate your advance. Allow the sandpaper of trial in your life to smooth out your rough edges. The end result will be polished and beautiful!

****

The moment you stop accepting challenges, is the time you stop advancing or moving forward.

****

Never use the opinions and failures of others to build your life. Somebody's stumbling block might be your opportunity to excel.

****

Those who are idle normally complain about how time flies, not knowing that their opportunities are also flying away with it.

****

Be sensitive and live sensibly. Each day is an opportunity exposed for grab. An opportunity missed may never come back again. Ambition is the first step. Action is the second step. Some people do find that one thing and dedicate their whole lives to it because they love it. In case you haven't got that one thing to stick to, I suggest that while you are waiting, you explore and experience different things in life. To me life is about exploring everything out there. It's trying different things and putting more attention on certain ones.

****

"Problems can be stumbling blocks or stepping block". Positivity is realizing that you can't control every circumstance, but you can control your attitude towards them. Problems can stop you temporarily, but you have the choice to allow them to stop you permanently.

****

Every person wants to get better but not to eat better. Watching what I put in my mouth completely changed my life for the better. Your health is your wealth. Don't ever take such blessings for granted.

****

Worrying is the giant killer of momentum. Do not worry of tomorrow because God is already there. Jesus gave us simple solution to the problem of worry. "Do not worry... Each day has enough trouble of its own" – (Matthew 6:34).

****

"Having a backup plan in your hip pocket can work to your disadvantage. It can deter your drive to succeed. If you always know in the back of your mind that you really don't have to work very hard to accomplish a business goal, you are less likely to attack your venture with fervor." - (Success Magazine)

****

People are going to put you to close scrutiny but there is no man so good that if he places all his actions and thoughts under the scrutiny of the laws, he would not deserve hanging ten times in his life. Legislation (or "statutory law") changes the society by regulating the lawlessness. Psychology changes the behaviors by changing the minds. Christ changes the heart in order to change the thinking and the behaviors.

****

An achiever's mentality assumes that things will get from bad to better as opposed from bad to worse every passing year. Such works as an investment magnet attracting various investors.

****

Purposeful living is discovering the work you were created to do for the glory of God. It is more than the normal choices of life and the natural things people do, like finding a good paying job to pay your bills. It is doing something and people see God's hand into what you do. God wants your best because He gave His best to us. He wants the whole of you. Surrendering to Jesus means laying down every area of your life. "Romans 6:13 say, stop offering the parts of your body to sin. Instead, offer yourselves as instruments of righteousness to God.' Live a life of purpose and be driven by purpose by being motivated by the Holy Spirit. Give yourself fully to God. Let Him use you for his glorious purpose. Surrender your burdens to Jesus but carry on your shoulder other people's burdens. This will cause you to leave a legacy on the earth and a fortune in eternity.

****

Philippians 4:19 - "But my God shall supply all your need according to his riches in glory by Christ Jesus." Being under God's grace means being under His provision constantly. It means being conscious not of your need, but of His supply. - Barbara Frone

****

Yes, give thanks for all things for, as it has been well said "our disappointments are but His appointments" - A.W. Pink

****

Aim high. Never settle for less. Where you are isn't your destiny but a filling station to gain momentum to reach your destiny. "A bird is safe in its nest - but that is not what its wings are made for." ~ Amit Ray,

****

"Passive inactivity, because you have not been given specific instructions to do this or to do that, is a serious deficiency" ~ George C. Marshall

****

"Success is not in-born. Success is made. Like a masterpiece, a successful life is to be constructed. Successful people have a set of core values in their hearts which guide them in all their decisions and actions as they travel on their journey to success and victory. They believe that the road to success is always under construction. So, they always learn. They know that, knowledge is power. Every day, all successful people have goals to achieve; plans to guide them; and, actions to make all their dreams come true."

****

"Anyone who desires to achieve success must have grit. The ability to do a great work is in the hands of many, but the grit to do a great work is in the hands of few. Having talent, capacity or ability doesn't mean you will automatically succeed, you must have grit. It is those who are consistent, persistent, faithful, focused, tenacious, and who have the most amount of grit that achieve greatness."

****

"One way of knowing God has changed you is when you go from being an angry person all the time without having any feelings or remorse when doing wrong to others, to having a heart for other people. I mean a heart that rejoices when others rejoice and weeps when others weep. A heart that wants nothing less than to see others well, full of joy and being everything God created them to be."

****

Never be jealous about another person's blessing. You have no idea what they had to go through to get it. Though they have a smile on their face and full of joy, they fought battles in tears and pain to be what they are. God is no respecter of persons. What He does for one He certainly can do for another. Just be faithful and obedient to God and trust and seek Him.

****

If material prosperity was a success, then Jesus would have been a failure. Jesus said that "Foxes have holes, and birds of the air have nests; but the Son of man has nowhere to lay his head" (Luke 9:58). Jesus sent us to win people as opposed to gold. The people around you are therefore the greatest asset at your fingertips.

****

This earthly life is compared to the ship on troubled waters. When the ship is rocked by hurricane - force winds, it is likely to tip side to side but eventually, it will stabilize. Don't let the storms stop you from taking your voyage. It doesn't matter how long it might take you to get there, you will get there because God sent you there. If you are afraid of the storms you will preserve the ship on the harbor forever without the possibility of sailing. "I am not afraid to sail in the storms of life because I know the maker of the storms."

****

There are certain characteristics that separate the successful from the unsuccessful in every walk of life: It takes humility, teachability, integrity and commitment to be successful. "Don't seek just to look successful but seek to actually being successful."

****

"Success, as with most things, starts with attitude. When you're struggling, a small burst of inspiration can make a huge difference." Frustration is our emotional response after repeated failures to achieve the anticipated results to succeed. Ironically, the things we yearn for and fight tooth and nail to achieve are at times the same things others are struggling to get rid of. Instead of despair, frustration should bring awareness that life is more than what it can offer; life sets us a challenge to look beyond this life for fulfillment.

****

Success usually comes to those who are too busy to be looking for it."If you set your goals ridiculously high and it's a failure, you will fail above everyone else's success" ~ James Cameron

****

"Success is walking from failure to failure with no loss of enthusiasm."
Winston Churchill

****

Success has a brother, his name is Struggle. Success has a price tag. Success comes from heaven where there is no tag swapping.

****

"If you're not failing, you're probably not really moving forward. Those who hardly fail, are those who are hardly succeeding. Know that in life you will make mistakes and you will fail, this however doesn't mean you're a failure. Remember this: Failure is simply a price we pay to achieve success. The more you do, the more you fail. The more you fail, the more you learn. The more you learn, the better you get. Therefore, In order to succeed in life you must learn that failure is part of success. Embrace it. Learn from it. Grow from it and keep moving forward."

****

If you want be successful in any area of your life you must be patient and diligent. Success is uphill, the journey is long, and tough. It is likely to take you longer than you anticipated.

****

"Courage doesn't happen when you have all the answers. It happens when you are ready to face the questions you have been avoiding your whole life" ~ Shannon L. Alder

****

Experience is the best teacher. No one is born a great cook, one learns by doing. I mean doing and doing.

****

The difference between rich people and poor people is: Poor people always talks about what they have…..... Rich people always talk about what they would like to have!

****

"When you can't change your predicament... change your perspective" ~ Donna

****

A little bit of wealth earned by a fraudulent scheme will fault all of your resources including the clean hard-earned money. Remember that just a little bit of salt will spoil the entire pot of milk. When you can't have what you want, start wanting what you have instead of manipulating others to get what you don't have. The more principle-centered and faithful you become, the more unselfish you will be, and hence, caring for the good fortune of other people as you care for yourself. It is a warning to pursue virtue before you pursue wealth.

****

Our culture encourages all of us to always put our best foot forward. Let us do it by being considerate of others. "The world is the difficult realization that something other than oneself is real."

****

The road to success isn't straight. There is a curve called Failure, a rope called Confusion, speed bumps called Friends, red-lights called Enemies, caution lights called Family, and you will have flat tires called Jobs. But if you have a spare wheel called Determination, an engine called Perseverance, insurance called Faith, and a driver called Jesus, you will make it to a place called Success. (R. Ziwa)

Dr. Myles Munroe preaches ten words of wisdom:

1. Understand crisis and use it to solve a problem. Every business is a response to a problem.
2. Initiate something; do not wait for things to be done.
3. Identify and refine your talent, skill, idea, service or knowledge to create wealth.
4. Whatever makes you angry, you must solve it.
5. Poverty is not the lack of money, but the lack of ideas.
6. God does not give cash, but ideas on how to create wealth.
7. Be in control of your mind, thoughts, perception and mentality to respond to change.
8. Be keen and take advantage of changes brought about by technology and globalization.
9. Leave your legacy, but in the people you train, not in products or buildings.
10. Every human being was born with a treasure. Your greatest secret to success lies in discovering your treasure. Secure your future, stop blaming every sitting president of your country for your destiny.

Tips to effective leadership

True leadership comes from God. A leader must have confidence that he is where he is positioned by the divine appointment. Be assured that if God has selected you, it doesn't matter who rejects you. God's favor outweighs all oppositions. Do your work with confidence and awareness that God knows the end of your story. Avoid insecurity because it is the recipe for disaster.

Self-confidence grows with confidence. Build a sense of balanced self-confidence, founded on a firm appreciation of reality. "As a leader, first, work on yourself- increase your self-awareness. There shouldn't be any other urgent agenda than this. Get enlightened! Know very well who you're including your strengths, weaknesses, and blind spots!"

Leadership involves climbing up through the ranks. The reality is everybody wants to be promoted. However, we should not ignore the fact that opportunities come with responsibility. "Every right implies a responsibility; every opportunity, an obligation, every possession, a duty" ~ John D. Rockefeller

High destiny callings always require time and effort to develop. Most people give up during the training and testing season. Most probably because all training and testing involve some kind of resistances. Yet, that resistance is necessary to prepare you to step into leadership.

Trust is the most valuable resource of Heaven! "There are no oil drills or water wells in Heaven, only storehouses of trust. Storehouses full of dependency on the promises. And every time you turn a failure, a mistreatment, something unfair, over to Jesus, you are making a deposit into those storehouses."

Technically, every person is a leader because people are watching you curiously to learn something from you. Leadership does not depend on age. Paul instructed Timothy that, "Let no man despise thy youth; but be thou an example of the believers, in word, in conversation, in charity, in spirit, in faith, in purity" (1 Timothy 4:12).

I am going to specifically discuss profession leadership. Education is the only panacea to both human & national development. It stirs the ship of developmental research and problem-solving issues. However, in Africa, we've not yet seen the need to create a new national bourgeoisie to give birth to new creative entrepreneurs, investors & even new elites with the traits to take the mantles of leadership.

People are attracted to professionals that specialize into a particular professional rather than a jack of trade who knows a little bit of everything. For example, if I own a Ford car, I opt for a mechanic that specializes in Ford cars alone instead of the one who claims to repair all kinds of brands.

Professionalism is essentially necessary for effective delivery. A professional approach involves appreciating etiquette, knowing how to do things properly, good inter-personal skills and customer care, competence, reliability and respect for the different parties one deals with. It further combines honesty and integrity.

Most of the time leaders are gifted with talents to do certain things. A talent is a natural ability to do something. However, they should take some time to study other skills that will support their talent. A skill is a learnt ability and may be acquired e.g. communication skills, public etiquette, playing musical instruments i.e. A professional approach involves appreciating etiquette, knowing how to do things properly, good inter-personal skills and customer care, competence, reliability and respect for the different parties one deals with. It further combines honesty and integrity.

Professionalism will not let one's talent, skills or knowledge become outdated; they will always seek out ways of staying current or upgrade. Leaders must, therefore, learn to acquire and equip themselves with relevant resources such as books and attending appropriate training among others.

****

A leader is committed to nothing less than efficiency. However, a professional leader also appreciates that they can at some point err. Therefore, when counsel or correction comes their way, they take it positively or in good faith and may change their course of action where necessary and applicable. This attribute amplifies trust, humility and obedience as earlier observed.

****

A leader must have respect in order to be respected. Respect is earned by virtuous people. Character and integrity are the virtues that determine a good leader. Integrity is what people say about you. Character is what you are in the absence of people (when you are alone). "Integrity is the state of being of sound moral principle and takes into account personal values like honesty, truthfulness, reliability and discipline which encompass one's lifestyle" ~ (Prince N. Nyombi

****

"Life is not linear; you have ups and downs." There is promotion at every stage of life. You are either climbing up or down. It's how you deal with the troughs that define you. "The best way to predict the future is to create it".

****

A leader must have a vision and follows up to pursue it. A vision outlines your goals. Specifics would be easier than having your emotions all over the road. The world has the habit of making room for the man whose words and actions show that he knows where he is going.

****

To be a leader you must have followers. People will not follow you blindly unless you have an appealing vision. Short-term thinking without Long-term strategy almost always leads to the same thing: "Long-term Failure".

****

A leader doesn't just create followers. He creates more leaders to do what he is doing.

****

"A leader is the one who knows the way, goes the way and shows the way"
~ John C Maxwell

****

A leader is meant to be a prism refracting the policies and values of the company to the workers. The rules of the company apply to you before they are embraced by the people you lead.

****

Leadership involves a chain of command and also a chain of responsibility. It is the responsibility to serve others. Jesus, the greatest servant ever lived said that "Whoever wants to become great among you must be your servant" (Matthew 20:26).

****

You are a leader, not a boss. A leader is not called to control the people whom he is over. He is called to enforce the rules with love. He helps people to control themselves because the only person you can control is yourself.

****

True leaders grow with their people. They strive to make individuals in the organization or society grow to their full ability. They teach and guide just like the mother eagle does. They never stop giving challenges but never-give-up empowering and directing.

****

Eagles are the only birds that love the storm. When all other birds try to flee from the storm and hide its fierceness, eagles fly into it and will use the wind of the storm to rise higher in a matter of seconds. Leaders love to take challenges as the eagle does when the storm comes.

****

There are two types of employees: In the first group are the seasonal workers who are there temporarily. Then there is the second group involving the committed employees who have made up their minds to settle and to stay with you in spite of the ups and downs. The second group has exceptional qualities which you should treasure. All employees begin in the first group with the potentiality to roll into the second group.

****

The priority of a good leader is to train the employees so that they acquire the required experience, and then making sure that he doesn't lose the experienced ones. "When employees leave a job, of their own volition or not, employers lose the institutional knowledge or history that they take with them, and many organizations lack sufficient transfer programs to stem the loss."

****

Any serious organization must have and should implement an employee exit policy where the human resource department engages the outgoing employee in the exit interview and the staff formally hands over all institutional property. This is where an employee is either retiring or has resigned. Where the staff is leaving due to disciplinary issues, still the institution should be able to complete the exit details with respect to their privacy. People should only be put in newspapers only where the formal procedures and measures have failed.

****

They say that clients come first. But in reality employees come first because when you take care of your employees, they will take care of the clients.

****

Giving people what they need does not necessary mean that they want it. A good leader has the charisma to sell good ideas to the people he leads.

****

"Work for a cause, not applause. Live life to express, not to impress. Don't strive to make your presence noticed, but your absence felt."

****

We are fighters by nature. Competition is the byproduct of fighting. We are obsessed with winning, yet nobody goes undefeated all the time. Then comes frustration after a crushing defeat. Repeated frustrations may result in strife which is a vice behavior. Strife makes you stiff, stubborn and is contagious because it creates strife with others. It can affect your relationship with your family, church, friends, neighbors, employees and even with the vanquished or the dead. I advise you to strive to have an environment that is free of strife. In Christ there is no loser because we are all winners.

****

Self-control concedes to the control of God. Self-control restrains over-reacting and under-reacting by regulating your emotions. When you are out of control you give yourself permission to misbehave and to do what you think regardless of its validity. You deny your conscience an opportunity to accuse or excuse you. The people who are out of control are irritating. They do not weigh the consequences of their actions, and they are carried by the stigma of gambling and manipulation. On the contrary, self-control allows a pause to properly study the situation and to respond appropriately. Such characters always have a dialogue with the people they interact with. Self-control and self-discipline are the qualities of the incredible leadership.

****

Never be afraid of resistance if you know that you are doing the right thing. If people can't see your worth it's because they have never been exposed to quality before. There is going to be opposition because not everyone is ready or worthy of the gifts you bring.

****

At times "Good management is the art of making problems so interesting and their solutions so constructive that everyone wants to get to work and deal with them" ~ Paul Hawken

****

You need to find something to hold onto, something to motivate you, and something to inspire you. You have to be inspired in order to inspire others. "There is no knowledge, no light, no wisdom that you are in possession of, but what you have received it from some source." Freely you received, freely pass it on to others. It is only as we develop others that we permanently succeed in our careers.

****

"Precision is your friend. The more precise you can be in your intentions and requests, the better. You can avoid misunderstandings by being clear and direct in your communications" ~ Sunny Smith-Lowery

****

"If you don't love what you do, you won't do it with much conviction or passion." Passion is the energy that keeps us going, that keeps us filled with meaning, and happiness, and excitement, and anticipation. Passion is a powerful force in accomplishing anything you set your mind to, and in experiencing work and life the fullest extent possible. Ultimately, passion is the driving force behind success and happiness that allows us all to live better lives.

****

Appreciation is a catalyst that motives others into better performance. Try to appreciate even the little things done. There is a saying that, "Even the smallest stone, still causes a ripple effect in the water."

****

Criticism will certainly come, the difference is how you handle it. Constructive criticism is good. Not all criticism is intended to minimize you. Handle criticism in a mature way, with awareness that at times the people who criticize others do not know that they don't know!

****

You want something to be done exactly your way? Then get involved in doing it...

****

"The best job goes to the person who can get it done without passing the buck or coming back with excuses" ~ M. Trevelyan

****

You have to do what you have to do before you can do what you want to do. It is called prioritization.

****

"Remember, a chip on the shoulder is a sure sign of wood higher up."

****

"You have a fingerprint that nobody else has, to leave an imprint that no one else can leave".

****

If you are a leader, you teach people by how you treat yourself and by what you reinforce.

****

Leadership is about responsibility, reliability, availability and obedience.

****

Royalty is my identity. Servant hood is my assignment. Intimacy with God is my life source.

****

"It is not a will to win, but a will to prepare to win that makes a difference.

****

When you get little, you want more, when you get more, you desire even more, but when you lose it, you realize little was enough! It is called contentment.

****

It is good to do what you enjoy to do, but at times good things happen when we do what is not exciting. "Your purpose is more important than your pleasure."

****

Leadership is taking a risk to do what others are not willing to do. It is the will to make a difference.

****

A leader readily accepts his or her mistakes. A self-absorbed person only can see the faults of others but they are often color blind to their own.

****

Leadership takes counsel from the wise and consults reliable sources before implementing.

****

"Minds are like parachutes; they work best when open" ~ Lord Thomas Dewar

****

"A truthful evaluation of yourself gives feedback for growth and success" ~ Brenda Johnson Padgitt

****

There is that tendency in us to do the seemingly important things and neglect the important things. Good leaders have their priorities right. True leadership is knowing what to do and when to do it. Then doing it right at the right time.

****

"Time management is an oxymoron. Time is beyond our control, and the clock keeps ticking regardless of how we lead our lives. Priority management is the answer to maximizing the time we have" ~ John C. Maxwell

****

Without God, mankind is out of control. We are left at the mercy of fate. Fate is a one-way street to destruction. We know that animal populations need to be managed, but we counterproductively haven't yet figured out how to manage our own.

****

Our churches should be environments of grace, so we can stay connected to the vine and bring forth real and genuine fruit so that the world will see Jesus in us and not self-righteousness.

****

Leaders are transparent. Trust is earned when people can see through you, and see no dark sports. A leader is careful not to leave unanswered questions regarding his or her characters.

****

Identify your weaknesses and correct them or else people will manipulate the situation and use it against you.

****

Leaders deliver rather than talking. Talking tough with a litany of deadlines and speculative projections does not necessarily translate to progress.

****

When you are a leader, you are in a higher position. You are an exposed target for those below you to shoot down. There will be people spinning outrageous fabrications to ruin your reputation. "Do not be overcome by evil, but overcome evil with good" (Romans 12:21).

****

Whether your God-given assignment in life seems large or small, you can grow into it. A vocal teacher once told Mary Martin, the famous American singer, that she had an inferior voice and would never make it in the field of music. But she determined otherwise and, for over half a century, she reigned as one of the country's most loved and popular singers. Mary overcame her seeming deficiency through determination and self-discipline. The Greek statesman Demosthenes had such a speech impediment as a boy that he was embarrassed to speak before a group.

But he invested long hours by the sea in unrelenting practice to overcome his problem - and as a result became one of the most famous orators of all time. You may not have a natural aptitude for leadership, but under God's guidance you can develop into a leader. Why? Because even though you may be limited, the God who lives within you isn't!

****

Leadership does not depend on size but on knowledge and wisdom. A leader when given an audience of any kind has the incredible gift of impacting them positively.

****

Be strong because you never know whom you are inspiring. Focus on yourself as opposed to others because the people you are focusing on are focusing on you.

****

If you can lead yourself right in private, you can lead others in public.

****

The only power people have over you is the power you give them.

****

God is the beginning of wisdom. The moment you begin seeing as God sees, even if it's just little by little, everything starts to change.

****

Leadership is determined by the concept of Teamwork. It is the process of working collaboratively with a group of people in order to achieve a goal. Teamwork is often a crucial part of a business, as it is often necessary for colleagues to work well together, trying their best in any circumstance. It is the concept of teamwork.

****

You hear it over and over when the leaders of various institutions are appealing to the people they lead to work together in order to create a good working environment and relationship. But working together does not create a good relationship. On the contrary, it is the good relationship that creates the desired working together. The relationship comes first then the good works follow. The same applies to our salvation. Wishing you a great week at work.

****

You are the CEO of your life. Evaluate the people in your life then promote, demote or terminate. The bottom line is that people are going to judge your values by looking at your closest friends.

****

"Power does not corrupt men; fools, however, if they get into a position of power, corrupt power" ~ George Bernard Shaw

****

"A leader should always be open to criticism, not silencing dissent. Any leader who does not tolerate criticism from the public is afraid of their dirty hands to be revealed under heavy light. And such a leader is dangerous because they only feel secure in the darkness. Only a leader who is free from corruption welcomes scrutiny; for scrutiny allows a good leader to be an even greater leader."

****

"How you handle conflicts speaks volume of your characters. Some things won't be worked out of us until we learn to work well with others; whether it be in a workplace, in friendships, with family members, or of course relationships. I believe that even the best of people will always have issues and things that need to be worked out. Simply because we're humans and have faults."

****

A leader imparts constructive criticism out of love and is open to constructive criticism. "Unlike those who are threatened or defensive upon receiving correction, a leader should receive it with a grateful heart. The LORD always tells it like it is to HIS people. Those who whitewash sin and do not tell you the truth about yourself are actually contributing to your destruction. It is better to be rebuked openly if it causes your repentance and restoration. Surround yourself with friends who are willing to wound you with correction, rather than enemies who multiply kisses!

****

A leader is never afraid of competition because competition is part of the game. Many people want to be in your position or where you are. They will try to poke and challenge you in anticipation to pull you down. Never see people as a threat. Regard it as a normal process to be challenged, ignore the people and do your job right; their schemes will certainly fail.

****

A leader is stable but flexible. He adjusts to win all people. It is a virtue to be real but the problem is that people are being hated when they are real and are being loved when they are fake. Paul said that: "To the Jews I became like a Jew, to win the Jews. To those under the Law I became like one under the Law (though I myself am not under the Law), to win those under the Law. To those without the Law I became like one without the Law (though I am not outside the law of God but am under the law of Christ), to win those without the Law. To the weak I became weak, to win the weak. I have become all things to all men so that by all possible means I might save some of them." (1 Corinthians 9:21).

****

Unlike a ruler, a leader is a servant. In order to be over somebody you must be under somebody. Every good servant does not sit down to eat but first serves his master, standing by beside the dining table. And when his master is belching, having had his full, off goes the servant out to hunt his own game. Assuredly, no man will ever be able, or come close to successfully snatching such hard earned game from your hands!

****

Charity is expecting the best of each other while at the same time respecting our differences. Charity is accepting someone's weaknesses and shortcomings. Also, having patience with someone who has let you down or resisting the impulse to become offended when someone doesn't handle the situation the way you anticipated. It is acknowledging that I'm not in this world to live up to your expectations and you're not in this world to live up to mine. When it comes to the crusty behavior of some people, don't rush into judging and condemning them. Give them the benefit of the doubt. They may be drowning right before your eyes, but you can't see it.

****

It is hard to qualify what makes a good leader, but many people would agree that some of the most successful business heads are those who consistently make the right decisions.

****

"There are no extraordinary men... just extraordinary circumstances that ordinary men are forced to deal with" ~ William Halsey

****

A leader is never afraid to take on responsibility for his mistakes. "The difference between maturity and immaturity is in who you blame for what's going on in your life"

****

"Management is about persuading people to do things they don't want to do, while leadership is about inspiring people to do things they never thought they could do" ~ Steve Jacobs

****

Influence skills are so critical to success in the business world. They help leaders get people on board with them, which is pivotal in the long-term to getting people to follow through with decisions that have been made.

****

If it ain't broke, don't fix it; if it's not complicated, don't complicate it.

****

If questions don't make sense neither will the answers.

****

There are no perfect people and perfect answers. Wisdom is knowing what to do next, virtue is doing it!

****

Leaders always study to increase their knowledge capacity.

****

Loyalty is flattered commitment. The greatest gift you can give to your leader is loyalty.

****

Success is getting what you want, Happiness is liking what you get.

****

People may doubt what you say but they will believe what you do!

****

Generosity has two hands: The receiving hand and the giving hand. A true leader is willing to serve whether they are liked or not. They serve whenever there is a need. They serve even those who rejected them.

****

Attitude is a little thing that makes a big difference.

****

Self-pity and navel-gazing will drain you. Avoid wandering in a barren land. A despaired heart leads to a depressed heart.

****

Negative people destroy self-esteem. When the people around you give you every reason to be negative, think of one good reason to be positive. There's always something to be grateful for.

****

It's easier to condemn someone when you are not in their position.

****

"Close scrutiny will show that most "crisis situations" are opportunities to either advance, or stay where you are." ~ Maxwell Maltz quotes

****

Experience is the best teacher, but also a school that a fool will not attend!

****

Don't worry about the degree of your individual prominence achieved; worry about the individuals you have helped become better people. True Success is not about selfish achievements, it is about service.

****

Not everybody can be famous but everybody can be great because greatness is determined by service; all you need is a heart full of grace and a soul generated by love.

****

There is a need to be compassion but compassionate truth and principled as opposed to pleasers of men. Have a bit of a people-pleaser in you, but not so much so that it's out of control.

****

Values involve characters. The quality of our Characters is determined by our beliefs. The difference between the human kingdom and the animal kingdom is discipline. Practicing discipline involves subjection of all areas of your life to morality. Also, making deliberate choices, such as controlling your appetite, desires, emotional reactions, and obedience to the rules or laws of the social set up where you stay. Arguably, the most important thing is to acknowledge that you and I were made to live in harmony with others. "One of the most transcending outlooks is seeing others from a framework of love, God's love. Each one of us is a beautiful creation of God. We are precious to Him". As for believers, we are one body of Christ (Church). The Body of Christ is the living temple of God. We are interdependent. There is no such thing as an independent Christian or congregation. Instead of thinking of those who don't share your passions as not 'real Christians,' recognize the beauty of diversity within the body of Christ.

****

Often, you hear people say that "I am happy to be me". Strategically, they mean to say that "I am free to do what I want, the way I want it to be done." The issue of who is in charge does not resonate with their wisdom. It is an open defiance against the civil, social and spiritual authorities and the laws in place. Antinomianism comes from the Greek meaning lawless. Whenever we reject those people who are sent to be over (above) us, we automatically reject those who sent them. Rejecting your leader means rejecting the executive authority. Jesus said that ""Whoever listens to you listens to me; whoever rejects you rejects me; but whoever rejects me rejects him who sent me" (Luke 10:16).

****

Trust in God in order to be consistent. When Jesus is the conductor of your Orchestra, all the music makes sense... you can hear it with the ear of God instead of the ear of the world.

****

Promotion comes from God. When you promote yourself, you are most likely to take a dive and hit the base.

****

These qualities will make you an effective person in your career:

Determination: the refusal to let anything prevent you from doing what you have decided to do.

Perseverance: A determined attitude that makes you continue trying to achieve something difficult.

Ambition: Something that you very much want to do, usually something that is difficult to achieve.

Will: someone's determination to do what is necessary to achieve what they want.

\# Dynamism: energy, enthusiasm, and determination to succeed.

Motivation: a feeling of enthusiasm or interest that makes you determined to do something.

\# Resolve: Firm determination to do something.

\# Aspiration: Something that you want to achieve, or the wish to achieve something.

Drive: Must be vision driven in order to achieve your goals.

February – Romance

To fall in love with God is the greatest romance; to seek Him is the greatest adventure; to find Him is the greatest human achievement.

****

Your boyfriend is not a sexual partner but a prayer partner. "Women of God desire a Queenly Anointing from God, and your Father (God) will attract to you the right chosen one and he will have that Kingly Anointing... only a queen will stand beside the king." ~ Julie Hampton

****

Ever wonder why a drawing of a heart doesn't look like an actual human heart? The heart symbol we use today came from the idea of two human hearts being fused together as one, forming the iconic heart-shaped symbol we know as Love.

****

Love exists, regardless of our opinions of what it ought to be. Love is different than society's fabrication. It never sleeps, and it knows no limits. It defies all reason and differs from what the ego wants. It will always rush in where pain has left a scar, it has the power to move mountains, people, and it debases death. It doesn't boast, and it's not jealous. Never let your pride or hatred silence your heart. Love is always worth fighting for, if it's not, it is never worth anything at all and we don't deserve it. (Posted by Rose Queener).

****

Romance leads to deep intimacy. Men are eye-creatures. They are attracted by what they see. Women are ear-creatures. They like it when you say nice things about them.

****

We (the bride) love Jesus (our bridegroom) because He first loved us. When it comes to romance, a man is supposed to take the initiative. In fact, in the past times before the era of feminism, a woman that took initiative advance towards man, asking for love, was considered to be a prostitute.

****

The difference between the hopeful and hopeless romance is the difference between selfish lust and sincere love.

****

"The man of God, not perfect himself, but he sees perfect in you, because he has a perfect GOD. He puts a necklace of righteousness and faithfulness, and leads you to JESUS. He brings you commitment, Joy, forgiveness. Makes you feel wanted and special... Priceless~ Lisa Lorraina

****

If a man loves a woman's soul, he'll end up loving one woman, but if he loves a woman's face, all the women in the world won't satisfy Him ~ Muganwa Dorren

****

The early days of our marriage when we just made our vows were characterized with romantic language. But later on, after we settled down the functioning language replaced the romantic language. Instead of saying "I love you, it is who does what." This week decide to rekindle your romance with your spouse.

****

Remember love is the richest of all treasures. Without it there is nothing, and with it there is everything. Love never perishes, even if the bones of a lover are ground fine like powder. "Just as the perfume of sandalwood does not leave it, even if it is completely ground up, similarly the basis of love is the soul, and it is indestructible and therefore eternal. Beauty can be destroyed, but not love." ~ Adibiyi Kolawole

****

Let your life lightly dance on the edge of time like dew on the tip of a leaf.

****

"Love is like the wind; you can't see it but you feel it".

****

"Diamonds are hidden and you are a bright shiny jewel underneath this earthly façade" ~ Tamarrah Ann

****

There is no remedy to love, but to love more.

****

"To love someone is to learn the song in their heart and sing it to them when they have forgotten it!"

****

When you fish for love, bait with your heart, not your brain ~ Mark Twain

****

"Make a man dig into God's heart to find yours."

****

"Like oil upon your feet. Like wine for you to drink. Like water from my heart. I pour my love on" ~ Jesus

****

It is possible to love somebody and at the same time dislike him or her. Agape love is unconditional and is of the transformed heart of the integrity of God. It is deeper and stronger than emotional feelings and reaction. While like is more of a tender feeling towards what people do (their personalities, attitudes, behaviors, policies and etc.), love is a matter of the heart involving the will. Disliking someone is not necessarily hating them. It is disapproval of their conducts. There is that special person you love and like, you are happy being with that person, and you absolutely cannot bear to be without that person. Loving others (including our enemies) is mandatory to all of the believers, but when you like the person you love, it gives you the proverbial butterflies in the stomach and the experience is not superficial.

****

"Show me a man who is smiling from ear-to-ear and living a beautiful life, and I'll show you a man who is grateful for what he has and utterly in love with his wife." ~ Fawn Weaver

****

"If a man expects a woman to be an angel in his life, he must first create heaven for her. Angels do not live in hell!"

****

There is a big difference between love and lust. If there is no trust, love, and communication, then it's not a relationship, it's something else. Pure love is the willingness to give without a thought of receiving anything in return! True love has ups and downs. You can complain because a rose bush has thorns or rejoice because a thorn bush has roses!

****

"Love was a willing sacrifice. Love suffered and died and now brings us on high to feast on this love. Since love has conquered all our foes, why not let it conquer us?" ~ 1 Corinthians 13:4-7

****

"No, we don't date unbelievers but it's so much more than that. Just because they say they are a Christian doesn't make it so. You must learn to observe their character before you fall in love with their words. Just because we think "he" is what we want doesn't mean he is what God has for us."

****

February 2nd is my birthday. Thank you all for my birthday cards and wishes. A person has two birthdays: The day you were born by your mother, and the day you were reborn by God (born again). On the day on which we were born we began our countdown. The countdown should not be just numbers of years but a life lived and invested wisely. The countdown to eternity begins when you experience a new birth. It is when you make up your mind to take a giant step to accept Jesus Christ as your personal Savior. This is the greatest decision you can ever make in your lifetime. Make a decision and follow through it by your commitment to live for Christ the rest of your life. Remember that the consequences of the decision you make now will follow you even after this life.

End of February for Spiritual Growth

John 1:1- "In the beginning was the Word, and the Word was with God, and the Word was God." In Christ, God has executed and given to us His Word. He equipped us with everything we need in order to live in His grace and purity. The Word is living. It comes to us teamed with life, renewing the minds. Focusing on God is making the Word not just relevant but central to each and every activity. It is the Word that pulls us together in this world that pulls us apart.

****

The mind can be the harshest battleground. It can be the place where the greatest conflicts are carried out. Satan wins his battles in the minds. It is in the minds where all sorts of imaginations take place. It's where half of the things you thought were going to happen, never came to be. But if you allow those thoughts to dwell in your mind and fester, they will succeed in robbing you of peace, of happiness, and of everything that is beautiful in this world. Transformation is when God brings about regeneration. It is simply an exchange of life. It means we are showing forth and manifesting Christ's Life instead of our own. We are called to renew our minds in order to facilitate our sanctification. Renewing the minds is putting off the garbage in our own thinking and putting on the Mind of Christ. It's the Holy Spirit's mission, with our consent, to produce the Mind of Christ in us, so that we can be converted and live by the truth.

****

Everybody has a worldview; most people simply don't realize this – not even most Christians. A world view is a mental model of reality — a framework of ideas & attitudes about the world. Distorted world views jeopardize our sense of humanity, eventually killing the positive attitude. Negativity is the expression of criticism of or pessimism about something regardless of its authenticity. It is the major cause of arguments and then bitterness. The difference between better and bitter is the letter "i". It means I alone can turn my bitter life into better. Understanding your own worldview involves a positive attitude; it is coming to the end of yourself and coming out of the way to let God's purpose and plan to take their course. In a certain sense, this is the sum and substance of what it means to be a Christian.

****

Water baptism is a commandment which we must obey. Water baptism is symbolic of the death, burial and resurrection of Jesus Christ. Water baptism is not the cause of our justification but a sanctifying action. Since sanctification is part of salvation, I can say that baptism is a post-salvation action which follows the forgiveness of sins. Christendom insists that the remission of sins (justification) is an absolute work of God done on the human soul. It is imparted to the sinner the very moment a sinner "believes and repents" (i.e., accepts Jesus as personal Savior). This reception of Christ is internal, involving the surrendering of the will and a genuine commitment to receive Jesus as Lord and Savior. Water baptism is an external work of obedience; it is the evidence of the internal transformation that is already in place. Water baptism signifies that we were crucified, buried and raised with Jesus through faith (Colossians 2: 11-14). When Jesus was on the cross, you were there; your name is on His death, burial and resurrection! He died for you and with you. His resurrected life is in you. Paul Said that, "I am crucified with Christ: Nevertheless I live; yet not I, but Christ liveth in me (Galatians 2:20).

****

Jesus gave the story of the prodigal son (Luke 15:11-32). Basically, the son spat in the face of his father by asking for his inheritance before his father died. After squandering his inheritance, he went and worked on a pig farm. This was another insult to the father because it was a taboo for a Jewish man to come into contact with pigs. But when he made up his minds to return to his father, he was accepted as he is. The father hugged him and kissed him taking on himself the stench of his son. This story is the perfect illustration of the grace. Jesus took on our sins (stench) to save us. He received as we are without pre-condition.

****

Three places of the Holy Spirit: He is in you (John 14:17). He is with you (Matthew 28:20). He is upon you (Acts 1:8). He regenerates you. He comforts you. He works for you (anointing).

****

The Spirit of God (Holy Spirit) is ultimately the One who is supposed to be in control of your life, and He is determined that you be conformed to Christ (not to some straitjacket TULIP doctrine or some sloppy sentimental suffocating 'mysticism). You were created for His glory. You are a reflection of Him. Let your life, words, thoughts and actions honor Him so that He may be glorified in you. If there is no Christ-likeness in you, then probably you are not a born again Christian!

****

"What is to be filled with Holy Spirit?" The Bible says that, "And be not drunk with wine, wherein is excess; but be filled with the Spirit" (Ephesians 5:18). The instruction and responsibility to be filled with the Holy Spirit is given to us, not to God. God baptizes us with the Holy Spirit and gives us the responsibility to be filled with the Holy Spirit. He gives us the Holy Spirit without measure (all we need), and He asks us to walk in the fullness of His power. To be filled with the Holy Spirit is not a one-time event but a perpetual process or lifestyle. Everything in excess, including wine, money and food is bad but the Holy Spirit in excess is good. To be filled is a term that was used during biblical times in reference to the ships. The sails of the ships were filled by the wind and driven in the direction of the wind. To be filled is to be driven by the Holy Spirit in the direction of God.

****

Ephesians 5:18-19 – "Do not get drunk on wine, which leads to reckless indiscretion. Instead, be filled with the Spirit. Speaking to yourselves in psalms and hymns and spiritual songs, singing and making melody in your heart to the Lord." The scripture says that keep on drinking and be filled continuously but not with wine but with the Holy Spirit. To be filled with the Spirit is to yield to the divine guidance. The knowledge of God invites us to praise God regardless of the situation -- that is, doxology. We have such assurance that nothing happens to a child of God without being filtered by the hands of God. The more we know God, the more we trust Him, and the more we are compelled to praise him, awestruck at His greatness. "A child of God should always be a visible beatitude for joy and happiness, and a living doxology for gratitude and adoration." Indeed, the joy of the Lord is our strength (Nehemiah 8:10). The paradox of the prosperous spiritual living is solved when we acknowledge that we owe our being and existence to God in whose image we are made (Genesis 1:27). His image in us is His manifested glory in us. God's glory is His heaviness, goodness, majesty, splendor, and beauty. Christ in us is the hope of all glory. It is His love pouring into us and manifested through us. We need to acknowledge this fact in order to avoid being superstitious instead of supernatural.

****

The spiritual gifts are called gifts of grace because they are works of God manifested in and through us undeservingly. They are perfect gifts operating in the body of Christ (Church) in faith and love.

****

Somebody asked, "What is the difference between the anointment in the Old Testament and the New Testament?" The difference is the same because He is same God that anoints. The only difference is that in the Old Testament there is the limitedness of the working power of the grace among God's chosen people. In the old covenant, God anointed a few people chosen to work in the sanctified offices of the High priest, prophet, and king. In case they lost the favor (grace) of God, the anointing moved to another person. For example, when God rejected Saul as king, David was anointed, and the Spirit of God moved from Saul to David. When Jesus died on the cross, He opened up an account of grace for whosoever believes to draw from. According to the new covenant, all of us have unlimited access to the grace of God such that every believer can be anointed to serve. The word 'grace' (*Charis* in Greek) also means gift. Normally, a gift is not given indiscriminately to all people. It is given deservingly to those who are worthy to receive it. But Jesus became a sacrifice so that on His merits, whosoever believes, might receive the gift of grace. In this case, the gift is for those who cannot give something back. Jesus did more than give *charis* to the unworthy dregs of society. He made it His mission to seek them out. "For the Son of Man came to seek and to save the lost" (Luke 19:10). All kinds of sinners are refreshed by Jesus' declaration: "It is finished!"

****

Jesus fulfilled the Law because any spiritual law not fulfilled creates disharmony and the absence of divine love, thus ripple effects that bring "death". "Because the spiritual laws govern the outcomes of our choices; if we are aware of them they can illuminate the cause and effect dynamics occurring in our lives. Understanding these laws help us to "see" our consciousness and in contrast the divine consciousness. Through them, we see how the consciousness operates, functions and expands."

****

Somebody asked that "Does the Epistle of James contradict the teaching of Paul on grace and faith?" The Bible has no contradiction at all. God revealed to Paul the doctrine of the saving grace - It is the gospel of justification by faith in the finished works of Jesus Christ (Ephesians 2:8-10). Paul's teaching is not different from the teaching of Jesus in the gospels. The grace is God's faithful act to fulfill His promise of salvation at the expense of Christ. Faith is our good work that connects us to the promise of God. The Epistle of James emphasizes the working faith (not grace plus works) that is proven by good works (James 2:17). Salvation is divided into three parts: Justification, sanctification & glorification. Justification is of God and by God alone. But sanctification involves our good works of obedience to the moral commandments of God. Our good works implicate our loyalty, trust, commitment and submission to God. Again, our good works are not the cause of our justification but the proof that we are justified. It is the invisible inward transformation manifested to the outside (good works) that constitutes to faith. Look at the following teachings of Paul: "This is a faithful saying, and these things I want you to affirm constantly, that those who have believed in God should be careful to maintain good works." (Titus 3:8); "And let our people also learn to maintain good works, to meet urgent needs, that they may not be unfruitful" (Titus 3:14). ; "And let us consider one another in order to stir up love and good works" (Heb. 10:24).

****

Repentance cannot exist without faith, and faith cannot exist without repentance. We need to repent in order to be saved, and we need to repent regularly in order to stay saved. The saving faith is supposed to grow into the sanctifying faith until glorification. Repentance is such a vital portion of our sanctification.

****

The world says that "I will believe when I see. Faith says that "I believe, so I see."

****

The Law says "Do and live". The Grace says "Live and do".

****

Luke 7:28 - "I tell you, among those born of women there is no one greater than John; yet the one who is least in the kingdom of God is greater than he." Every person, apart from Adam, was born of a woman. The greatness of John the Baptist depends on the task (vocation) entrusted to him. Unlike the Old Testament prophets, he did not point to the future coming of Messiah but he introduced Jesus by baptizing Him. But our greatness depends on our faith in Christ. Faith is trusting in what Jesus can do on our behalf. By faith, His perfect works of obedience become ours. The grace of God made it possible for the Spirit of Christ to dwell in our bodies. We are the sanctified (separated or set apart) vessels (temple of God) in which and through which He reaches out to the lost world. We live every day in His presence, and He lives in us!

****

1 Corinthians 3:2 – "I have fed you with milk, and not with solid food: for until now you were not able to bear it, neither yet now are you able." There are several places in the New Testament when the Holy Spirit describes God's Word (doctrine) as both "milk," and "solid food" (meat). And since a new-born Christian is directed to grow to spiritual maturity, he or she should understand that it is necessary to transition from the "milk" to the "solid food" ("strong meat" in the King James Version) of the Word. Such growth does occur automatically. It involves the daily devotion of a believer. Furthermore, it is only by feeding on the "solid food" (meat) of the Word that a Christian may fully discern both good and evil (Hebrews 5:14). It is not a sin to be an infant if you are an infant but it is a sin for a mature person to be an infant.

****

1 Peter 3:15 – "But sanctify the Lord God in your hearts: and be ready always to give an answer to every man that asketh you a reason of the hope that is in you with meekness and fear". To sanctify is to set apart your heart and life for Christ. In order to be ready with an answer, we must be deeply immersed in the Scriptures. Peter's instruction is a direct challenge to us to study and to heed the Word of God. Be ready so that you don't have to get ready.

****

When your appetite for the Word is greater than your appetite for food then you are maturing spiritually. Your Mind is as sound as the measure of the Word of God in you. The calories from the food of the soul (Word) starve the flesh. The mind is your control center where resentment for the corrupt world is activated or negated. Your appetite for the Word obliterates your appetite for the world so that you are satiated and satisfied spiritually. "A true believer is not geared toward fighting the world that is, but toward creating the world that could be." We are contending with this world because it is not our home. It is the eternal world that we call home.

****

"Don't feel guilty when you haven't read the Bible. Feel hungry."

****

Change what you believe and change the course of your life.

****

If you are born once you die twice; if you are born twice you die once.

****

If the Bible is stepping on your toes, it is because your feet are in the wrong place.

****

His grave became my place of hope. His death certificate became my birth certificate!

****

It is the truth that you know that can set you free. The truth exposes the lies. However, knowing what is wrong does not make a difference, what makes a difference is making it right by acting on the revealed truth. Knowing without applying what you know leaves you in bondage. Think about it!

****

Faith does not deny a problem's existence; it denies it a place of influence.

****

The great faith does not depend on the expressions of your physical capabilities but on acknowledging your weaknesses, and inviting God to work on your behalf.

****

All of us have the circumstantial faith. Such faith is ignited by feelings and circumstances around us. For example, answered prayers, people's messages, life experiences and etc. The problem with circumstantial faith is that life is the inconsistency of life and the randomness of the world. The faith that depends on circumstances flips up and down depending on circumstances like feelings and experiences. Circumstances can shape our faith but should not be allowed to be the reason for our faith. Our faith is supposed to depend on Jesus. He is the dependable object and masterpiece of our faith. The Bible says that "Therefore, since we have such a great high priest who has passed through the heavens, Jesus the Son of God, let us hold firmly to what we profess" (Hebrews 4: 14).

****

The health minds flitter the emotions. The mind rather than the emotions is the right barometer to determine what is right. We fight with our brains because our spiritual battles are fought in our minds. The minds make us the most powerful creatures on the face of the earth, but we are vulnerable to the spiritual powers of darkness (blind) unless we are redeemed and renewed by acquiring the minds of Christ. Renew your zeal and passion by renewing your minds. "When you have the mind of Christ, you become Unstoppable."

****

Galatians 3:28 - "There is neither Jew nor Gentile, neither slave nor free, nor is there male and female, for you are all one in Christ Jesus." The grace is the ultimate equalizer, building bridges between God and man, and between us. The equalizing effect of the grace is that, regardless of the level of our spiritual growth and knowledge of the Scriptures, we are all equally related to God by our intimate relationship with Jesus Christ, and the fellowship of the Holy Spirit. The grace levels the ground such that not your color, not your ethnic background, not your gender, not your education and not your social status matters. In Christ, we all have the same opportunities and destiny!

****

Isaiah 64:6 - "But we are all as an unclean thing, and all our righteousnesses are as filthy rags; and we all do fade as a leaf; and our iniquities, like the wind, have taken us away." If our own righteousness is so bad, how bad is our unrighteousness? The eyes are infected with lust. The heart is polluted with pride. The flesh is corrupted with worldliness. Without salvation, we are doomed because God demands nothing less than His perfect righteousness in which He originally created us. Jesus, the only righteous One, exchanged His righteousness with our sins and paid in full the wages for our sins. We can now stand before God in the very righteousness of His Son without guilt.

****

Mark 12:41-44 – "Jesus sat down opposite the place where the offerings were put and watched the crowd putting their money into the temple treasury. Many rich people threw in large amounts. But a poor widow came and put in two very small copper coins, worth only a few cents. Calling his disciples to him, Jesus said, "Truly I tell you, this poor widow has put more into the treasury than all the others. They all gave out of their wealth; but she, out of her poverty, put in everything—all she had to live on." God looks at the motives rather than the actions. People may be pure in our eyes, but the Lord that examines their hearts knows exactly the level of their purity.

****

Galatians 4:9 - "But now, since you know God, or rather have become known by God, how can you turn back again to the weak and bankrupt elemental forces? Do you want to be enslaved to them all over again?" To know God is to be known by God. Being the beloved of God constitutes the core truth of our eternal existence. Our identity is in Christ. Armor yourself in it, and don't allow to be identified by the past old nature of sin. Accept no one's definition of you but define yourself by living right. The Word of God is the mirror that reflects your right image.

****

Ephesians 4:10 – "He that descended is the same also that ascended up far above all heavens, that he might fill all things." We are sculpted after Christ. We are heading to where we came from. "A Christian is not just a person going to Heaven. Shouldn't a Christian also be a person coming from Heaven, with the goods, power and virtue of Heaven? —Spiritual Discernment and the Mind of Christ" ~ Francis Frangipane

****

Ephesians 3:20 – "Now unto him that is able to do exceeding abundantly above all that we ask or think, according to the power that worketh in us". Child of God, you are not the super power but it is His power working in you. When things become tough you should become tougher by running to Jesus. He will wrap His arms around you. To be full of power is to be full of the Spirit of Christ.

****

The judge doesn't send a crime to prison but the criminal. God doesn't send the sin to hell but the sinner.

****

"A mind that is stretched by a new experience can never go back to its old dimensions."

****

Joy is the glimpse of heaven. Commitment is fulfillment that overlooks the circumstances. Happiness is emotional feelings as results of a sanctified heart.

****

Sometimes the truth that liberates offends before it liberates. Don't discard a good message just because it is uncomfortable to you.

****

Faith is trusting in God. The evidence of faith is laboring in love.

****

Faith, hope, and love; love is the greatest of the three. The problem is that we often brag about faith and hope, and we forget that it is love that makes our faith and hope binding. Faith brings hope but without abounding love faith and hope cannot thrive.

****

Fear has two contradictory meanings. *Phóbos*: Means "terror, horror, dread, fright, panic, or to flee from." Fear is the major factor influencing our decision making. Making decisions out of fear "phobéō" leads to making wrong decisions. Fear, doubt, and unbelief are the opposite of faith. Faith eliminates the negative fear and ignites the positive fear of God. *"Eulábeia*: Reverential fear. This references the fear we are expected to have towards God. The Bible says that "The fear of the LORD is the beginning of wisdom: and the knowledge of the holy is understanding" (Proverbs 9:10). Look at the yearning of the Psalmist: "Come, my children, listen to me; I will teach you the fear of the LORD" (Psalm 34:11). Faith is stepping out of the limited You, and stepping into the unlimitedness of God. Faith is to line up with the promises of God for provision and protection (Psalms 91). The eye of faith sees the invisible God at work on our behalf. Faith finds hope and discovers love. The Christian's hope is the "hope of glory," a hope with expectation and anticipation which enables us to endure the sufferings and groanings of this life with confidence and genuine optimism.

****

Matthew 18:3 - "And said, Verily I say unto you, Except ye be converted, and become as little children, ye shall not enter into the kingdom of heaven." Compare the calm characters of little children with the tensions and restlessness of your life. The kids have the qualities which adults lack: They are perfectly content to be themselves. They can easily adjust because their minds have not yet been programmed as ours. They are fulfilled by the little they have. They have the strong urge to be like their parents. The absence of grudges and inner conflict is only found in little children.

****

John 4:29 - "Come, see a man who told me everything I ever did. Could this be the Messiah?" God knows everything about you, and there is nothing you can hide from him. The woman believed because Jesus precisely foretold everything concerning her. The Bible accurately predicted the unfolding events. Will you believe?

****

"Jesus will always hold you up when life makes you feel like you haven't the strength to stand".

****

Heaven's sound of a rushing mighty wind is dependent on the element of resistance. The Wind never makes a sound unless there is resistance. The sound of the wind is also caused by the resistance of ears sticking out of your head, by the wheat stalk standing from the ground or by the trees and leaves standing firm. Man in his unredeemed state stands as resistance to the wind of the spirit. A man's spiritual state determines the sound coming out of his life ~ Nyesiga Catherine

****

Trials and tribulations prove the authenticity of our faith. As we endure and remain true to Christ, we demonstrate the authenticity of our trust in the Savior by which we lay hold of the "crown of life". It is easy to do what is right when everyone applauds it. What about when there is opposition and popular opinion is not in our favor? Are we emboldened in keeping the Lord's commandments? Our faithfulness to Christ even when it seems no one else stands with us will reveal the true state of our hearts, whether we are people of integrity.

****

Revelation 3:20 - "Behold, I stand at the door, and knock: if any man hear my voice, and open the door, I will come in to him, and will sup with him, and he with me". Some denominations and people openly claim to be Christians but when they have locked Jesus outside. He is knocking and they won't let Him in! Next time when somebody claims to be a Christian please ask him if Jesus Christ is in him. The Bible says that the fullness of God was in Christ, and is in Christ dwelling in us. Salvation is our union with Christ. Christ in us, is the hope of all glory (Colossians 1:27). We are made perfect (complete) by Christ. No system of beliefs centered on man's efforts at pleasing God, no matter how outwardly pious they appear, will ever satisfy God's righteousness and His perfection. Without Christ, we will never have the perfect knowledge or ability to rise above our own imperfection. Human resources at its best will still fall infinitely short of God's perfection.

****

Luke 19:1-10 – "A man was there by the name of Zacchaeus; he was a chief tax collector and was wealthy. He wanted to see who Jesus was, but because he was short he could not see over the crowd. So he ran ahead and climbed a sycamore-fig tree to see Him since Jesus was coming that way. Not only did the tree help this short man to see Jesus but most important is the fact that the Rabbis used to teach the Torah (Law) under the shades of the trees. Remember that Jesus told Nathanael that, "I saw you while you were still under the fig tree before Philip called you" (John 1:48). It means that Jesus saw Nathanael when he was being instructed in the Law under the tree. The Law is the spiritual tree we climb to see Jesus who saves us. Jesus provided already the prerequisites necessary for you to see Him.

****

Our salvation constitutes of a double lock: Jesus in us, and Jesus in God. It is the assurance we have that we destined to eternity. Jesus holds your hands and He will never let your hand go! We are like little kids crossing the street full of traffic with our hands in His hand. At times, your grip may not be in place to hold on but His grip is ever in place to sustain you and to make you cross over safely to the other end (eternity).

****

Legislation (or "statutory law") changes the society by established rules regulating unlawfulness. Psychology changes the behaviors by changing the minds. Christ changes the heart in order to change the thinking and the behaviors.

****

"Sin leaves you empty and powerless, even lifeless. But that's not the message. The message is that Jesus fills the emptiness and gives you life in abundance. That's the greater message. The Message of Love" ~ Ade Dayo

****

Humility is acknowledging that your life belongs to God to be used as He wills. It is celebrating the life of Christ by living as He lived.

****

Jesus is the good shepherd armed with a rod and staff in His hands. He uses the staff to draw the lost sheep back into the sheepfold. God draws you with gentle cords, with bands of Love. These Love-cords keep you connected to Him; they also help you to discern the way you should go. Though His bands of Love are unbreakable, they do not curtail your freedom. These highly elastic bands allow you to go your own way for a while. However, even if they are stretched out for a long time, as you seek to live independently of God, they retain their drawing power. Eventually, when you grow weary of worldly ways, the cords draw you gently back to Him. No matter how far you have roamed, God welcomes you with unfailing Love (Hosea 11:4). ~ Rhona Nansiima

****

Agape love is the unconditional love of God. It is spiritual and experiential in nature. We do not learn it, it is from the benevolence of our new nature (salvation). It is born into us when we are regenerated. True believers are supposed to recommend their faith by deeds of benevolence. But everything we do must be wrapped in love. Love is manifested in continuous formation through the choices of actions we make daily. We are supposed to love others in Spirit and truth as Jesus loved us. It means to love others not as we want but as God wants. Loving people unconditionally is to love people in spite of themselves. It is ignoring their natural personalities and relating to the image of God in them. Love in its practicality goes deeper than a mere confession. This kind of love cares about what others are going through and does something about their deteriorating conditions. Meditating on the scriptures of love daily and confessing them without swinging into actions won't cut it. In fact, even the people who hate Jesus and others quote the scriptures to justify their vice behaviors.

****

Without God, mankind is out of control. We are left at the mercy of fate. Fate is a one-way street to destruction. We know that animal populations need to be managed, but we counterproductively haven't yet figured out how to manage our own. The only person that can manage you is you! To be wisely directed and steered safety into the desired destiny is your reserve, and yours alone.

****

Self-righteousness people are selfish too. Some people conceal their own sinfulness by judging others. It is easier for them to fix the lives of others than fixing their own lives. Our churches should be environments of grace, so we can stay connected to the vine and bring forth real and genuine fruit so that the world will see Jesus in us and not self-righteousness.

****

Somebody posted this message: "How tempting it is to remind someone of a past offense! But when God forgives our sins, he totally forgets them. Isaiah 43:25 says "I-yes, I alone will blot out your sins for my own sake and will NEVER think of them again". So we never have to fear that He will remind us of them later. Because God forgives our sins, we need to forgive others! Let's stop judging and forgive!" My comment: Ignore the people who look at you in the old depiction before you were saved. Every person has the past from which they were saved. The Holy Spirit convicts rather than accusing us. Satan always points to the past because that is where the blame is. God wants you to look forward. You can't drive forward safely while your eyes are focused on the side mirrors looking behind.

****

To be born again is to encounter a new beginning. A born again believer starts off on the right foot and is expected to continue that way. Like a well-prepared soil, ready for sowing, God waters and ploughs forth from the soil of the heart. Out of the heart saturated with faith comes forth the incorruptible fruit of the Spirit, being the manifestation of spiritual maturity, and seeds to plant in the lives of others. The seeds never die. They always hold the germ of life - the germ of His Spirit within themselves.

****

When a person is born again, his passion for God is rekindled and is very counterproductive to any deception. A prepared heart has always made up minds with the assurance of salvation. He knows what to believe and why to believe so. This advantage enables him to grow and to obtain the desired result. "The restored fellowship with God should be marked by the overflowing joy. Avoid putting one foot in the world and the other in the church. "Be sure you put your feet in the right place, then stand firm." The most miserable person is not a person who is not born again but the one who is born again but lacks fellowship with God and hence the joy of the Lord due to their lifestyle. The reason is because they simultaneously miss the temporary pleasures of the world and the eternal benevolences.

****

Galatians 5:16-18 - "So I say, walk by the Spirit, and you will not gratify the desires of the flesh." It is imperative (command) to be led by the Spirit. The Spirit of God is the only faultless leader that cannot error when leading you. There is nothing as hopelessly as to be guided by the crooked or those who falsely believe that they are free. There is a saying: "To error is human". Human resources at its best will excuse evil because the natural mind (our carnal thoughts and reasoning) is enmity toward God. But the Holy Spirit is perfect and flawless. The Holy Spirit is the glorious display of the divine infinite wisdom on the earth. The validity of wisdom and knowledge depends on the truth. He is called the Spirit of truth because we depend on Him to know the truth. He reveals the truth through the scriptures to passionate seekers of the truth for the advancement of the Kingdom of God on the earth. God did not create us to depend on our natural wisdom without His guidance. The guidance of the Holy Spirit brings about the required revelation and inspiration, this being the congruence needed to reveal God's purposes on earth as it is in heaven.

****

Matthew 5:5 - "Blessed are the meek, for they will inherit the earth." This world is not what we are fighting for but what we are fighting against. Our real citizenship, our true commonwealth, is in the heavens. God is in the process of redeeming this world for our inheritance. If at all people knew this truth, nobody would kill another person for this world which is passing away!

****

The word 'unbelief' common in the New Testament but it is not directed quoted in the Old Testament but its meaning is there. Unbelief is the oldest of the many spiritual diseases by which fallen human nature is afflicted. It is deliberately refusing to believe in spite of the overwhelming evidence provided. For example one of the thieves on the cross said to Jesus mockingly that, "If you are truly the Son of God come off the cross (save yourself). This is a good example of unbelief at its best. But the other thief out of humility said to Jesus that, "Remember me in your kingdom. Likewise, one of the Roman soldiers saw Jesus at the cross and confessed that "Truly this is the Son of God".

****

Matthew 16:26 - "For what is a man profited, if he shall gain the whole world, and lose his own soul? Or what shall a man give in exchange for his soul?" There is an eternal humanity that crosses through all people. The life you have lived and the rest of the life you will live is just a very tiny portion of eternity. We are naturally wired to seek happiness and prestige but never do it at the expense of your soul. "Nothing on earth is worth going to hell for." Everything in this world is in transit. "Nothing stands still - everything is being born, growing, dying - the very instant a thing reaches its height, it begins to decline." True happiness is initiated in another dimension (eternity). Enter into the everlasting joy of the Father by allowing the Holy Spirit to activate your spirit. Live every day as if there is nothing to lose but heaven to gain!

****

Hebrews 8:10-11- "This is the covenant that I will make with the house of Israel after those days, saith the Lord; I will put my laws into their mind, and write them in their hearts: and I will be to them a God, and they shall be to Me a people. And they shall not teach every man his neighbor, and every man his brother, saying, Know the Lord: for all shall know Me, from the least to the greatest." This promise is the new covenant of grace. Under the old covenant the Moral Law was engraved on tables of stone; under the new covenant the law of God is put into the Christians' minds and written on their hearts so that a believer living under the grace may not deliberately transgress the Moral Law with impunity. It is written upon his mind and heart that he cannot escape the responsibility of obedience. It is the law of love and loyalty to Jesus because we know God by our intimate relationship with Jesus. Remember that Jesus was loyal to all that was written in the Scriptures concerning Him, and He fulfilled all the prophecies that applied to Him before the eyes of those who heard Him. Likewise, we must be loyal to every word concerning us. Jesus said that His words are Spirit (John 6:63). The Holy Spirit cannot be separated from the Scriptures. No man can possess the fullness of the Holy Spirit while living in known disobedience to the written Word of God.

****

Ezekiel 36:26 – "A new heart also will I give you, and a new spirit will I put within you: and I will take away the stony heart out of your flesh, and I will give you a heart of flesh." When you get down to the heart of the matter the heart is what matters.

****

Luke 9:23- Then he said to them all: "Whoever wants to be my disciple must deny themselves and take up their cross daily and follow me. For whosoever will save his life shall lose it: but whosoever will lose his life for my sake, the same shall save it." This scripture is given in the imperative form. It is not a casual statement. Self-denial has to do with rejecting the secular mentality of worldliness. Also, we are called to embrace His values at any cost, even death. Jesus laid down His life for us, and we must be willing to lay down our lives for the sake of the gospel. After giving His disciples the above instructions, Jesus took Peter James and John to the mountain, which we call the Mount of Transfiguration, to give them a preview of the Kingdom. They had a glimpse at what they will gain by giving up what they have. Nothing in this world is worthy of missing the future glory.

****

Matthew 25:14-30 – "And he who had received the five talents came forward, bringing five talents more, saying, 'Master, you delivered to me five talents; here I have made five talents more.' His master said to him, 'Well done, good and faithful servant. You have been faithful over a little; I will set you over much. Enter into the joy of your master.'" Faith is about multiplication. God requires you to be productive by multiplying everything He put in you. After God created man, He instructed them to go and multiply. God wants to bless you and enlarge your territory. Your territory can be your sphere of influence or your realm of responsibility or authority. Press on to your intended destiny with a stewardship mentality. Your spiritual journey has only one valid direction - moving forward: No turning backwards, no retreat and no standing still. If you are not moving you are stranded, and you need a jump starter so that you can make a good ending. It means standing before God without any unused talent in you.

****

But he said to me, "My grace is sufficient for you, for my power is made perfect in weakness. Therefore I will boast all the more gladly about my weaknesses so that Christ's power may rest on me." The grace is God's power for us to pursue holiness. The power of the grace works for us in our weakness. It is that moment when we realize that we can't do it on our own, we need God's help to do it. The quality of life does not depend on what we can do but on what God can do in us and through us.

****

Where you stand today will determine your eternal status. You are better off when you stand for something instead of nothing. Stand for the truth, and do not fall for the deception of the corrupt nature and the corrupt world.

****

John 5:31 - "If I testify about myself, my testimony is not true." Jesus came to glorify the Father. The Holy Spirit was sent not to testify for Himself but to testify for Jesus: "But the Advocate, the Holy Spirit, whom the

Father will send in my name, will teach you all things and will remind you of everything I have said to you (John 14:26). The Holy Spirit guides us through the words of Jesus. The Holy Spirit gives us assurance that we belong to God: "The Spirit itself beareth witness with our spirit, that we are the children of God" (Romans 8:16).

****

Ebenezer wasn't called so until after the Israelites finally defeated the Philistines, and took back the Ark of the Covenant. To commemorate the victorious battle, Samuel set up a marker-stone, named it "Stone of Help," and thereby the site became identified with the stone and with the place where God's miraculous help aided them in their victory over the Philistines (1 Samuel 4:1-11 and 5:1). The stone, standing up-right, was called "Ebenezer," and the site naturally took on that name as well. "Ebenezer." The etymological roots of the word, thus defined, should demonstrate that an "Ebenezer" is, literally, a "Stone of Help." God sees your failure as an opportunity to lift you up.

****

Revival is not calling God to come down to the earth because He did that on Pentecost Day. When we call for a revival, we are not calling for another Pentecost because God poured out already His Spirit in His fullness on the earth. We are calling for the awakening of the church. We pray and cry out to God to open the eyes of the saints to see the Holy Spirit that is already in place. Revival is cultivating His presence to manifest intensively so that the people acknowledge it with tears of joy.

****

Jesus did not die just to take you to heaven but so that heaven comes into you. Christ's nature became your nature. God sees you in the image of Christ Jesus. To see yourself anything less than how God sees you is synonymous to spiritual dwarf. Spiritual strength does not come from physical capacity. It comes from an indomitable will to surrender. It is when we are week physically that we are strong spiritually. Even the weakest saint can become the strongest spiritually when he begins to see himself in Christ Jesus. Put your feet in the right place, and stand firm on your conviction that your new assigned identity is in Christ.

****

Psalm 51:17 - "My sacrifice, O God, is a broken spirit; a broken and contrite heart you, God, will not despise." Jesus instructed us to carry our cross and follow Him. The way to the cross is brokenness and a contrite heart. Humbleness is the means of accessing the grace. Humility is the opposite of ego. Ego is a small word with many derived meanings. Ego implements delusion and makes life dissatisfactory without a possibility of fulfillment. You kill your ego by surrendering your will to Christ. Broken people are self-conscious. They allow the Holy Spirit to steer them in the right direction, and to hurl them into their intended divine destiny. Also, they extend to others the same opportunity to hurl themselves into their divine intended destiny.

****

Egoism affects sincerity. The more our egoism is satisfied, the more robust is our belief. Selfish Christians are ever learning, but they never grow into the character of their Savior... If your opinion does not agree with the Word of God, then you have no right to your opinion!

****

Matthew 7:1-3 - "Judge not, that ye be not judged." In this scripture, the word 'judge' does not mean discerning but the presumptuous judgmental attitude that ends up into condemning. We are called to judge ourselves but at times we go beyond our limits. We prefer judging others to judging ourselves. There is that tendency in us to look more spiritual by criticizing others. Such criticism is driven by ego, envy and jealous, and portrays a distorted character of Christ. This is most probably the deception which the devil is deploying to tear up the body of Christ today. We have a situation whereby God's people hurt God's people in the name of piety! Judging others results into a crisis and eventually schism. We are not called to be fruit inspectors but fruit preservative. If truly we are one body then caring for the spiritual welfare of others shouldn't be a problem - it is not self-indulgence, it is self-preservation. Given the fact, constructive criticism is healthy when the intention is to preserve the integrity and unity of the church. It is wrong when it tends otherwise.

****

Godfrey Nsubuga responded to the above article in this way: "It is a great snare! Talk about being, "Fruit inspectors." The goal should always be to reconcile one with God rather demonstrating to the one 'limping' how we can walk perfectly."

****

James 1:19 – "My dear brothers and sisters, take note of this: Everyone should be quick to listen, slow to speak and slow to become angry". It is a calling to pause before reacting and dying to your own self and logic. It is bypassing your emotions, filtering out all of your thoughts, and going with what feels instinctive and true to your heart. The Bible says that "Above all else, guard your heart, for everything you do flows from it." (Proverbs 4:23). Expressed anger is being out of control. It is typically an attitude that is unable to contain what is given. It is impossible to think right when you are unable to control your thinking. An activist who goes on a rampage without auditing his information academically, rationally and intuitionally becomes fanatic. Fanaticism focuses on what you know and what you do regardless of the factual reality. It is a failure to cultivate and to address your problems from your point of weakness. Fanaticism ignores the opposite views of others. God is not an ally to partisan fanaticism. Whether it be in politics or religion, fanaticism is an extremely dangerous derange of otherwise sane and goodhearted people. "Fanaticism obliterates the feelings of humanity."

****

Proverbs 18:21 - "Death and life are in the power of the tongue, and they that love it shall eat the fruit thereof." Doctors say that the nerve controlling the tongue is connected to all of the body organs. The words you speak to yourself have a great impact on your health. The negative words you say to yourself hurt you more than the negative words others say to you.

****

We are saved and secured in our salvation by God. The grace saves and sustains us in Christ. Union with Christ means we are in Christ, and Christ is in us. He made us without us, and He saves us without us. The freedom we have is not to do what we want but not to do what we didn't have to do.

****

John 16:7 - "But very truly I tell you, it is for your good that I am going away. Unless I go away, the Advocate will not come to you; but if I go, I will send him to you." How can it be good to the disciples for Jesus to be separated from them? It is better for them because Jesus is going to be in them by His Spirit.

****

The Holy Spirit was given to us to help us do what we couldn't do by ourselves. Your inadequacy is, therefore, an asset if you know how to use it. Your inadequacy is what leads you claim your adequacy by faith. Contentment comes with the Holy Spirit. Humility is admitting that you can't. It is when you say you can't that God steps in to help you. Your trials are therefore good for you because anything that helps us to know God is good.

****

2 Peter 1:16 – 17 - "For we did not follow cleverly devised stories when we told you about the coming of our Lord Jesus Christ in power, but we were eyewitnesses of his majesty. For He received honor and glory from God the Father when the voice from the Majestic Glory said to Him, "This is My

beloved Son, in whom I am well pleased…" The glory (Shekinah) literally means "he caused to dwell," signifying that it was a divine visitation of the presence or dwelling of the Lord God on this earth. The Shekinah was first evident when the Israelites set out from Succoth in their escape from Egypt. God's presence was manifested by the intense light that filled the Tabernacle and even in the wilderness where He was a light during the night and the Shekinah cloud of His glory shaded Israel in the scorching sun of the desert. God's glory filled the Temple. Jesus' glory as God was veiled in human flesh but at times His glory, the so-called Shekinah glory, was revealed like in the Transfiguration. Peter saw the glory of the Lord with his own eyes, but we have an equivalent of the glory of God before our eyes, compared to what Peter saw, in form of the Holy Spirit. He reveals the glory of God in the Scriptures. Therefore not to read the Bible is as immoral as not doing what the Bible says.

****

The Christian living is compared to fasting. When you fast you deny your body the food that it likes much. Likewise, spiritually, we are vulnerable to deception. We overcome by denying those things which our old nature desires. It is called the spiritual warfare. The Word of God makes it very clear that the devil is against all that God is. He has waged war against the people of God whom he hates. "Whenever you decide to go after God, the devil will go after you." Satan fights us in our minds. Walking by the spirit is starving the flesh. It is by the mighty power of God, pulling down the strong holds; Casting down imaginations, and every high thing that exalteth itself against the knowledge of God, and bringing into captivity every thought to the obedience of Christ (2 Corinthians 10:5).

****

The gifts of the Holy Spirit are called gifts of grace because it is Jesus directly working through our corrupt bodies. The gifts of the Holy Spirit are the manifested perfect works of the Holy Spirit (1 Corinthians 12:8-11). The fruit of the Spirit is the manifested evidence of the work of the transformed heart that cannot be faked by any natural means (Galatians

5:22). Our greatest achievement in this world is leaving behind the monuments of His grace.

****

Romans 1:1 – "Paul, a servant of Christ Jesus, called to be an apostle and set apart for the gospel of God". The word 'servant' means to be sealed in the will of another person. The word 'called' means invited. To be 'set apart' is to be separated to be used by God (sanctified).

****

Somebody asked "I have been actively serving in my church whenever there is a need but I don't know my specific calling. How can I know my specific calling?" God calls all of us to salvation and to serve in various ministries. God is willing to use all of us because He did not create a useless person. A ministry is your vocation assigned by the Holy Spirit. The calling to serve is instant but it might take long to be recognized. God uses the ordained elders and various people around us (laity) to discern our callings. Given the fact, you can know what you are called to do. I usually compare it to falling in love. How do you know that you are in love? You just know it. The same thing applies to your calling. God puts into your heart the passion for the people and the places where He wants you to serve. Your vocation is your love of Jesus. Normally, God uses our natural talents to determine our callings. Continue serving faithfully as you have been doing. Eventually, God will show you where He wants you to specialize. Keep on shaking those branches, in case there is a fruit hidden in the leaves, it will drop right into your hands.

****

John 3:16 - "For God so loved the world that He gave His one and only Son, that whoever believes in Him shall not perish but have eternal life." The world that God loved includes you. God loves you so much that He sent His Son, Jesus Christ, to be born on earth and die on a cross. Even if there was just one sinner in the whole world, He could have sent His Son to die for you!

****

They say that striving to be excellent is man's duty. We're constantly striving in pursuit of success. But our spirituality involves less striving and more yielding. The anticipated full blessings will come your way when you allow God to be in full control of your life instead of you controlling your life. Yielding comes with conviction. To yield is to surrender to a force greater than your own, in order to become part of the whole. It is killing your pride and ego, which are the enemies of submission. Let them die!

****

Inactivity is death. Inactivity is contrary to the antagonistic Christian life. The Bible instructs us to seek and continue seeking by knocking that door until it opens (Matthew 7:7). Choosing your priorities and sticking to them until you get the anticipated results is the evidence of a disciplined heart. Likewise, commitment is the Key to receiving from God.

****

When you deliberately break (violate) God's will, you will definitely be broken by the same will you broke.

****

The 'Breaking News' is intended to emotionally entice you but there is the backlash of breaking your faith replacing it with anxiety. Turn to the Bible for spiritual insight; it is anxiety reliever. In the Bible, there is neither bad news nor grievances for redressing. The Bible revokes and replaces the 'Breaking News' with the 'Good News'. Jesus never breaks hearts but He picks up the broken pieces of our lives and put them together. There is an art to brokenness. The knack lies in humility, throwing yourself at the Rock (Jesus). "The Lord is close to the brokenhearted and saves those who are crushed in spirit" (Psalms 34:18).

****

"The goal of Bible study is not simply observation and information, but application and transformation" ~ Steve Lawson

****

Acts 17:11 – "These were more noble than those in Thessalonica, in that they received the word with all readiness of mind, and searched the scriptures daily, whether those things were so." The scriptures they had were the scrolls of the Old Testament. They searched them to prove that the words preached to them were prophetic. Check out every word spoken to you to prove that it does not contradict the Scriptures. Use the scriptures as your point of reference. It is when we search the Scriptures that God searches our hearts. Searching is testing, and it involves doubting the spoken words (not the Scriptures). This is positive doubting because it ignites cautious optimism. In this case, your doubting becomes your greatest ally in your life's search for the truth and wisdom. Doubting when searching for the truth is understandable but refusing to search the scriptures is refusing to understand. It is called unbelief!

****

Mark 10:18 - "Why do you call me good?" Jesus answered. "No one is good--except God alone." Jesus meant that by calling me good you are acknowledging that I am God. The religious leaders ignored the Scriptures and searched for God by the wisdom of this world. They used the scriptures to justify their insubordinations. They flattered people in their sins, because they loved to be flattered. Jesus is the embodiment of the Word (John 1:1;5:39). We are good compared to other human beings but not compared to God because God alone is absolutely good, and He only accepts His goodness in us through Jesus Christ.

****

Somebody asked "I have been actively serving in my church whenever there is a need but I don't know my specific calling. How can I know my specific calling?" God calls all of us to salvation and to serve in various ministries. God is willing to use all of us because He did not create a useless person. A ministry is your vocation assigned by the Holy Spirit. The calling to serve is instant but it might take long to be recognized. God uses the ordained elders and various people around us (laity) to discern our callings. Given the fact, you can know what you are called to do. I usually compare it to falling in love. How do you know that you are in love? You just know it. The same thing applies to your calling. God puts into your heart the passion for the people and the places where He wants you to serve. Your vocation is your love of Jesus. Normally, God uses our natural talents to determine our callings. Continue serving faithfully as you have been doing. Eventually, God will show you where He wants you to specialize. Keep on shaking those branches, in case there is a fruit hidden in the leaves, it will drop right into your hands.

****

The difference between the Christians and the rest of the world is that the rest of the world is made up of orphans, without the Father. Jesus promised that He will not leave us as orphans: "And I will pray the Father, and he shall give you another Comforter, that he may abide with you forever." (John 14:16). Why a Comforter? We go through the same trials like the rest of the world. The difference is that we are not alone; God is with us. The Holy Spirit does for us everything that Jesus would do if He was here on the earth. The ministry of Jesus is that of comforting, and He extends the same ministry to us. The Bible says that: "Grace and peace to you from God our Father and the Lord Jesus Christ. Blessed be the God and Father of our Lord Jesus Christ, the Father of compassion and the God of all comfort, who comforts us in all our troubles, so that we can comfort those in any trouble with the comfort we ourselves have received from God" (2 Corinthians 1:3-4).

****

Prophetic message to you: The things you are going through are not accidental. The Bible says that everything that can be shaken will be shaken until only the ones that can't be shaken remain. Trust and allow Jesus to walk you through the process. I can see a flashing yellow signal light warning you to get ready to move on because the red light that has been holding you hostage is about to change to green. The pain you are experiencing is for the sake of others. God wants to use you as an example. Your testing today will be your testimony tomorrow so that you may teach others about the amazing power of God that delivered you.

March - Apologetic

Apologetic is intended for the Christians to become thinkers, and for the thinkers to become Christians. Jesus was confronted by people with a lot of questions and He had answers for them. Even when He was at the cross, one of the thieves asked Him if He will remember Him in His kingdom (Luke 23:39-43). The Holy Spirit is Jesus in us to answer all questions from the biblical prospective.

****

Just because you can't see the air, doesn't mean you stop breathing. And just because you can't see God doesn't mean you stop believing.

****

The Bible says in the beginning God (time) created heaven (space) and earth (matter). Time, space and matter all of them have to come into existence at the same time (simultaneously). The reason is because if there was matter and no space where will you put it? If there was matter and space and no time when will you put it? The God of the Bible is not limited and is not affected by time, space and matter. The God that created the universe is not in the universe, in the same manner the guy that created the computer is not in the computer. All things existed in God as ideas and He spoke them into existence. God preexisted and is self-existence.

****

YHWH is expressed as HaShem (השם), which is Hebrew for "the Name" (cf. Leviticus 24:11 and Deuteronomy 28:58). The consonants represent the secret name of God. God said to Moses, "I AM WHO I AM (Exodus 3:14). Meaning that He exists in such sort that His whole inscrutable nature is implied in His existence. He exists infinitely eternally; there is no time He has never been and He will never be. There are multiple titles for God, each describing a different aspect of His many-faceted character and attributes. The Son is called Jesus - meaning Savior, and Christ - meaning the Anointed. The Holy Spirit has no given name because He takes on the name of the Father and the Son whom He represents. Jesus said that "But when he, the Spirit of truth, comes, he will guide you into all the truth. He will not speak on his own; he will speak only what he hears, and he will tell you what is yet to come" (John 16:13). To take the name of God in vain is denying the Holy Spirit an opportunity to do what He was sent to do.

****

The Trinitarian God is One (Father, Son and Holy Spirit). He is one God with one will. There is no contradictory will between the First, the Second and the Third persons of the trinity. Except that the will of the Jesus was separated from the will of the Father after He put on the human flesh (Luke 22:42).

****

Somebody asked that "When God said that let us make mankind in our image (Genesis 1:26), isn't this Jesus talking to the angels?" I have two reasons to reject the idea that God was discussing with the angels. If the term "in our image" is in reference to the angels then we could have been made in the image of the angels. But the scripture goes on to say that, "So God created mankind in his own image, in the image of God he created them" (verse 27). Angels are creations rather than the agents of creation. I believe that the above conference of creating involved the persons of the Godhead. God the Father initiated, the Holy Spirit implemented as an agent of creating through the Son. The Bible says concerning Jesus that,

"For in him all things were created: things in heaven and on earth, visible and invisible, whether thrones or powers or rulers or authorities; all things have been created through him and for him. He is before all things, and in him all things hold together" (Colossians 1:16-17). The term "all things" is inclusive of all created things including the angels but is exclusive of the Creator (Godhead). The story of creation presents the Godhead (Father, Son, and Holy Spirit) as the Creator. The last part of the scripture says that "in him all things hold together". Jesus holds the entire universe together.

****

Matthew 16:13-17 - ""Who do you say I am?" Simon Peter answered, "You are the Messiah, the Son of the living God." Jesus replied, "Blessed are you, Simon son of Jonah, for this was not revealed to you by flesh and blood, but by my Father in heaven." The apostles had been with Jesus for almost three years yet they did not know who He is. Of course, they knew His earthly parents (Matthew 13:55), but because of the miracles which He did, they were reluctant to say that He was a mere man like them. Elsewhere, Jesus challenged the Jewish religious leaders that if they doubt what He claims to be, they cannot doubt what He does: "But if I do them, even though you do not believe me, believe the works, that you may know and understand that the Father is in me, and I in the Father" (John 10:38). Jesus warned them that you shall die in your sins: for if you believe not that I am He (John 8:24). Peter's confession that Jesus is the Christ (Messiah) was not a product of intellectual research but a direct revelation from the Father who is in heaven. The proper name of Messiah is Adonia Tzidekunu meaning the Lord our Righteousness (Midrash Lamentation 1).

According to the Rabbinic writings, from the time of creation, there is a constant reference made to the coming of Messiah as hope to Israel. "'The Spirit of God moved upon the face of the waters'; the Spirit of God means Messiah" (Midrash Genesis Rabbah 2; Leviticus Rabbah 14). Jesus lamented over Jerusalem that ""Jerusalem, Jerusalem, you who kill the prophets and stone those sent to you, how often I have longed to gather your children together, as a hen gathers her chicks under her wings, and you were not willing" (Luke 13:34). The act of the hen gathering her chicks under her wings is brooding. In Hebrew, brooding and hovering are delivered from the same root word. Let us look at the parallel scripture in Genesis: "The Spirit of God was hovering over the waters" (Genesis 1:2). The Spirit of God hovered (brooded) over the waters instead of the earth because the earth was void. In the same way, the Spirit of Jesus would not brood (hover) over Jerusalem because the people were wicked. When Jesus died on the cross, an account of the grace was opened on our behalf. On Pentecost, the Holy Spirit moved from Christ and hovered (brooded) over the Church. All saints (dead/alive), make up the spiritual body of Christ because we are partakers of His Spirit; He indwells us. The Spirit of God is also called the Spirit of Christ: "However, you are not in the flesh but in the Spirit, if indeed the Spirit of God dwells in you But if anyone does not have the Spirit of Christ, he does not belong to Him" (Romans 8:9).

****

We are God's anointed purposely to serve others. The word Messiah (Mashiach) comes from the verb Mashach, which means to smear oil usually for the purpose of dedicating or consecrating something (such as a vessel temple) or someone (such as a priest, prophet or king) for the service of Adonai.

****

Jesus said that "My sheep listen to my voice; I know them, and they follow me. I give them eternal life, and they shall never perish; no one will snatch them out of my hand. My Father, who has given them to me, is greater than all[a]; no one can snatch them out of my Father's hand. I and the Father are one" (John 10:27-30). We are naturally selective listeners. Unless we are regenerated, we have no antenna to pick the signal of the voice of the Savior. The hearing sheep are the ones that are following the Savior. The scripture says that Jesus gives them eternal life. Jesus is the source of eternal life. The saved souls are safe and secure in the Son's hands because they are given to Him by the Father. Jesus concludes with these words "I and the Father are one". It means that the Father and the Son are alike and are in agreement. The Spirit of God working in the Son is the Spirit of the Father. Remember when Philip asked Jesus that "Lord, show us the Father, and that will be enough for us." Jesus replied, "Philip, I have been with you all this time, and still you do not know Me? Anyone who has seen Me has seen the Father. How can you say, 'Show us the Father'? The words I say to you I do not speak on my own authority. Rather, it is the Father dwelling in Me, carrying out His work" (John 14:9). Jesus introduced the Holy Spirit to His disciples in this way: "And I will ask the Father, and he will give you another advocate to help you and be with you forever—the Spirit of truth. The world cannot accept him, because it neither sees him nor knows him. But you know him, for he lives with you and will be in you--- Because I live, you also will live. On that day you will realize that I am in my Father, and you are in me, and I am in you." (John 14:16-21). Jesus called the Holy Spirit another one of the same kind as Jesus. He told them that "You know Him already". How could they know Him without being taught about Him? Because He has been at work in Jesus; all of the works of Jesus during His earthly ministry were the works of the Holy Spirit. In the same way all of the supernatural works of the Apostles in the early Church were works of Jesus through the Holy Spirit. Jesus specifically said concerning the Holy Spirit that: "He lives with you" - Jesus with them in the present. "He will be in you" - Jesus in them in future.

****

John 5:22 – "For just as the Father raises the dead and gives them life, so also the Son gives life to whom He wishes. Furthermore, the Father judges no one, but has assigned all judgment to the Son, so that all may honor the Son just as they honor the Father. Whoever does not honor the Son does not honor the Father who sent Him.…" The Father and the Son give eternal life but the Father assigned the duty of judging to the Son. Jesus shared the glory with the Father before He emptied Himself of the heavenly glory in order to save us: "Who, being in very nature God, did not consider equality with God something to be used to his own advantage" (Philippians 2:6). At the end of His mission of saving us He prayed to the Father to restore to Him His glory: "And now, Father, glorify me in your presence with the glory I had with you before the world began" (John 17:5). Because of His perfect obedience even unto the cross, the Father exalted the Son as the ultimate judge. God rules and judges from His heavenly throne. The Bible specifically says that there is only one throne from which God rules and judges (Revelation 4:2). Jesus is seated on the heavenly throne at the right hand of the Father. 'Right hand' is symbolic of authority. This is the enthronement of our King in preparation for His coming kingdom on the earth. Jesus preached the message of the kingdom of God of which He is the King. When Jesus called God His Father, his ancient enemies accused Him of blasphemy, and making himself equal with God (John 10:33). The term 'Son of God' means being of the same nature and character as God.

Atheism is, in a broad sense, the rejection of belief in the existence of deities. Anti-theism is a conscious and deliberate opposition to the true nature of one God who has revealed Himself in three persons. "The word Elohim is the plural of El (or possibly Eloah) and is the first name of God given in the Old Testament: "Let us make man in our image." (Genesis 1:26). Also, "And the LORD God said, "The man has now become like one of us" (Genesis 3:22). Jesus used the same plurality in reference to God: "Anyone who loves me will obey my teaching. My Father will love them, and we will come to them and make our home with them." (John 14:23). We cannot study God with our finite minds but we are called to believe even when we do not fully understand.

****

Somebody asked that "If Jesus is God why didn't He tell us to worship Him? The Bible says that if any man sees God he must die. Why didn't all of the people who saw Jesus die if He was God?" True, no man can see God and live. That is why Jesus had a veil of the human flesh. Look at the transfiguration when Jesus was changed into his glory (Matthew 17:1). The apostles were overcome by the glorious sight. But that was just a minor glimpse to prove to them that He is more than the man they see daily. Was Jesus worshiped? Jesus was worshiped after He walked on water Matthew 14:33; A healed blind man worshiped Jesus John 9:38; The Bible gives an occasion after the resurrection of Jesus when all of the disciples worshiped Jesus. We are told, "When they saw him they worshiped him"

(Matthew 28:17). Jesus did not turn down the worship or even rebuke them for worshiping Him when God alone can be worshiped. The reason is because He is God. Jesus forgave sins when God alone can forgive sins. The Pharisees reacted in this way: "Why does this fellow talk like that? He's blaspheming! Who can forgive sins but God alone?" (Mark 2:7). More important God alone can save. The name Jesus in Hebrew means Jehovah saves.

He who descended is the very one who ascended above all the heavens, in order to fill all things" (Ephesians 4:10). The scripture says that He ascended from where he descended. Where? At the heavenly throne. He emptied Himself and put on the human flesh to save us. God exalted Him by putting Him where He was before coming to the earth. The Bible says that, "And being found in appearance as a man, He humbled Himself and became obedient to death—even death on a cross. 9Therefore God exalted Him to the highest place, and gave Him the name above all names, that at the name of Jesus every knee should bow, in heaven and on earth and under the earth (Philippians 2:9-10).

****

Somebody asked, "If Jesus was truly the Son of God why did he call himself the Son of man?" Son of man was a popular slang among the Hebrews. In fact, God called Ezekiel 'son of man' numerous times (Ezekiel 2:1) and called him Ezekiel only two times. The only difference with Jesus it was also one of the Messianic titles. It was Jesus' favorite designation, in referring to Himself, was the "Son of Man." The Gospels record some seventy-eight times that Jesus used this title for Himself. For example, when He asked His disciples the question about His identity (Matthew 16:13). The term "Son of man" implies His deity and His humanity as well depending on the context of the scriptures. For example, Daniel called the promised Messiah the Son of man: "In my vision at night I looked, and there before me was one like a son of man, [a] coming with the clouds of heaven. He approached the Ancient of Days and was led into his presence. He was given authority, glory and sovereign power; all nations and peoples of every language worshiped him. His dominion is an everlasting dominion that will not pass away, and his kingdom is one that will never be destroyed." (Daniel 7:13-14). Also, "And Jesus said, 'I am, and you will see the Son of Man seated at the right hand of Power, and coming with the clouds of heaven." (Matthew 24:30).

****

Is the Holy Spirit God? Jesus said that "Truly I tell you, the sons of men will be forgiven all sins and blasphemies, as many as they utter. But whoever blasphemes against the Holy Spirit will never be forgiven; he is guilty of eternal sin" (Mark 3:28-29). The word 'blasphemy' can only be applied to God. When Jesus said that whoever speaks evil against the Holy Spirit, it a blasphemy, He was emphasizing that the Holy Spirit is God!

Jesus meant that God the father appeared to Moses and handed him the Ten Commandment but you broke the covenant. God the Son came with the new covenant, and the message of salvation and you rejected Him. There is one last chance of the grace available for you when the gospel inspired by the Holy Spirit is preached. Rejecting the gospel means no more chance. Therefore blasphemy against the Holy Spirit means your fate is sealed eternally.

****

Somebody asked that, "So you mean that Jesus came as God and then he said he was God's son? Would that be a lie?" God's Son means in the nature of God. Compared to a dog producing after its nature a dog; a cat producing after its nature a cat: Look at this scripture: "I and my Father are one. Then the Jews took up stones again to stone him. Jesus answered them, Many good works have I shewed you from my Father; for which of those works do ye stone me? The Jews answered him, saying, For a good work we stone thee not; but for blasphemy; and because that thou, being a man, makest thyself God." (John 10:30-33). Jesus was persecuted and killed by people who denied that He was God as He claimed to be.

****

"Faith is not about knowing what the future holds but who holds the future "Time is divided in AD / BC, after Jesus Christ. The terms anno Domini (AD) and before Christ (BC) are used to label or number years in the Julian and Gregorian calendars. The term anno Domini is Medieval Latin and means "in the year of the Lord", but is often translated as "in the year of our Lord". The destiny of every human being that ever lived on this universe depends on this one man, Jesus Christ. As longer as you are still breathing and conscious, you still have a chance to receive Him as your personal Savior. Your defiance won't last for a long time and won't take you far. It is compared to trying to drive fast while at the same time your foot is pressing hard on the brakes!

****

Romans 1:18 - "For the wrath of God is revealed from heaven against all ungodliness and unrighteousness of men, who hold the truth in unrighteousness". A culture without the future locks God out. The consequence of which is living a life without purpose, and having a future without hope.

****

1 Peter 3:15 - "But sanctify the Lord God in your hearts: and be ready always to give an answer to every man that asketh you a reason of the hope that is in you with meekness and fear:" This is an apologetic calling to all believers intended to win souls. Our objective is not just to win an argument but to win a soul to Christ. Stand for the truth in love. If you do not do it in love, you may as well be against your apologetic.

****

Science now agrees with the Bible concerning the origin of life. The lead to a recent article in the U.K.'s Telegraph newspaper sums up a remarkable discovery by researchers at Northwestern University near Chicago: "Human life begins in bright flash of light as a sperm meets an egg, scientists have shown for the first time, after capturing the astonishing 'fireworks' on film. An explosion of tiny sparks erupts from the egg at the exact moment of conception." God's active act of creation, as described in Genesis 1, begins with those familiar words "Let there be light," or, as my Latin-loving colleagues prefer, "fiat lux." Throughout the Scriptures, God's presence and power is associated with light. This is most obviously true in all of the writings the Apostle John. 1 John tells us, "God is light and in Him there is no darkness at all." John specifically uses the metaphor of light to describe the life of Christ that is given to the fallen man as a divine act of regeneration. He says concerning Jesus that, "In him was life, and that life was the light of all mankind" (John 1:4).

****

The historical accuracy of the Bible: The Bible is the most accurate of ancient writings. There are 25,000 archaeological findings that back it up. There are nearly 25,000 manuscripts and portions of manuscripts that attest to its accuracy. There are several writings by scholars, who lived during the times of Jesus but were not followers of Christ supporting the biblical story of Jesus.

Acts 19 starts with Paul leaving Apollos in charge of the church in Corinth while he continues his missionary journey. It ends with Paul's encounter with an angry mob. But for the Gentiles, the problem was literally closer to home: their pocketbooks. What Acts calls "a serious disturbance" broke out when a silversmith named Demetrius told his fellow silversmiths that Paul's monotheism was bad for business. To understand why, it helps to understand what made Ephesus famous: a shrine to Artemis, also known as "Diana," the goddess associated with, among other things, childbirth, children, virginity and the hunt. Actually calling the temple to Artemis in Ephesus a "shrine" is a gross understatement. The temple was one of the Seven Wonders of the Ancient World. At 425 feet long by 200 feet wide, it was four times the size of the Parthenon. The structure was held by 127 columns that were 60 feet tall and 7 feet in diameter.

As the article shows, the account of Paul's adventures in Ephesus is filled with details that demonstrate intimate knowledge about Ephesus and its way of life. For instance, the reference to silversmiths. In 1984, a monument was discovered that corroborated Luke's account of their prominence in Ephesus. The inscription stated that the monument had been paid for by the silversmiths and called their city the "greatest metropolis of Asia, [and] the thrice-honored temple guardian of the venerable Ephesians."

In others words, theirs was a status quo worth rioting to preserve. Note that both the inscription and Acts 19 uses the same Greek word, neokoros, "guardian," in describing Ephesus's relationship to the temple cult.

Then there's the seemingly-obscure reference to "the great Artemis and of her image that fell from the sky." As Biblical Archaeological Review tells readers, "The origin of Ephesian Artemis is traditionally associated with a meteorite that was worshiped in early Ephesus."

As the article concludes, "Luke knew what he was talking about in recording the riot in the theater. His claim at the outset of the two-part work (Luke and Acts) to have 'investigated everything accurately and reported them orderly' is substantiated in Acts 19."

****

Seventy years ago, a Bedouin shepherd boy shattered those doubts when he threw a rock into a cave, breaking some clay pots containing the Dead Sea Scrolls. These ancient manuscripts of the Old Testament were near matches to the medieval text, confirming our modern Bible's antiquity and pushing the earliest known evidence for the Hebrew Scriptures back a millennium.

Now, thanks to another discovery on the shores of the Dead Sea, and an exciting technological breakthrough, that date has moved back even further. This story begins in 1970, when archaeologists at En-Gedi found a burnt scroll that was little more than a lump of charcoal. A fire in 600 AD had destroyed the synagogue there, leaving its ancient documents so brittle that a touch would cause them to disintegrate. Unable to read the scroll, curators merely preserved it, hoping that someday, the technology necessary to peek at its contents would be developed.

Well, that day has arrived. The New York Times reports that computer scientists at the University of Kentucky partnered with biblical scholars in Jerusalem to pioneer a technique for "unfurling" this badly-damaged scroll. Thanks to traces of metal in the ancient ink and a new method for reconstructing 3-D surfaces, known as "volume cartography," these scientists were able to read the charred parchment, without ever opening it.

The results were stunning. Dr. Michael Segal of the Hebrew University in Jerusalem marveled: "Much of the text is as readable, or close to as readable as actual unharmed Dead Sea Scrolls."

That text is the first two chapters of Leviticus—ironically, a set of instructions for burnt offerings to the Lord. But what's really amazing is that the fragment is identical—letter for letter—to the Masoretic text that forms the basis of modern Old Testament translations.

And how old is this incredibly accurate copy? Experts in Hebrew paleography say the script style strongly suggests an origin in the first century A.D., around the time of Christ. And that, reports the Times, would make it the oldest fragment of the Hebrew Pentateuch—aka, the first five books of the Bible—ever discovered.

"Never in our wildest dreams did we think anything would come of it," said Pnina Shor, head of the Dead Sea Scrolls Project at the Israeli Antiquities Authority. Yet despite being burnt itself, this chapter about burnt offerings is now as visible to us as it was to the scribe who copied it two-thousand years ago. (As narrated by Eric Metaxas).

****

The Bible is not just another book. It is unique – it's a diverse collection of 66 thoroughly harmonious books with one single theme that contains a broad variety of genres: historical, narrative, epic, law, poetry, prophecy, wisdom, gospel, apocalyptic and letters. Many Christians are not aware of this fact, let alone non-believers. The Bible was written over a span of 1500 years, by 40 different authors, yet without contradictions. These authors came from a variety of backgrounds: shepherds, fishermen, doctors, kings, prophets, tax collectors and scholars. Most of these authors never knew one another personally. To be certain, not one had a Facebook account, Myspace page or a blog to collaborate with fellow co-conspirators on a "fake left, go Divine" book of the ages. There many factors supporting that the Bible is inspired Word of God. There are 353 prophecies accurately fulfilled in Jesus Christ. The Bible has survived centuries of persecution.

****

Somebody asked that "If there are no contradictions in the Bible why is the number of angels at the tomb of Jesus different in the accounts of the Gospels?" Angels are personal spiritual beings who appear in the physical realm to humans at their will. There might be multitudes of angels surrounding you but you can see only those who choose to appear to you. One must see two, and another three depending on their manifestations but there always a lot more than what you can see.

****

If Jude quoted Enoch why don't we read the book of Enoch? The scripture reads: "And to these also Enoch, the seventh from Adam, prophesied, saying, 'Behold, the Lord came with ten thousands of his holy ones, to execute judgment upon all, and to convict all the ungodly of all their works of ungodliness which they have wrought, and of all the hard things which ungodly sinners have spoken against him'" (Jude 14-15). Observe further, by way of contrast, what is not contained in this text. Nothing is said about a "book of Enoch." There is no phrase such as, "it is written in the book of Enoch." Nothing at all is indicated about any literary production. The book of Enoch is not credible. The book of Jude is a powerful little treatise that warns the children of God of the dangers of apostasy from the faith.

****

The beauty of nature reveals the wisdom of the Creator. By observing stars that are invisible except during an eclipse, astronomers were able to watch the sun bend their light, making them appear out of place in the sky, and confirming Einstein's prediction. Einstein's theory of relativity, predicted that gravity bends light. Eclipses were also how man first observed solar flares and coronal mass ejections on the surface of the sun. These phenomena are normally invisible to the naked eye, but appear briefly around the edges of the moon during an eclipse. It turns out the conditions for this dazzling display are incredibly rare. The moon has to be just the right size, orbiting a planet just the right distance from its host star. And it so happens that although the sun is 400 times bigger than the moon, it's also (coincidence?) 400 times further from us, meaning that the two objects appear roughly the same size in the sky. This allows the moon to block the sun in precisely the right way for scientists to study the solar atmosphere.

****

The human heart is a factory for all kinds of evil—including the evil of racism (see Jeremiah 17:9 and Matthew 15:18–19). Still, while Darwin certainly didn't invent racism, his ideology of evolution has fostered it. Consider the case of Ota Benga—a pygmy from Central Africa, who in 1906 was caged in the Bronx Zoo with an orangutan. Remember the Jews in the gas chambers devised by Hitler to advance the Aryan "master race." Reflect on the Australian aborigines hunted down in the 1800s by evolutionists in search of the "missing link."

****

If there are other ways to Heaven, then why would God send His Son to die? The ultimate truth based on the biblical truth is that Jesus is the only way to heaven (John 14:16). The truth is embraced by all (regardless of their religious background), who make a decision to receive Jesus as their Lord and Savior. Nobody is born from their mothers' womb when they are children of God. We choose to be born of God, the Father, through Jesus Christ. The Bible says that when you shall know the truth, the truth shall set you free (John 8:32). Our priority is not to fill the pews with people but to fill the pulpit with the truth. We must stand for conviction even when it hurts those close to us. "It is better to tell the truth that hurts but heals than to tell the lie that comforts but kills." It is better to stand alone on the truth

than to be wrong with multitudes. Those who go to heaven are modeled after Christ. "For we are God's handiwork, created in Christ Jesus to do good works, which God prepared in advance for us to do" (Ephesians 2:10).
****

Humanism says that the truth depends on man. Relativism says that the only truth you can know for sure is that there is nothing for sure. On the contrary, Christianity maintains that there is an absolute truth that does not depend on human opinion. Jesus said that, "To this end was I born, and for this cause came I into the world, that I should bear witness unto the truth. Every one that is of the truth heareth my voice" (John 18:37).

****

Somebody asked that, "Why do you think that Christianity is different from other religions?" The world religions (apart from Christianity) worship the impersonal gods. They want a god made in man's image instead of a man made in God's image. Christians are worshippers of a personal God. I mean the God that left eternity and stepped into time and space to relate to us and save us. All religions of the world (apart from Christianity) trust in their abilities to clean up their mess (sins) and be accepted by God. Yet they acknowledge that nobody is perfect! I wish they knew the consequences of not being perfect. But Christians believe that no man can clean himself and be sinless. They invest their faith in Jesus Christ to clean up their past, present, and future sins, and to present them before God the Father in His very perfectness. Jesus teaches His followers to obey not as a means of earning salvation but in order to maintain the already established communication with the perfect God.

****

What influence did the exhibition of the scars on the hands and feet of Jesus (John 20:21-29) have upon His disciples? Secondly, why is it that Jesus Christ, now in heaven, bears with him the scars on his resurrected body? Wounds are the triumph marks of the intruder but scars are the triumph marks of the victor. Christ wears His scars on His body in heaven as his ornaments of glory. They are His trophies—the trophies of His sacrificial love. It is because of His scars that Death sucked in its own death, and hell was destroyed. The scars on his body signify that by His stripes we were healed and we are whole. Jesus put on mortality so that we might put on immortality (John 11:26). We, whom He saved, we will never know what hell is like but the scars of Jesus will remind us that hell is real and we will recall what He saved us from. It is an eternal reminder that Jesus is the Savior! If you rejected Him, those scars on His body will be witnesses against you.

****

You've probably heard the phrase "he's my right-hand man" but where does this phrase come from? During my youthful times, to be left handed incited cordial hatred. It was considered to be disgraceful to receive something from somebody when using your left hand. No wonder the teachers, beginning from the elementary grade, were sanctioned to rectify the defect with an iron hand. The words "right hand" occur 166 times in the Bible so it is no accident that the words "right hand" are used. The words have significant meaning. God inspired Isaiah to write "For I, the Lord your God, hold your right hand; it is I who say to you, "Fear not, I am the one who helps you" (Isaiah 41:13). We cast out fear by our awareness of our surrounding. He that is for us is greater than those against us. God raised [Christ] from the dead and seated Him at his right hand in the heavenly places. The right hand signifies strength, blessings, and protection (Luke 20:42-43). He put all things under his feet and gave Him as head over all things to the church, which is his body, the fullness of him who fills all in all."- Ephesians 1:20–23. All of His enemies are being put under His feet as His gospel is preached and His kingdom expands (1 Cor. 15:20–28).

****

Somebody asked that "If Adam knew good and bad after sinning why did God give us the Ten Commandments?" When God made Adam and Eve he said they could eat anything except from the tree of knowledge of good and evil. It seems like the tree granted the knowledge of bad. Adam and Eva experientially knew good because when they were in the Garden of Eden everything was "very good" (Genesis 1:31). It wasn't the evil side of tree of the knowledge of good and evil that Eva was attacked to but the good side of the tree: "When the woman saw that the fruit of the tree was good for food and pleasing to the eye, and also desirable for gaining wisdom, she took some and ate it. She also gave some to her husband, who was with her, and he ate it (Genesis 3:6). But Adam and Eva did not know of evil experientially until after their disobedience.

Before sin, Adam depended on the revealed truth from God and obeyed God's prohibition. Adam had a free will to choose from good and bad but evil was outside him, embodied in the serpent. The serpent was not a creature of the Garden but of the wilderness outside the Garden of Eden. Partaking of the Tree of Knowledge was the beginning of the mixture of good and evil together in man. Before that time, the two were separate, and evil had only a nebulous existence in potential. The consequence of sin (death) terminated the fellowship and communication between God and Adam. When they were expelled from the Garden, the corrupted human conscience replaced the conviction by God. Then good and evil were determined by the corrupted minds according to the human standards instead of the divine. God gave the Moral Law to man to reveal His standard of righteousness. The Law represents everything Adam lost before becoming corrupted by sin. Obeying the entire Law was a condition to restore the broken communication between God and man. The Law causes us to flee to the salvation that God has given us through Jesus Christ because no man was able to keep the whole Law, in their lifetime, without a possibility of breaking one of the laws. Jesus saves us from the consequences of our sins and restores our lost relationship and fellowship with God.

****

Genesis 3:6 - "When the woman saw that the fruit of the tree was good for food and pleasing to the eye, and also desirable for gaining wisdom, she took some and ate it. She also gave some to her husband, who was with her, and he ate it". It wasn't the evil side of the tree of the knowledge of good and evil that Eva was attracted to but the good side of the tree. We are vulnerable because sin corrupted our emotions. Learning to recognize the signs of damaged emotions allows you to identify problems sooner and alter the behaviors that perpetuate them. On the contrary, making choices out of emotions leads to deception. Most times the things appealing to our emotions are not necessarily good as they appear to be. Everything which glitters like gold is not necessarily precious. There are utterly valueless things that look like gold and taking them on their face value is unwise. Goodness and perfection do not go with gaudiness.

****

Somebody asked, "What is the difference between the old covenant and the new covenant?" The word 'covenant' is also translated as testament. Both the old and new covenants are about the holiness of God. Both covenants demand from man the holiness of God, but in the new covenant, God provides to man the means of acquiring God's holiness to the satisfaction of God. Basically, the new covenant is sealed in the old, and the old is revealed in the new. The old (Moses - Law) prepared man to enter into the Promised Land. The new (Joshua – Grace) ushered man into the Promised Land (salvation). The new covenant is a completion of the old covenant that Yahweh made with the Jews. Essentially, the old and the new are one covenant, but with several distinct connotations; it is a sacred agreement instituted by God in the person of Christ. "Mercy and truth are met together; righteousness and peace have kissed each other" (Psalm 85:10). Jesus came to fulfill the old covenant, not to destroy it (Matthew 5:17-18). In this case, 'fulfill' means to satisfy its demands.

****

Somebody asked that "My pastor does not believe in reading from the Old Testament. What is your view?" The Bible is the Word of God from cover to cover. I want to radically say that even the covers are part of the Bible. "The new is in the old concealed; the old is in the new revealed." This famous statement by Saint Augustine expresses the remarkable way in which the two testaments of the Bible are so closely interrelated with each other. The key to understanding the New Testament in its fullest is to see in it the fulfillment of those things that were revealed in the background of the Old Testament. The Old Testament points forward in time, preparing God's people for the work of Christ in the New Testament. I suggest that the Old Testament scriptures should be interpreted in the light of the four Gospels. When we read the Gospels, we are privileged to hear the author of the Scriptures (God) rightly interpreting them to us.

****

"Now we'll be told that truth and love cannot really fit together, that we choose one at the expense of the other. We must not allow that thinking in our hearts and minds. Jesus Christ, the center of history, is Himself truth and is Himself love. The tension between the two is resolved in Him."

****

The tabernacle and later the temple represented God's presence with Israel. There was a cloud above the tabernacle signifying the presence of God. Whenever the Israelites saw the temple, they could feel the comforting hand of God wrapping around them. They could hear God saying that "You are not alone; I am with you here". Jesus said that He is the true temple. Jesus came to glorify the Father. The Holy Spirit is to us everything that Jesus was to His disciples during His earthly ministry. The Holy Spirit glorifies the Father. Jesus said that He will not leave us as orphans, He will send the Holy Spirit to comfort us. He said that He will be with us up to the uttermost ends of the world. The Holy Spirit wraps His arms around us; He is God with us.

****

Somebody asked "Why are the preachers of today obsessed with hell? I am Jehovah Witness. We don't believe in hell." First of all, our believing or not believing in something does not make that particular thing to exist. It is either there or not there regardless of our beliefs. The Jehovah's Witnesses believe death is a state of non-existence with no consciousness. They say that there is no Hell of fiery torment; Hades and Sheol are understood to refer to the condition of death, termed the common grave. Contrary,

Jesus talked more about hell than about any other topic. Amazingly, of the 1,850 verses in the New Testament that record Jesus' words, 13 percent of his sayings are about hell and judgment. Hell is God's way of purging this universe of sin. We cannot get around this fact. The Jehovah's Witnesses are considered to be a cult because they deny the central teachings of the Bible. They deny that Jesus Christ is God. Instead, they teach that Jesus Christ is a created angel. Jesus said that there cannot be salvation without acknowledging who He is (John 8:24). They deny the bodily resurrection of Jesus Christ. Instead, they teach that Jesus' body was dissolved into gasses. Charles Taze Russell, founder of the organization taught, "The man Jesus is dead, forever dead" (Studies in the Scriptures, Vol. 5, 1899, p. 454). Without the resurrection of Jesus, His death has no meaning! The Jehovah's Witnesses deny the Holy Spirit is God. Instead, they teach that the Holy Spirit is an impersonal force, like electricity. I advise you to put aside the Watch Tower Bible, which is opinionated biased commentary on the Scriptures, and read the real Bible translation for the sake of your soul.

****

Somebody asked that, "How can Satan accuse us before God when he was kicked out of heaven?" Satan's fall from heaven is symbolically described in Isaiah 14:12-14 and Ezekiel 28:12-18. These passages describe why Satan fell, but they do not specifically say when the fall occurred. What we do know is this: the angels were created before the earth (Job 38:4-7). Satan fell before he tempted Adam and Eve in the Garden (Genesis 3:1-14). The book of Job tells us, at least at that time, Satan still had access to heaven and to the throne of God. "One day the angels came to present themselves before the LORD, and Satan also came with them. The LORD said to Satan, 'Where have you come from?' Satan answered the LORD, 'From roaming through the earth and going back and forth in it'" (Job 1:6-7). Satan was dethroned from his original duties in heaven but he was sent to earth as a negative force to test our loyalty to God. Without the cross we wouldn't know of the unconditional love of God. For it is not a big deal for someone to love the people who love them. But it is amazing grace for God to love his enemies to, and give His begotten Son to die for them so that they might be saved. On the other hand, Satan presents to us emotionally appealing things like traditions and religions, which we value much but we must give up in exchange for loyalty to God. Satan's work on earth is not accidental; it is sanctioned by God for such a period of time. God gives us a protective mechanism to overcome Satan. Remember that Satan is a creation and he has no power over God. The name of Jesus given to us is the power of the divine.

****

Somebody asked me to clarify on the grace. Everybody knows that grace is the unmerited favor of God. But this is not all that grace is. Often, I am tempted to believe that the grace cannot be fully contained in our finite minds, in the same manner, we cannot contain God in our tiny minds. My professor used to compare various definitions of the grace to three blind men who were asked to define an elephant by touching it. One blind man touched the trunk and came to the conclusion that an elephant is like a tree. The second blind man touched the belly and said that "Now I know an elephant is like a huge wall." The third blind man touched the tail and said, "I am convinced that an elephant looks like a rope". None of the three blind men had the true definition of the elephant. The grace is much bigger than we tend to define it. Everything that God does for a fallen man is by His grace. The best definition of the grace is that it is the divine influence on the human heart: The grace transforms the heart by the Holy Spirit. Then the grace sanctifies the human heart by teaching us to obey the commandments of God. Jesus divided the Ten Commandments into two parts – Loving God and loving your neighbor (Matthew 22:37-40). Because the first four commandments define how to love God, and the last six define how to love your neighbor. I want to emphasize that we are justified by grace alone (not by our works), but we are called to grow in the grace (2 Peter 3:18). Our good works are the proof that we are saved. Remember that salvation is divided into three parts – Justification (by faith in the finished works of Jesus); sanctification (God working with man's obedience to clean the minds); glorification (by God).

****

Somebody asked "Paul wrote one-third of the New Testament. My friend who is critical of the Bible uses Peter's warning in 2 Peter 3:16 to justify his criticism. What can I say to him?" The scripture says that: "Paul also wrote you with the wisdom God gave him. He writes this way in all his letters, speaking in them about such matters. Some parts of his letters are hard to understand, which ignorant and unstable people distort, as they do the rest of the Scriptures, to their own destruction." Peter says that Paul was moved by God to write. Peter has no problem with what Peter wrote but he has a problem with the readers that misinterpret Paul's writings for their destruction. As Paul was moved by God, we need to be moved by the Holy Spirit to understand what he wrote. Peter warned the people who took the grace for granted in form of a license to be disobedient to God. Paul never instructed us to ignore the Ten Commandments. Exegesis is a critical explanation or interpretation of a text. The best way to rightly divide the Scriptures is to use other scriptures to interpret your scripture. You don't have to go outside the Scriptures to find out what is inside the Scriptures. Paul emphasizes internal holiness unto the Lord that manifested by external obedience. Throughout his epistles he is defining how to live holy without breaking God's commandment: He teaches how to worship God, honoring God, honoring parents, not stealing, not committing adultery, not to tell lies, and etc. The grace of God teaches us to be obedient and covers for the consequences of our disobedience.

****

1 Corinthians 12:3 – "Therefore I inform you that no one who is speaking by the Spirit of God says, "Jesus be cursed," and no one can say, "Jesus is Lord," except by the Holy Spirit." The spirit of deception rejects the Lordship of Jesus. But the Spirit of God acknowledges the Lordship of Jesus. Acknowledging is not mere reciting but it is the conviction brought about by the Holy Spirit. Every person can be convicted depending on their beliefs but the Holy Spirit convicts with the gospel, purposely, to save and to clean the conscience. The Word of God is the absolute standard of righteousness. Jesus said that the Holy Spirit will testify on His behalf: "But the Advocate, the Holy Spirit, whom the Father will send in my name, will teach you all things and will remind you of everything I have said

to you" (John 14:26). Therefore cursing Jesus is rejecting the conviction of the Holy Spirit to be saved because Jesus is the substance for salvation.

****

Religions are the invented human organized institution to mobilize us to worship, but not a means of reaching God. God created a place for Himself to be worshiped and that place will crave for other things till the rightful occupier is found. The word 'God' means the creator of all things. He did not create the universe and stayed anonymous. There is a label of trademark on each and every creation pointing to Him. Also, He revealed the way (Jesus) to know Him.

****

Somebody asked that, "Why did God instruct Noah to take with him seven pairs of all clean animals, the male and his mate, and a pair (two) of every kind of unclean animal?" The reason God instructed Noah to take in the clean animals in a bigger number (seven pairs of clean animals) is because they were needed for sacrifice (Genesis 8:20). Later on, after the flood, the clean animals were suitable for consumption (Genesis 9:3).

****

Somebody asked, "Is it a sin for women to wear short hair and pants?" I want to say that the Bible is against men behaving like women and women behaving like men. God made it very clear that women are to "act feminine" and dress modestly (Deuteronomy 22: 5). There is nothing wrong when a woman wears the ladies' pants, designed for ladies. Remember that during biblical times, Jewish men wore robes cloaks and coats and wrapped rags inside to cover their loins and their thighs completely. Paul wrote that "I also want the women to dress modestly, with decency and propriety, adorning themselves, not with elaborate hairstyles or gold or pearls or expensive clothes" (1 Timothy 2:9). Did Paul mean that wearing jewelry (gold rings, necklaces, and earrings) is a sin? No! Peter, who wrote later on after Paul defined Paul's instruction in this way: "Your beauty should not come from outward adornment, such as elaborate hairstyles and the wearing of gold jewelry or fine clothes. Rather, it should be that of your inner self, the unfading beauty of a gentle and quiet spirit, which is of great worth in God's sight" (1 Peter 3:3-4). Peter elaborated that our primary focus should be put on internal cleanness as opposed to the external beauty that is fading away. This means you can take care of your hair but don't waste all the time on the hair and forget your spiritual well-being. Do not covet the opposite sex, and do not be seductive to the opposite sex.

****

Do you know that according to Hebrew history, Abraham was 137 years-old and Isaac was about 36 years-old when they ascended to Mount Moriah to worship God? Abraham volunteered to sacrifice his son Isaac, and Isaac volunteered to be bound as the burnt sacrifice because he did not resist his father act which literally looked like human sacrificing.

****

Somebody asked that, "Didn't Jesus preach violence in Matthew 10:34?" Jesus said that "Think not that I am come to send peace on earth: I came not to send peace, but a sword." During biblical times, people had a ritual of exchanging the swords when they were establishing a covenant of peace between two parties. The exchange of the swords was symbolic of exchanging foes: "Your enemies become my enemies." I think it is from this background that Jesus said that "I came to bring sword". Jesus meant that His enemies will be our enemies. Even your close relatives might decide to disown you or persecute you the moment you are converted to follow Jesus.

****

Somebody asked that "Hitler burned millions in the oven and they called him a sociopath. Why should God be called a loving God when He is sending billions to burn in hell forever?" The holy God is justified to send all sinners to hell because it is the righteous means of getting rid of the dented and unwanted souls from the face of the earth. Hell is a pit compared to the jails of this world where the offenders are incarcerated for the safety of the public. God is preparing a new world (regenerated souls and new city coming down from heaven) that is not corrupted by sin. Hell is a place reserved for the fallen angels and the souls which rejected the salvation of God. The killings by Hitler were unjustified killings. God's righteous judgment demands death to every soul corrupted by sin. For God to save one soul that deserved not to be saved is amazing grace!

****

Somebody asked a question: "A friend told me that unless you have the faith, to believe for a Physical Healing, God 'will not or won't be able' to heal you. I personally believe it is true to a certain extent, however, is that not works? And just for the record; the account of "Lazarus" won't be considered as an example. Thanks for posting supporting scripture. Answer: Psalms 103: - "Praise the Lord, my soul, and forget not all his benefits— who forgives all your sins and heals all your diseases. Jesus atoned for our sins and our infirmities. Sickness is the byproduct of sin leading to death. We shall never be condemned for the same sins for which Jesus died. Also, we shall put off the corrupt bodies in exchange with the incorruptible bodies at the resurrection. God heals us in the same way he forgives our sins. It is by His grace alone. Our faith connects us to God's provision. The Bible says that everyone is given a measure of faith. Faith is, therefore, a gift from God that must be nurtured to maturity. The divine healing of our physical bodies in this world depends on the will and timing of God. When people are not healed it is not because of lack of faith. Look at the miracles of Jesus in the four Gospels. The majority of the people who were healed did not even ask for healing. Some were taken by friends, whereas others were healed because Jesus had compassion on them. Jesus performed other miracles to teach His disciple some moral lessons. Again, I believe in divine healing but the ultimate healing is in future when all believers will put on the incorruptible bodies.

****

Somebody asked that, "Why did Jesus heal and forbade the people He healed to tell others?" There are two reasons. The first one is that He did not want to stir up the public and incite them to crown Him prematurely before His prophesized time at Calvary had come. We know that the miracle of Lazarus provoked the crowds to want to crown Jesus at the triumph entry in Jerusalem. The second reason is because His message of deliverance was not yet complete. The real atonement for our sins and sicknesses took place at the cross. After resurrection, Jesus, sent His disciple to go all the way to the utter most ends of the world telling all people what He has done. It is called the Great Commission.

****

Somebody asked, "Why did Jesus perform the miracles?" I am going to answer with the help of the scriptures. Jesus said that, "For the works that the Father has given Me to accomplish--the very works I am doing--testify about Me that the Father has sent Me" (John 5:36). The miracles were done to testify that Jesus is the promised Messiah. John said that the miracles of Jesus were written to us so that we might believe in Jesus as our Savior: "Jesus performed many other signs in the presence of His disciples, which are not written in this book. 31But these are written so that you may believe that Jesus is the Christ, the Son of God, and that by believing you may have life in His name" (John 20:31). Jesus performed miracles for the following reasons: 1) To prove His identity. 2) Out of compassion. 3) To teach us some moral lessons.

****

Luke 5:8 – "When Simon Peter saw this, he fell at Jesus' knees and said, "Go away from me, Lord; I am a sinful man!" We have a built in allergy to sovereignty" - R. C. Sproul

****

Somebody asked that "Why are there so many hypocrites in the Church who pretend to be perfect?" A hypocrite is a person that pretends to be something that he is not or behaving in a way that suggests one has higher standards or more noble beliefs than is the case. The word "perfect" when used in reference to God it means holy (sinless), but when used in reference to man it means complete. Jesus makes us perfect (complete). There is no such a thing as a sinless human being apart from Jesus Christ who is God/man. The Church is made up of repented sinners, who were transformed, and called out of the corrupt world to embrace the kingdom of God (under God's rule). These are sinners who accepted forgiveness and whose target is the righteousness of God. At times, they fail to hit their intended target (it is called sin), but the grace of God covers their failures. The world can judge them as hypocrites but God will never condemn them because Jesus was condemned for their sins.

****

Somebody made this comment: "I don't go to the Pentecostal Churches because the pastors are fake." I replied: Fake money is made after real money. You don't reject all the money just because there is fake money in circulation. You look for genuine one. The same applies to pastors.

****

Oneness Pentecostalism denies the triune nature of God. According to this theology, God is not three distinct persons in one. He is not the Father, and the Son, and the Holy Spirit (Matthew 28:19). God simply has different "moods," sometimes manifesting himself as a Son, sometimes as a Father (Isaiah 9:6 is the passage they use to justify this belief), and sometimes as the Spirit (most often referred to by Onenists as the Holy Ghost). This teaching also called Modalism or Sabellianism, goes back to the false teacher, Sabellius, in third century Rome. Tertullian called it "Patripassianism" from the Latin words for "father" and "to suffer," because it implied that God the Father suffered on the cross. Sabellius taught that God the Father was the only true manifestation of the Godhead. Modern Modalists will say that God is only Jesus. T.D. Jakes is perhaps the most famous Modalist of today.

****

Somebody asked that "Why believe in the Catholic doctrine of the trinity?" The word trinity does not appear in the bible but its meaning is everywhere in the Bible. Trinity is a Latin word meaning three. There are many other Latin words we use in our language because the Roman Empire had a big influence in the early church. In fact, the word Catholic is a Latin word simply meaning the universal church. But later on, it was called 'Roman Catholic' due to the impact of Rome and their doctrines, some of which were not biblical. God is one but in a team of three persons. The Bible refers to the Father as God; the Son as God and the Holy Spirit as God. It is not coincidence that man was created in God's image as a triune – spirit, soul, and body; family is divided into three parts – husband, wife, and children; matter was created in three parts - solid, liquid, and gas; an atom is divided into three parts - a nucleus of protons and neutrons; time is divided into three parts - past, present and future; the end time adversary is divided into three parts – Satan, antichrist, and the false prophet.

****

Never be afraid to be a Christian just because there are many hypocrites in churches. The fact that there are fake people is the reality of the genuine. They don't counterfeit the worthless but the worthiness.

****

Somebody asked, "Does this world belong to Satan?" No. This world belongs to our Father (God). However, Satan controls the system (values) upon which this world operates. Satan corrupted mankind in order to control this world. That is why Satan is called the god of this world (2 Corinthians 4:4). Definitely, those who are idolizing things of the world, worship Satan, whether they know it or not. Jesus defeated Satan, and He is the rightful owner of this world. He came to establish the kingdom of God on the earth. The kingdom of God is in the past, present and future. Your choice is either Jesus or the world; you can't be neutral or stand on the fence because Satan owns the fence.

****

Somebody asked that "If Jesus defeated Satan why do Christians say that they are still fighting a spiritual war?" True, Jesus defeated Satan when

He defeated death. The spiritual warfare is not between us and Satan but between the corrupt nature and the corrupt world. We are vulnerable to Satan because he corrupted our human nature and the world. Satan is called the prince of the air and of this world because he established the system and the principles on which this world operates. His influence also encompasses the world's philosophies, education, and commerce. The thoughts, ideas, speculations and false religions of the world are under his control and have sprung from his lies and deceptions. We are exposed to them and we resist them daily. That is why the Bible says that we are in this world but not of this world (2 Cor. 4:4). We physically live in this world but by faith, we live in eternity. We die physically but with hope. So, when the Bible says that Satan is the "god of this world," it is not saying that he has ultimate authority. It is conveying the idea that Satan rules over the unbelieving world in a specific way. Satan sets the agenda which the unbelieving world follows, and mankind continues to be deceived. We are in spiritual warfare not against flesh and blood but against powers and principalities that exalt themselves against God. The good news is that we fight from victory to victory. How do you like to go to war with victory already on your belt? We fight Satan by fleeing to Jesus where victory is. He gives us His armor of victory. As long as we are in Christ's armor, we are not worried of Satan.

****

Somebody asked that "Where did pain come from?" God cursed this body of sin (physical body) to die the day Adam sinned. As for Eva God added pain experience when she is giving birth. Pain or sickness is death in slow motion. It is experienced by every person born after Adam. The good news is that a born again believer has a new nature that has passed over death!

****

Judges 21:25 – "In those days there was no king in Israel: every man did that which was right in his own eyes." Israel was a theocracy. God ruled Israel directly - the nation was unified through the Torah. God's plan was to use judges as overseers over Israel as opposed to kings because God was

118

the King. The book of Judges records Israel's progressive unfaithfulness and refusal to live as God intended. God established a visible structure, the tabernacle, and later the temple to centralize the worship. He chose a place (Jerusalem) and put His name on it (2 Chronicles 6:6). The most significant thing about Jerusalem is the temple. The most significant thing about the temple is that it is the dwelling place of God. Jesus said that He is the true temple (John 2:19-21) Jesus predicted the destruction of the temple at Jerusalem (Matthew 24:1-25; 46) because its role had ended with the old covenant. The prophetic words of Jesus came to pass when Jerusalem was plundered by the Romans in AD 70. The Jewish people migrated to Europe and North Africa. 10 Bible prophecies were fulfilled at midnight May 14th, in 1948 when Israel became an independent, united nation for the second time in history, and for the first time in 2,900 years. Interestingly, Israel controls Jerusalem but the Temple Mountain is still in the hands of the gentiles (Arabs).

****

Somebody asked that, "Does the Bible say anything about Islam?" I have tried to read through the prophetic scriptures but found none directly referring to Islam, except this one verse: "You who have escaped the sword, leave and do not linger! Remember the LORD in a distant land, and call to mind Jerusalem." (Jeremiah 51:50). I know from history that Israel has been a traditional enemy of Islam because they refused to accept Muhammad as a prophet. The sword has been used throughout the history of Islam to forcefully convert people. The sword is an icon of conquering among Muslims.

****

Somebody asked, "Do Muslims worship the same God as we do?" Christians don't worship the same God as Moslems. The God of the Bible has the Son called Jesus Christ. The god of Islam doesn't have a Son, and even the thought of that would be sacrilegious to Muslims. The God of the Bible sent His Son to the earth to die in our place to save us from our sins. The god of Islam requires you to die for him to be sure that you go to heaven.

****

Orlando massacre has once again shown that the terrorists are prepared to stop at nothing in creating human victims. The weakness of the terrorists is that they are fighting from the point of hate. On the contrary, we are called to fight with love to preserve our values, as opposed to violence and revenge. Love is the greatest power. God is Love, and all things are held together by the power of His love. Christianity propagates to win the world by the power of love. The gospel is the story of love. When you receive Jesus, love finds you, attends you, and blesses you so that you become a blessing to others. The return of love received is the beginning of the process of sanctification. Through the gospel, the Holy Spirit helps us to build the bridge of love together for others to cross over to eternity.

****

Somebody asked that "Doesn't the Bible, in Leviticus 20:13, say that homosexuals should be put to death?" True, the Old Testament condemned the people involved in all kinds of adulterous relationship and idolatry to be stoned to death. Given the fact, according to Galatians 3:24, the Mosaic Law was instituted as a schoolmaster or tutor to train the Israelites into obedience to the coming Messiah. One of the ways Jesus fulfilled the Law is by rightly interpreting it for us. He taught the Law with authority as the Lawgiver. For example "You have heard that it was said, 'Eye for eye and tooth for tooth.' But I tell you not to resist an evil person. If someone slaps you on your right cheek, turn to him the other also" (Matthew 5:38-39). When the woman who was caught in adultery was brought to Him, instead of prescribing to her the capital punishment, Jesus said that: "Let him who has no sin cast the first stone." All of her accusers walked away, and Jesus said, "Neither do I condemn you" (John 8:11). Jesus came not to condemn the world but to save it (John 3:16-17). The Law teaches us to identify sin. But the grace teaches us to obey and helps us to get rid of sin at the expense of Christ's sufferings and death. Therefore, the Old Testament should be interpreted by the New Testament for us to implement.

****

Enock Bugimbi responded to the above posting: "But Sodom and Gomorrah was destroyed because of homosexual" My Reply: True, but God alone can and will condemn all sins. The Second Coming of Jesus is the Day of God's vengeance and wrath against all sins including homosexuals. If you were judged in Christ you don't need to worry because you were saved from God's wrath against sin. The Bible says that, "Do you not know that the wicked will not inherit the kingdom of God? Do not be deceived: Neither the sexually immoral, nor idolaters, nor adulterers, nor men who submit to nor perform homosexual acts, nor thieves, nor the greedy, nor drunkards, nor verbal abusers, nor swindlers, will inherit the kingdom of God" (1 Corinthians 6:9-10).

****

Jesus told the woman that was caught in adultery that "Now" go and sin no more" (John 8:11). The words of Jesus are given in the imperative form. Jesus basically instructed her not to continue sinning, by embracing His ministry of the grace. This time, Jesus was her Savior but in future He will be the ultimate judge to condemn her for her sins unless she repents. Repenting is completely turning around from your ways and turning to God's ways. No matter how disappointing you believe your life currently is, it is never too late to let Jesus reshape it into an amazing testimony!

****

Somebody asked "Some Christians go for plastic surgeries; why do they consider transgender to be a sin?" Transgender people are people who experience a mismatch between their gender identity, or gender expression, and their assigned sex. They are sometimes called transsexual if they desire medical assistance to transition from one sex to another. Transgenderism is a concept of "gender fluidity," or the belief that one can "choose" their gender. I believe that we do not have the right to choose our gender, in the same way, we can't choose our race. Transsexual involves genital mutilation. The Bible says that "No one who has been emasculated by crushing or cutting may enter the assembly of the LORD" (Deuteronomy 23:1). I want to add that switching your genitals does not change your gender. You are a male with or without the male genitals. According to history, some men serving at the courts of the kings became eunuchs in order for them to be fully devoted to their duties. The eunuchs were castrated (had their sexual organs removed) but they were still men. Rejecting your gender is an insult to God. It is yapping to God that "You made a mistake to create me this way." Never seek to be somebody else, be proud that you are the only you God made...

****

Somebody asked that "If Jesus was here today, will He be on Facebook?" It is not a coincidence that Jesus came to this world during the era of the Romans, at the peak of their civilization. The Romans ruled the known world. Rome was the center of the world communication as the Internet is today. There is this old adage: "All roads lead to Rome". Paul's ministry was mainly centered in the synagogues and marketplaces because that is where people were gathered. We don't choose where to be or go but God sends us where people are. The internet provides an opportunity to pass on a message to friends, strangers, and the world at large. It's worth saying that the internet itself is neither good nor bad. It is how people use it that determines whether it is an effective force for good or bad. I compare it to going to the beach. People go to the beaches with different motives. Some go to have fresh air and to swim whereas others go with lustful intentions to look at half naked ladies. The issue is not that you are at the beach but why are you there. Jesus defined sin in intents as opposed to actions (Matthew 5:21-22; Matthew 5:27-28; Mark 12:43-44). The Bible says that "A good man brings good things out of the good stored up in his heart, and an evil man brings evil things out of the evil stored up in his heart. For the mouth speaks what the heart is full of" (Luke 6:45).

****

The Bible is the only book that calls God's name 'Love.' Other religious books call Him just a god of mercy. When mercy is the primary cause of salvation there is a subtle touch of reciprocation. Mercy is initiated by the condition of the recipient. When one great sinner finds mercy, another great sinner (who is without awareness of an awful guilt in having sinned against a Holy and Righteous God) is encouraged to hope that he may also find mercy. On the contrary, it is not mercy that moved God but the enduring love of God caused God to move in the direction of mercy and grace. Love caused Him to exercise mercy and grace. Love is the heart of the gospel call. Salvation stems from the love of God, however, God does not save by His love but by His grace. God did not so love the world that He saved the world — He didn't do that. God so loved the world that by His mercy He provided a Savior for the world. By grace, He can now save without contradicting His character and attributes. God is committed to saving a sinner on account of who He is as opposed to what we are. John wrote: "Grace, mercy, and peace from God the Father and from Jesus Christ, the Father's Son, will be with us in truth and love" (2 John 1:3). The Grace of Jesus - the way God saves you; the mercy of God- which provided a Savior; the peace of God - the condition of the redeemed. When you have all this, then the peace of God that passeth all understanding is going to keep your heart - this being the evidence that you are saved. The last part of the scripture says that everything is given in truth and love. Salvation is the unconditional love of God but the grace is given on God's terms as opposed to your terms. Why? Because God is sovereign and He is the center of the universe, and you are not.

****

Uwase Daphine made this comment: "Muslims are the peaceful and Sympathetic people in this Holly Month". My reply: God seeks the holiness of His Son (Jesus) in us, nothing less and nothing more. The Pharisees were the most righteous people during the biblical times but Jesus taught that, "For I tell you that unless your righteousness surpasses that of the Pharisees and the teachers of the law, you will certainly not enter the kingdom of heaven." (Matthew 5:20). Christ's righteousness, imputed to us by faith alone, is needed by every one that enters the kingdom of grace or of glory.

****

Nakanwaji Mwajibu said, "And it's too late to change me, I was born a Muslim and will die a Muslim, inshallah". I am just delivering a warning. You are compared to a person who is in a house but who is not aware that the house is on fire. But you won't take heed, you are just relaxed and enjoying your ice cream! Ignoring the fire won't stop the fire. We don't hold on traditions just because we were born into them. You were born naked but you learn to put on clothes because nakedness is bad. Jesus does not need anybody but saves a few who are willing to escape the flames of hell. He said the way to heaven is narrow, and few find it! What if your parents made wrong choices, are you willing to sacrifice your soul and follow them into hell?

****

"It is easier for people to believe that Mary could produce a Son without a man, than to believe that God has a Son without a woman!!! Luke 1:30-35. Genesis 18:14. Moreover, they contend about the same SON! Saying that " Jesus is Mary's Son, but He cannot be God's Son. A paradox of unbelief!" ~ Jonathan Zake

****

Somebody asked: "Slaves, obey your earthly masters with respect and fear, and with sincerity of heart, just as you would obey Christ" (Ephesians 6:5). Does the Bible support slavery?" The biblical times slavery was either voluntary or prisoners of war. In case a person failed to pay back the debit, they could volunteer to pay back in form of service (slavery). Even in this case the Mosaic Law sanctioned that all slaves should be freed in the seventh year, and the year of Jubilee. The God of the Bible is a liberator of slaves. He liberated Israel from slavery. Jesus came to declare the year of jubilee to set the captives free (Luke 4:18). The American slaves started off in form of trade and then when it blossomed, it became kidnapping. The Arabs, serving as middle men raided the African villages, and forcibly took the Africans to sell them as human cargos on the coast to the Whites. The Bible condemns kidnapping: "If a man be found stealing any of his brethren of the children of Israel, and maketh merchandise of him, or selleth him; then that thief shall die; and thou shalt put evil away from among you"(Deuteronomy 24:7).

****

Somebody asked that "I grew up in a denomination that believed that children born out of wedlock were illegitimate. What do you say?" I want to say that God intended marriage to be a lifetime covenant between a man and a woman. Children are victims of circumstance because they do not choose how they are born. The Bible says that "Fathers shall not be put to death because of their children, nor shall children be put to death because of their fathers. Each one shall be put to death for his own sin" (Deuteronomy 24:16). Therefore, there are no illegitimate children but there are illegitimate parents. Jesus came to reconcile all of us to God because we were all strangers to God. Reconciliation is the restoration of a relationship that went sour. "The gospel is the story of God covering his naked enemies, bringing them to the wedding feast and then marrying them rather than crushing them."

****

Hebrews 2:7 – "You made them a little lower than the angels; you crowned them with glory and honor". Evolution and immorality reduce a man that was created a little lower than angels to be a little lower than an animal.

****

Somebody asked, "Regarding abortion, why can't Christians respect the woman's right to control her body?" A woman has the right to control her body but a fetus is not her body. It is another body within her body. A fetus is another human being in development. It is a baby's body within a mother's body. A woman has a right to control her body by deciding whether to have sex or not. Abstinence and contraception are the only legitimate abortion pills. After pregnancy, she has no control of another person treasured in her body as a dependent. She is left with one option: To let nature take its course. She should try her best to deliver that new life formed in her womb rather than destroying it. She is the custodian of another life in progress with a mandate to nurture it to growth. Remember that God always vindicates the weak and the voiceless.

****

Somebody responded to the above topic on abortion in this way: "Have you ever been raped? Or met someone who has gone through that, how they are traumatized?" Answer: True, rape traumatizes but two wrongs do not make a right. Billy Gram's mother was raped; he doesn't know even his father. But look at how great a gentleman he is. What if his mother decided to abort him? We wouldn't have had Billy Gram! If a fetus is not human, why is murdering a pregnant woman considered to be a double homicide? When the heart stops beating, a person is declared to be dead. Why isn't a person declared to be alive when the heart begins to beat in a fetus?

****

Somebody asked that "Why do conservative Christians are against the distribution of condoms?" A recently released study by University of Notre Dame researchers Kasey S. Buckles and Daniel M. Hungerman has found that access to condoms in schools actually increases teen pregnancies by about 10 percent—that's right, increases it! Buckles and Hungerman selected 22 school districts in 12 states that started such programs back in the 1990s, including New York City, Los Angeles, and San Francisco. The study analyzed teen-fertility data from nearly 400 high-population counties over a span of 19 years.

Among the contributing factors Buckles and Hungerman cite is the possibility that condom-distribution programs can crowd out efforts to encourage young people to delay sexual activity. Condom-distribution programs may actually encourage more teenagers to have sex. Is this really that surprising? If adults tell teens that the decision to engage in sex is theirs and give them condoms, what message do they receive? It makes sense, especially given another finding of the study. Buckles and Hungerman found that sexual activity, along with STDs, increased in counties with condom-distribution programs. This puts a lie to all those lofty assurances from the Sexual Left that condoms would prevent all that. No, more likely, they encouraged it!

Michael J. New, an assistant professor of political science at the University of Michigan at Dearborn, notes that this ugly outcome likely is a result of increased sexual risk-taking as a result of condoms in the schools. All at taxpayers' expense. Now Buckles and Hungerman are quick to point out that they believe the effects of teen fertility would be less alarming if the condom-distribution programs were also accompanied by mandatory sex counseling.(Special thanks to John Stonestreet for contribution of these facts).

****

Matthew 16:13-20 – When Jesus came to the region of Caesarea Philippi, he asked his disciples, "Who do people say the Son of Man is?" People had controversial opinions regarding the identity of Jesus. They replied, "Some say John the Baptist; others say Elijah; and still others, Jeremiah or one of the prophets." Then Jesus asked "But what about you?" he asked. "Who do you say I am?" Simon Peter answered, "You are the Messiah, the Son of the living God." The world has different opinions regarding who Jesus is. The question is: "What is your opinion? Who is Jesus to you?" Acknowledging who Jesus is, is the first step towards Salvation. Jesus promised to build His church upon the confession that He is Lord.

****

Somebody asked that "When God appeared to Moses at the mountain He told Moses to take off his shoes. Why do Christians go to Churches with their shoes?" Taking off shoes when entering a house was and is still a gesture of respect in the Middle Eastern cultures and African culture. Moses was asked to do it because He was standing on a holy ground before the Holy God. The power of the grace allowed God to indwell our human corrupt bodies by His Spirit. We are the temple of God (1 Corinthians 3:16). We respect God by respecting our bodies. The idea that "It's my body, and I can treat it any way I like" is not compatible with the renewed minds. The mystery of redemption is that Christ dwells in us and we are hidden in Him (John: 14:20 ; Colossians 3:2-4). We don't go to church to meet God but we go to church with God. We go to church to fellowship and to share His benevolences. Happy weekend.

****

Somebody asked, "Why don't Protestant Christians believe that the Pope is holy, as Catholics do?" The Pope (Latin: papa from Greek: πάππας *Pappas*, a word for "father") is the Bishop of Rome and the leader of the worldwide Catholic Church. The Catholic Church calls him the Pontiff or Holy Father. I respect the Pope very much but my respect does not escalate into reverence because this is a reserve for God alone (Psalms 111:9; Matthew 23:8-1). The root meaning of reverence in Hebrew is the word "yare" and it literally means "to fear, be afraid, or to revere." The use of religious titles, such as "Reverend," began when the great apostasy set in at the close of the first century. I want to emphasize that there is no human being born after Adam that is holy. Jesus alone is holy because He is God/man. He is the begotten Son because He was conceived by the power of the Holy Spirit and born of a virgin. The Catholics believe that the Pope is the ordained successor of Peter. Yet, Peter was not holy either. In fact, Jesus told Peter that get behind me Satan! (Matthew 16:23).

****

Have you ever heard the saying "a wolf in sheep's clothing"? We must remember that serious error can be extremely subtle. False teachers don't wear a sign proclaiming who they are - John MacArthur

****

Somebody asked "Jesus promised us to do greater works than Him. Why are there not more miracles today than during His earthly ministry?" The scripture says: "Very truly I tell you, whoever believes in me will do the works I have been doing, and they will do even greater things than these, because I am going to the Father" (John 14:12). According to the scripture, going to the Father is the cause of the greater works promised on the earth. Elsewhere, Jesus said that: "But very truly I tell you, it is for your good that I am going away. Unless I go away, the Advocate will not come to you; but if I go, I will send him to you" (John 16:7). How can it be good to the disciples for Jesus to be separated from them? It is good for them because Jesus is going to be in them by His Spirit. The greater works Jesus promised are His works in and through us. Jesus did not call us to imitate Him but to manifest His life treasured in us. Jesus said that when He is lifted up He will draw all men to Himself (John 12:32). Salvation is the greatest miracle available to all, experienced by whosoever is willing. Whenever we preach the gospel we proclaim the death and resurrection of Jesus Christ. The miracle of the death and the resurrection of Jesus Christ is supposed to be witnessed in the transformed lives of each and every believer. This is the multiplication of the works of Jesus on the earth. The same works qualitatively but greater works quantitatively.

****

Somebody said that "God does not predict the future." I believe that God can do all things including predicting the future as long as it is not a new revelation that is in contradiction to His will (written Word). The Bible says that "Surely the Sovereign LORD does nothing without revealing his plan to his servants the prophets." (Amos 3:7). The book of Acts is full of stories when God is directing His disciples in their day to day activities including where to go. Throughout the Book of Acts, the Spirit of God is portrayed as actively leading God's people. The apostles, for example, were led by the Spirit in dramatic and dynamic ways. There was a human side to the planning, planting, and development of the early church, but the leading of the Spirit was decisive for them (Acts 16:6-10). The Bible says that, "'In the last days, God says, I will pour out my Spirit on all people. Your sons and daughters will prophesy, your young men will see visions, your old men will dream dreams" (Acts 2:17). In the Old Testament God spoke through His prophets alone because He was a distant God separated from His people. But in the last days of the grace, God is not a distant entity, He is Emanuel God with us (Matthew 1:23).

****

You often hear this saying "A dead man walking". It has a significant spiritual meaning. God created the first man in His image (Spirit). But His image in us was tarnished by sin, the consequence of which is death. A person that is not regenerated (born of God or born again) is a dead man walking. The difference between them and a corpse is a coffin. God gives us a choice to be born again so that we might eternally be in His presence. "When you are born twice, you die once to the physical body but your regenerated person (spirit) will never see death. Listen to the words of Jesus: "and whoever lives by believing in me will never die. Do you believe this?" (John 11:26).

****

You hear people say that "God is everywhere". The truth is that dwells in sanctified places only. God is not in the shrines of the world religions. Certainly, God is not everywhere but He chooses wherever He wants to be. Everybody stands in the presence of God for accountability. I compare it to the popular saying that the sun rises. Literally, we mean to say that the sun is moving or rising up at certain times for us to behold. In reality, the sun is fixed in one place. It is the earth that rotates so that we can see the sun at certain times and angles. Every nature stands in the presence of God.

****

Somebody asked "Do you believe in talking in tongues?" Paul asked this rhetorical question: "Do all have gifts of healing? Do all speak in tongues? Do all interpret? But eagerly desire the greater gifts"(1 Corinthians 12:30). A rhetorical question is when you ask the audience or person a question when you don't want an answer but with an answer. He gave his answer in this way: "To one there is given through the Spirit the message of wisdom, to another the message of knowledge by the same Spirit, to another faith by the same Spirit, to another gifts of healing by that one Spirit, to another the working of miracles, to another prophecy, to another distinguishing between spirits, to another speaking in various tongues, and to still another the interpretation of tongues (1 Corinthians 12:9). The gift of speaking in tongues is different from the Pentecost experience. On Pentecost there were Jews from different parts of the world gathered to celebrate the Feast of Harvest. They spoke Hebrew with different dialects. Peter spoke in his dialect and all heard in their own dialect and responded in their own dialects. On Pentecost God undid what he did at the Tower of Bebel when He confused the languages of men. He reunited us into the oneness of the spirit of Christ (body). It is interesting to note that on the day Moses came down from the mountain 3000 were slain, but on Pentecost (the day the church was established in Mount Zion), 3000 were saved.

I want to say that the gifts of the Holy Spirit given in 1 Corinthians are perfect works of the grace distributed and controlled by God. They are called gifts because a gift is determined by the giver. They are gifts of grace because they are given to us undeservingly. They are distributed consistently to different members of the body so that we might depend on each other. They are given for our edification, and should unite us instead of dividing us. This is not what I am saying but what the Bible says.

****

Somebody asked that, "Why are there not so many miracles today?" The greatest miracle is the regeneration of man. Multitudes of people all over the world are experiencing this miracle. Other miracles like those of divine providence, healing, and deliverance still happen but not to the magnitude of the early Church. There are many reasons but the main one is that people seek miracles for wrong reasons. God does not perform miracles to benefit the miracle worker and the person receiving the miracle. God performs miracles for the sake of the kingdom of God. Remember Satan said to Jesus that "If thou be the Son of God, command that these stones be made bread." Satan was tempting Jesus to perform a miracle for Himself. Jesus did not come to perform miracles for Himself. I think the best way to expect a miracle is to understand the main reason why miracles happen. The right formula is to connect your faith with His will.

****

Somebody asked, "Why do you think that you have all answers?" Nobody has all of the answers. Even the Bible doesn't have the answers to all things except the answers pertaining to our salvation. For example, if you don't know how to build your dog a house, you don't go to the Bible but to the architect. Normally, counselors convince you to accept the very things you already know but you don't want to accept. All of us have the same access to the Scriptures. The truth does not come from our head to the scriptures but it comes from the scriptures to our heads. There is no such thing as 'the truth depends on how you see it.' The Christian life is not a race whereby we are competing against each other, it is a pilgrimage that we travel together - Quite a long pilgrimage all the way from the Garden of Eden to the new city (Jerusalem) coming down. We need Jesus for guidance and each other for encouragement. Together we will get there!

****

Somebody asked, "What is the difference between the brains and the minds. The brains are the physical organs in our skulls coordinating our thinking. The minds are the invisible thoughts involving our beliefs and influencing our reactions and attitudes. The spirit is seen as a function of the mind, whether it is God's mind, angel's mind, or man's mind. Just as we surely do not see the mind, but we do see what the mind does, so also we cannot see the spirit but only what the spirit does. As we understand it, the mind is more than the spirit, yet "spirit" can figuratively refer to a person's mind. Also, sometimes the scriptures use the minds and the heart interchangeably but they are two different words. Jesus said that "Thou shalt love the Lord thy God with all thy heart, and with all thy soul, and with all thy mind" (Matthew 22:37). We cannot acquire the new brains except by transplanting. But the minds can be renewed, and the heart can be transformed. Ezekiel 36:26 - "And I will give you a new heart, and a new spirit I will put within you. And I will remove the heart of stone from your flesh and give you a heart of flesh." Romans 12:2 - "Do not be conformed to this world, but be transformed by the renewal of your mind, that by testing you may discern what is the will of God, what is good and acceptable and perfect." Also, I Corinthians 2:16 - "'For who has understood the mind of the Lord so as to instruct him?' But we have the mind of Christ."

****

A common thread runs between English "spirit," Hebrew *ruach*, and Greek pneuma, even when a spirit-composed being is described. "Spirit" represents something non-physical and normally invisible. We can conclude, except in the one case where "spirit," ruach, or pneuma describes a being that has revealed itself, that spirit is never seen. All that is ever seen is what spirit causes, motivates, inspires, encourages, impels, triggers, stirs, provokes, stimulates, influences, or activates. Why? Because in every other sense, except where spirit clearly means a spirit being who has revealed himself, spirit is seen as a function of the mind, whether it is God's mind, angel's mind, or man's mind. Just as we surely do not see mind, but we do see what mind does, so also we cannot see spirit but only what spirit does. As we understand it, mind is more than spirit, yet "spirit" can figuratively refer to a person's mind.

****

Somebody asked "I planted a seed of faith in the ministry of my favorite preacher of television. I gave away part of my income but I don't see returns. Why?" Biblical giving is not in form of gambling. The only condition of giving and receiving from God is to give cheerfully. The Bible says that "whoever sows sparingly will also reap sparingly, and whoever sows bountifully[a] will also reap bountifully. Each one must give as he has decided in his heart, not reluctantly or under compulsion, for God loves a cheerful giver (2 Corinthians 9:6-7). Cheerful means "boisterously joyful" or hilariously. God rewards our giving in accordance to His riches and glory. He does not reward a dollar for a dollar because He has no currency. He may reward in joy, favor, good health and etc. Remember it is more blessed to give than to receive (Acts 20:35).

****

Which Bible is read most? It is the Revised Standard Version of the Gospel According to You? People might reject what you say but will never resist the new version of your life after transformation. "Read the Bible and allow the Bible to read you so that the Word may interact with your life today".

****

Recently, while filling my forms, I noticed that in the area where there is usually male and female choices, there was another choice for transgender added. Transgender insinuates crossing from one gender to another. Transgender people opt to have two identities. Therefore, transgender also means belonging to neither. As somebody said, "There are two sides to every issue: one side is right and the other is wrong, but the middle is always evil." It seems the liberals are massaging somebody's ego in the name of open-mindedness. We are called to accommodate all people regardless of their beliefs and sexual orientation. However, tolerance does not mean validating their immoral values and compromising our values. The moment we start compromising, we negate our responsibility, biblical principles, and moral authority. Also, we are dumping our common our common sense. Now we have transgenders (switching their gender), transracials (switching their races), and etc.

****

We are called the people of the book (Bible). But God is the hero of the book. Show me a hero, and I will show you someone who has given his or her life to something bigger than oneself. God wrote this book with the ink of His own blood!

****

Somebody asked that, "How do I know that I am anointed?" In the Bible, to anoint something meant to pour oil over it. Oil was an extremely common thing used for cooking and healing. The anointed person was set apart to be used by God to serve people. God instructed the kings, the prophets and the priests to be anointed to serve their respective offices. The New Testament Greek words for "anoint" are *chrio*, which means "to smear or rub with oil" and, by implication, "to consecrate for office or religious service"; and *aleipho*, which means "to anoint." Oil is symbolic of the Holy Spirit. As oil was available in every house, the Holy Spirit is available in every believer. The Bible says that, "Now He who establishes us with you in Christ and has anointed us is God, who also has sealed us and given us the Spirit in our hearts as a guarantee" (2 Corinthians 1:21-22). However, the word 'anointment' is literally used in reference to the spectacular work of the Holy Spirit manifested in the works of the anointed person. It is when people acknowledge that what you have done or said is beyond your natural capability and see the hand of God working through you or when they attribute your works to God.

****

Somebody asked, "When a Christian commits suicide, does he go straight to hell?" Committing suicide is judging your soul not worthy living by murdering yourself. Under normal circumstances, a true Christian who is born again, and who is in the right minds will never contemplate on deliberately killing himself. People who claim to be Christians and end up killing themselves were most probably never truly born again. However, under abnormal circumstances, like mental disorder, when a Christian kills himself, he goes to heaven. The reason is because his sins (past, present and future) were forgiven when he accepted Jesus Christ as His Savior. I want to emphasize that none of us goes to heaven because of our merits. The only résumé God requires of us is the résumé of Jesus Christ. That very moment when we experience transformation, our new nature in Christ is reconnected to God by His Spirit and our communication with the divine is established. Our holy living in obedience to the Word is the proof that we are genuine believers. The rest of the people who are not regenerated (not born again or born of God) are going to be the bundles of firewood fueling the flames of hell ablaze. This is how God is going to purge the world of the unwanted corrupted souls. It is scaring! But this is not what I am saying, it is what the Bible says.

****

Religion is literally man's way of reaching God. We are all religious in one way or another because there is a reserved place within us to communicate with God. There is that exigent demand within us to live forever in the presence of God. None of us is fulfilled without God. According to some estimates, there are roughly 4,200 religions in the world. People are free to join any religion of their choice, in the same manner, we choose our favorite political parties or football clubs. The greatest illusion is to believe that all people of different religions are actually praying to the same god, but simply using different names for that deity. Intrudingly, none of the world religions agree with the other on a uniform method of approaching their gods. Different religions have different religious books and dogma. Logically, it is impossible to have contradictory answers to the same question, and each be right in its own way. In the same way, God has an absolute standard regarding how He must be approached. Different religions with different standards of their own cannot all be the right way to reach God. Either the entire phenomenon of religion is a hoax or one of them is true. The uniqueness of Christianity is that it provides God's preferred way (as opposed to man's way) to worship God. Jesus claimed to be sent by God to show us the only way and truth we need in order to return to the true God. He said in one of His radical teachings that: "Very truly I tell you, unless you eat the flesh of the Son of Man and drink his blood, you have no life in you" (John 6:53). The word 'eat' means 'to partake of'. Jesus was not talking about dieting on His physical body. He meant that if there is any hope for us to acquire eternal life in the presence of God, His life must become our life. How? Jesus gave an answer: "Verily, verily, I say unto you, Except a corn of wheat fall into the ground and die, it abideth alone: but if it die, it bringeth forth much fruit" (John 12:24). Eternal life is partaking of His resurrected spiritual body. We do it symbolically whenever we partake of the substances of communion representing His body and His blood.

****

Somebody asked that, "Is it a sin to smoke?" I have no scripture directly saying that smoking is a sin. Except that the Bible instructs to keep our body holy. If God wanted you to smoke He could have created you with a chimney. Doctors say that smoking is not healthy at all. Every time you smoke a cigarette, you reduce five seconds from your life span.

****

Somebody asked that "In the Old Testament alcohol was forbidden why some people drink today?" I said the Old Testament Laws presented the character of God to the people that could not be merited by any natural man. The entire Mosaic Law functioned as one Law. Breaking one meant breaking all. The Law was given to make people thirsty for the Savior. Also to prepare the people to obey their coming Messiah. That is why Jesus taught that "You had in the old said ---- but I say to you---". He fulfilled the Law by rightly interpreting it for us. Everything in the old should be interpreted by the New Testament. Jesus said, "What goes into someone's mouth does not defile them, but what comes out of their mouth, that is what defiles them." (Matthew 15:11). We don't eat certain foods and partake of certain drinks for any spiritual significance but for health reasons alone. The New Testament condemns getting drunk (excess drinking); glutton (excess eating) and etc. Paul advised Timothy to drink a little for his stomach's sake (healing). Not to mention that most medicines have a certain percentage of alcohol in them. Given the fact, the danger of drinking a little bit is that in alcohol there are addictive chemicals. All alcoholics began with a little bit. Therefore the best way is not to drink at all.

****

Why Israel matters? The State of Israel ranks 154th among the world's nations in land size. Thirty-two Israels would fit in the state of Texas. Yet, this nation is such a fulcrum on which the lever of history moves. Israel matters because Jerusalem is the center of the world (Ezekiel 5:5). God promised to bless those who bless Israel and to curse those who curse Israel: "I will bless those who bless you, And I will curse him who curses you; And in you all the families of the earth shall be blessed" (Genesis 12:3).

****

Somebody asked that, "The first Scriptures were written in Hebrew to the Jews. Why did the Jews reject Jesus?" True, the Jews were the custodians to the Scriptures. Jesus said that He was sent only to the lost sheep of Israel (Matthew 15:24). The Bible says that "He came unto his own, and his own received him not. But as many as received him, to them gave he power to become the sons of God, even to them that believe on his name: Which were born, not of blood, nor of the will of the flesh, nor of the will of man, but of God(John 1:11-13). God always saves the minority. During the judgment of the flood, He saved just Noah and his family. When he destroyed Sodom and Gomorrah, only Lot and his two daughters were saved. When God judged Israel, the majority perished in exile, only the remnants returned to Jerusalem. When God sent the Jewish Messiah, He planned to save a few people. Certainly, the majority of the apostles and disciples of the early Church were Jews. All people who were baptized by the Holy Spirit on Pentecost Day were Jews speaking with different dilate (Acts 2:5). God blinded the eyes of the Jews temporarily so that we (the Gentiles) can be grafted in. But God will revisit Israel when Jesus returns. All those Israelites who will be alive at that time will recognize Him and accept Him as their Savior, and they will be saved(Romans 11:25-27).

****

Reformation Day (October 31) commemorates Luther's posting of his 95 Theses on the door of the Castle Church in Wittenberg, Germany on October 31, 1517. The Protestant Reformation was the 16th-century religious, political, intellectual and cultural upheaval that splintered Catholic Europe, setting in place the structures and beliefs embraced by the Protestants. In northern and central Europe, reformers like Martin Luther, John Calvin, and Henry VIII challenged papal authority and questioned the Catholic Church's ability to define Christian practice. The reformists headed by Martin Luther emphasized the "inerrancy" of the scriptures (Sola scriptura). They insisted that the Bible is the authority as opposed to the Pope. The church before the Reformation was riddled with abuse. Popes were worldly and abuses within the ranks of the church ranged from nepotism to financial excess to simony, immorality, and venality. The clergy tended to live scandalous and greedy lives. As a result of the Reformation, Christendom was broken into two areas: Protestant and Catholic. Whereas I am for reconciliation, I suggest that any reconciliation should put into consideration solving the demands that caused the reformation in the first place. Failure to do so means an urgent need of a fresh reformation to reform those who are claiming to be reformed.

****

Somebody asked "There were twelve baskets left after the miraculous feeding of 5000 men. Who took them home?" The Bible does not specifically say who took them home. There are a couple of possibilities: Either the little boy who brought the 'seed' that was multiplied or the disciples or the crowd. Aside from the resurrection, the story of Jesus feeding the 5,000 is the only miracle recorded in all four Gospels. Christ did not just meet the need; He lavished them with so much food that there were "twelve baskets full of broken pieces and of the fish" left over (Mark 6:43). It is noteworthy that Jesus fed the people through the agency of His disciples. He could have simply snapped His fingers and caused everyone present to have a meal, but He didn't. Instead, He "gave . . . to his disciples to distribute to the people". Twelve baskets of left overs, meant one basket for each of the twelve apostles to continue feeding the people. The church is built on the foundation of the apostles and the prophets, with Christ Jesus Himself as the cornerstone. (Ephesians 2:20). Also, "The wall of the city had twelve foundations, and on them were the names of the twelve apostles of the Lamb" (Revelation 21:14).

****

Somebody asked, "Why didn't anyone notice the miracle in Jesus addressing 5000 people without a microphone? Or is it only food that matters?" When I went to Israel, I saw the place where He fed the 5000. It is like a sloping mountain. People sat below and Jesus stood at the peak. In fact, we experimented it practically by placing somebody to stand where Jesus supposedly stood, and we could hear him clearly at any point beneath the mountain where the multitude supposedly sat to listen to Jesus. Given the fact, even if it was a flat place the miracle of people hearing without the microphone would have been possible. Remember that God changed the languages on Pentecost, Peter spoke with his accent and all people heard his message in different accents. It would not be a big deal if Jesus miraculously amplified His voice for all people to hear Him well.

****

Boldness is the high level of assertiveness that you need to win. Boldness can be naturally merited or faked as in the case of actors. This is true in particular when somebody spontaneously stands for a wrong cause. I saw this during the last presidential debate in the eyes of Hillary when she apologetically defended abortion. She blinked her eyes nervously in course of manipulating her audience. However, there is the ultimate boldness resulting from being filled with the Holy Spirit. This kind of boldness cannot be duplicated. It is the empowerment and strength that ignite radicalness for the right cause. To live spiritually in a culture of confusion is to live boldly. During this election, the biblical boldness, requiring standing for the biblical values, in spite of our political and social appetites has been tested. Lukewarm believers have the wrong notion about boldness. As for those standing on a solid rock, 'boldness' is being different from the world. It is standing without flexibility. Boldness is an identity-shaping element of the church. In the book of Acts, we see how the Holy Spirit empowered and equipped the apostles to speak fearlessly. The Apostles now full-fledged citizens of the Kingdom of God confronted the secular world with the truth (Acts 4:29-31, 13:46, 14:3, 19:8, 26:26). To be bold for the sake of the truth is divine.

****

While many people know that Oregon, Washington State, and Vermont have legalized assisted suicide, it is less well known that approximately half the states in the U.S. have either defeated bills to legalize it or have passed laws explicitly banning it. Such conflicts raise the old questions about the role of government, the role of religion, and the challenges of living in a diverse and free society. Humanism dictates that all answers come from man. We (Christians) believe that the truth comes down to us from God. The Liberals promote the idea of "Aid in dying" instead of saving a life. Unlike the Liberals, we believe in the sanctity of life. This current life is subject to depreciation and even death. Our only hope is in the comforting capability of the Holy Spirit. The greatest manifestation of the Holy Spirit is the authentic moral life lived day after day in spite of adversity. Please remember to vote, and vote for your values.

End of April - Temptation

Hebrews 4:15 – "For we have not an high priest which cannot be touched with the feeling of our infirmities; but was in all points tempted like as we are, yet without sin." The Savior had to be perfect in order to save us from our sins. Otherwise, if he had his own sins, he had to save himself first before qualifying to be our Savior. God alone is perfect, and God alone can save. The name 'Jesus' means Jehovah saves.

****

In order to understand evil, we must know the opposite of it (good). Good is an entity because God is the source of Goodness. Likewise, nothing evil exists in itself, but only as an evil aspect of some actual entity. Satan is the source of evil which polluted the hearts of the entire human race. "Take away all sin, and selfishness and you would have heaven on earth." Sanctification is a process of separating the redeemed from the corruption of sin. The process of sanctification will be completed in the future glorification. Sanctification involves the cooperation of a believer. God sets you aside for Himself but you must set yourself apart from evil. We run away from evil by running to Christ. The love of Christ compels us to disassociate ourselves from all of the wicked activities and people. "The easiest way of getting the wicked people out of your life is for you to get out of their lives"

****

Matthew 7:23 - "Many will say to Me on that day, 'Lord, Lord, did we not prophesy in Your name, and in Your name drive out demons and perform many miracles?' Then I will tell them plainly, 'I never knew you; depart from Me, you workers of lawlessness.'" This is the most scaring scripture in the Bible. To know Jesus is to be known by Him. Jesus saves us by His grace but our good works of obedience to His commandments is the value He uses to determine our authenticity. According to the above scripture, prophesying, casting out demons and working of miracles are good works but they are the works of Jesus manifested through us. In addition to the works of grace, Jesus demands from His followers their own works of obedience to His commandments. Lawlessness means antinomy or against His commandments. Jesus is the Word that became flesh (human) to be demonstrated for us to obey. The Word is not just informative but formative and transforming. I challenge you to make His life a masterpiece. Say what He said and walk as He walked.

****

1 Corinthians 10:13 - "There hath no temptation taken you but such as is common to man: but God is faithful, who will not suffer you to be tempted above that ye are able; but will with the temptation also make a way to escape, that ye may be able to bear it." Temptation is not something we can escape; in fact, it is essential to the well-rounded life of a person. Regardless of the magnitude of the temptation, God always provides an exit. It might be a narrow exit but it presents to you an opportunity not sin.

****

The greatest praising is not the shouting of the mouth but the calmness of the broken heart. It isn't what screams loud emotionally that scares away the demons, it's the silence whisper of the broken heart (our defiance). God always has the last word to defend you against the schemes of your enemies. That huge wall you are faced will collapse in a moment of time because of the whisper of God. We cannot stand unless the grace of God sustains us. We overcome temptation by whom we know as opposed to making resolutions regarding what we can and can't do. The more we love Jesus the more we are going to resist sin in our lives.

****

The two most precious things on this side of the world are our reputation and our life. Sin is the most contemptible whisper that may deprive us of the same privileges. "The only ones trying to justify sin are those living in habitual sin."

****

This is a prophetic message to somebody who has been called to do something but you are engrossed with fear. Fear is a weapon of Satan which he deploys to force us into insubordination, and hence making wrong decisions which are contrary to our divine appointment. The Bible says that: "For the Spirit God gave us does not make us timid, but gives us power, love and self-discipline" (2 Timothy 1:7). Decide to step out of fear, and to step into faith. Climb that ladder to your highest calling with such confidence that the same God who called you has the power to protect you, sustain you, and to enable you to do what He called you to do.

****

Hebrews 7:25 - "Therefore He is able also to save forever those who draw near to God through Him, since He always lives to make intercession for them". This verse (and others like it) tells us that although Christ's work to secure the salvation of the elect was completed on the cross, as evidenced by His cry "It is finished!" (John 19:30). His care for His redeemed children will never be finished. We can count on His prayers but you must pray also. Pray to overcome the evil one. Pray before temptation, pray in the midst of temptation, and pray after overcoming temptation. If you don't pray, you will be overcome by the evil one.

****

A person's inner nature, what he possesses in the inner, spiritual part of his being, determines what he is tempted by on the outside. The temptation fits the true nature of the person being tempted and reveals the possibilities of his nature. Every person actually determines or sets the level of his own temptation, because temptation will come to him in accordance with the level of his controlling, inner nature.

****

Today, at work we had the mandatory hearing testing. Hearing test results will tell if you should see a hearing professional for a hearing evaluation. We have five senses (sight, hearing, smell, touch and taste), all of them are important to us, and work in harmony to serve us effectively. The loss of one sense develops the others into extra performance to fill in the void. For example, a deaf man develops an exceptional vision, a blind man exceptional hearing, and etc. Spiritually, God tests our faith with the trials of life. God does not test us so that He might know the level of our faith. Certainly, He does not need to test us in order to know our faith. Our God is the mighty warrior of the hearts. He sees through the walls of our souls. All details of our hearts are transparent to Him. The testing is intended to expose to us the level of our faith and to create room for growth. Our confidence depends on the fact that God will not test us beyond our ability to bear and will always provide a way out (1 Corinthians 10:13).

****

"God crushes 'self' that sits on the throne of our souls so that He can mold us to be like Him. God is looking for someone willing to be crushed. Why do we have to be crushed, though, isn't there an easier way? No. Crushed grapes make the finest wine. Crushed olives make the best oil. Crushed petals of a rose make the rarest perfume. It is the crushed grain that produces the life-giving bread. God uses people who have been broken and when you are broken and crushed and you look like Him, then, and only then, are you ready to be poured out."

****

"We do not necessarily choose the attractions or temptations we have, but it is our choice to decide whether or not we are going to embrace them. We will always have temptations on this earth, but we run into problems when we include those temptations as part of our identity. Going our own way leads us to death, but when we embrace His ways, we will find life and true fulfillment." ~ Amy Riordan

****

Somebody asked "If the Garden of Eden was so perfect why was Satan there?" Satan was not a creature of the Garden, he walked in the Garden most probably as God did. God warned Adam of the consequences of the deception of Satan (disobedience). Adam willingly invited sin to himself when he chose to listen to Satan instead of God. Love gives us a choice of will. True, temptation was there in the Garden but temptation is not sin until you yield to it.

****

Being able to abstain from sinning in an area you struggle with is certainly very good, but it does not change anything in your heart all by itself. Look at God as your defense; take your weaknesses to Him and allow Him to direct your heart. He can fill your emptiness, create a new heart with new desires in you and renew your minds. Freedom is not in the act of abstaining from something but it is in allowing God to heal those areas of our hearts, redirecting your desires in the ways that glorify Him. Abstaining is a step forward as a result of the freedom found in Christ. Real freedom is when we fully recognize and embrace who we were created and redeemed to be.

****

If you are seeking God's protection from yielding to temptation, then never make decisions undermining His character.

****

The voice of sin is loud, but the voice of forgiveness is louder! ~ D.L. Moody

****

You can't defeat the demons you enjoy playing with!

****

Sometimes the real people you have to watch out are those calling themselves Christians.

****

If being hurt by people causes you to lose faith, then your faith was in people, not God.

****

"My scars show me where I've been; but His scars show me where I'm going" ~ Grace Ann

****

Be careful who speaks in your life and who pray for you, it might be for your down fall as opposed to your uplifting. As for me, I am covered by the blood of Jesus! ~ Marylou Evans

****

Be on offensive. "You are not a victim, you are a victor. You can't be docile and passive when it comes to warring against the devil, be defiant, ornery, unruly and have zero tolerance towards his attacks. The devil loves to see you discouraged and defeated; he laughs at you, and he thrives on it. He hates you and would love to tear you apart. So deny him his wishes.

****

Psalm 18:2 - "The Lord is my rock, and my fortress, and my deliverer; my God, my strength, in whom I will trust; my buckler, and the horn of my salvation, and my high tower." God's forgiveness is your fortress! No matter what this world flings at you today, you have a place to go where no one can touch you. ~ Barbara Flone

****

To me, Calvinism means the placing of the eternal God at the head of all things ~ Spurgeon

****

The higher the hill, the stronger the wind: so the loftier the life, the stronger the enemy's temptations. - John Wycliffe

****

Condemnation makes you feel guilty and ashamed. But conviction brings guilty with restoration.

****

A believer was redeemed from the power darkness but not from the presence of darkness. Carnality is allowing to be influenced by the darkness of the world. It is a decision that a born again believer makes to yield to the desires of the old (corrupt) nature rather than the Spirit of Christ. The flesh is evidently seen in the sins of envy, jealous, rumors, racism, adultery, fornication, lying, thievery, abortions, lies of omission, pilfering, addictions, and etc. Partaking in these things after one is born again is deliberately accepting the deception of Satan. Deception is when a Christian is swayed from the truth with prior knowledge of the consequences. Sin severs our communication with Christ.

****

"Pornography is designed to provoke a response in you. It's also designed to take you places you never thought you would go. You need to be aware that when you look at porn you are being baited. You are not just being baited by the porn industry, but you are being baited by the enemy of your soul."

****

"Money is the "God of this world", and it empowers millions of people to enjoy life living on substitutes. With money they can buy entertainment, but can't buy joy. They can go to the drugstore and buy sleep, but they can't buy peace. Their money will attract a lot of acquaintances, but very few real friends."

****

James 4:7 – "Submit yourselves, then, to God. Resist the devil, and he will flee from you." Submission and resisting are sandwiched together. We do not resist the devil by screaming at him but by submitting to God and by denying his desires.

****

Never mind when the whole world is against you. Chill out! And just smile, for you are against the whole world. The actual reality is that the world is not what you are fighting for but it is what you are fighting against!

****

When you can't defeat your enemy, the best idea is for you to join him. When the world is not hostile to you it is because there is no difference between you and the world.

****

"Now unto him that is able to keep you from falling, and to present you faultless before the presence of his glory with exceeding joy" (Jude 1:24). Surely, God will protect you from falling but you don't have to fall! The same God who sustains the galaxy in space is able to sustain you up. God sustains (upholds) universe by the power of His Word (Hebrews 1:3). There is transforming power in His Word. Whenever you fall, it is because you chose disobedience over obedience. You fall not because you have to but because you want to.

****

An idol is everything that takes place of God. Whatever has your heart has you. Whatever has you is what you worship. The most worshiped idol is 'self'. The people who worship themselves want others to worship them too."Everyone should be respected as individual but not idolized."

****

Genesis 3:8 - God walked in the Garden of Eden in the cool of the day or the time of the evening. The phrase literally reads the wind of the day. The Hebrew *ruach* means "wind," "breath," or "spirit." The corresponding Greek word is *pneuma*. Jesus compared the working of the Holy Spirit to the wind (John 3:8). God walked in the Garden of Eden by His Spirit, in the same way, He walks in the hearts of all born again believers today. In the Garden, there was a tree of life and a tree of death. In the Garden of your heart, there is only the tree of life because Jesus dismissed the tree of death from your soul. Your spirit is invisible but indispensable because your new nature is the nature of Christ. Your spirit is not limited by the physical laws; it is governed by the universal spiritual laws. Your spirit man is completely brand new, but your mind must be renewed to the kingdom principles so that you can operate at your full potential as a new person. Once you clearly recognize your new identity, you won't try to operate out of your old nature, and God will begin to manifest His will for your life.

****

Galatians 2:20 – "I am crucified with Christ: nevertheless I live; yet not I, but Christ liveth in me: and the life which I now live in the flesh I live by the faith of the Son of God, who loved me, and gave himself for me". Jesus took your position at the cross so that you may take His position in heaven. He took possession of you so that you may possess His life. This is the greatest bargain ever made.

****

When you hear the word 'Grace', people often think about free forgetting the price involved. The grace is a gift but never take it for granted. Because we forfeited our right to live, upon our first sin before our salvation, God doesn't owe us anything. We owe Him everything.

****

The greatest manifestation of the power of the Holy Spirit is not emotional excitement but an authentic moral Christ's life lived daily on earth.

****

We are saved from something to something. The Christian life has only one direction involving moving forward, without a possibility of turning back. Embracing the old lifestyle, from which you were redeemed, is like rummaging through the garbage dumpster for the unwanted thing you previously trashed. "You don't have a soul. You are a Soul." Rummaging in your soul is potentially dangerous because you are likely to dig up something that you ought not to have dug. Instead, ask God to search your heart. David lamented that "Search me, O God, and know my heart: try me, and know my thoughts" (Psalm 139:23). God scans your heart by His Word: "Your word have I hid in my heart that I might not sin against you" (Psalm 119:11).

****

Acts 4:13 - "Now when they saw the boldness of Peter and John, and perceived that they were unlearned and ignorant men, they marveled; and they took knowledge of them, that they had been with Jesus." Let the dignity of your nature and the brightness of your prospects constrain you to hold fast to holiness and to avoid the very appearance of evil.

****

"My granny used to say not everything that glitters is gold. She also said not everything that is spiritual is of God. The devil counterfeits spirituality so even the very elect will be deceived. Be careful what you expose yourself too" ~ Bishop Scott King

****

You need the faith of the mustard seed to overcome temptation. Your faith doesn't have to be the size of your mountain in order to move it. When you move your mountain, your testimony will move multiple mountains faced by others.

****

The Bible strongly condemns Spiritism, mediums, the occult, and psychics (Leviticus 20:27; Deuteronomy 18:10-13). Horoscopes, tarot cards, astrology, fortune tellers, palm readings, and séances fall into this category as well. These practices are based on the concept that there are gods, spirits, or deceased loved ones that can give advice and guidance. These "gods" or "spirits" are demons (2 Corinthians 11:14-15).

****

When you are on fire for God the world will hate you. "I have never as yet met a man or woman who is completely sold out to God, that wasn't considered to be "bizarre" in other people's eyes."

****

We live in the end times where people believe what they want regardless of the truth. We have a situation whereby those who claim to see are the real blind ones. Religion has turned out to be the Devil's Crucible, the great Melting-Pot where all kinds of heathen beliefs are melting and re-forming. Unfortunately, the erroneous doctrines have sneaked into our churches and have been embraced with two hands. The cause of the defect is ignoring the Holy Spirit; sidelining the Holy Spirit means sidelining the truth. There can be no Church without the presence of the Holy Spirit. Jesus warned that those who are not regenerated cannot acknowledge the Holy Spirit: "Even the Spirit of truth; whom the world cannot receive, because it seeth him not, neither knoweth him: but ye know him; for he dwelleth with you, and shall be in you." (John 14:17).

****

Matthew 12:36 – "But I say unto you, That every idle word that men shall speak, they shall give account thereof in the day of judgment." The law enforcement officers placed surveillance security cameras at every junction on the streets of the city, and the crime rate was reduced by 73%. The fear of God is the awareness that God monitors our actions, and that on the Day of Judgment we are going to be accountable for our actions. There is no mighty man before God except the might Savior. Everything in us, including attention seeking, was designed to drive us to Christ as opposed to ourselves.

****

"The beginning of anxiety is the end of faith, and the beginning of true faith is the end of anxiety."- George Mueller

****

"How do you feel when your children disrespect you? What do you think when you see children in the store that are totally disobeying and disrespecting their parents? Don't be that child in rebellion against God! Be obedient and show Him the utmost respect."

****

Somebody asked that "Did Jesus paid the penalties of the sins of all people in the universe?" If God intended to save everybody then everybody would have been saved. Because not all people are saved it would implicate that He failed in His ultimate plan to save. The right doctrine is that the Father sent the Son to die on the cross in order to make salvation available and affordable to whosoever is willing to be saved.

****

Somebody asked that "If Jesus won the war against His enemies, why do we say that we are in a spiritual warfare?" True. Jesus won the war on our behalf. The Bible says that "And having disarmed the powers and authorities, he made a public spectacle of them, triumphing over them by the cross" (Colossians 2:15). It is an ultimate victory. Not even death can cancel out the triumph He has already claimed for His obedient children. Yes, we are in a spiritual warfare involving to be renewed by God's mercy and grace, because Satan infected us with the sinful nature that we wrestle against as long as we are in this world. But we are fighting from the point of victory to victory. We are here to enforce the victory that is already in place, and that will be fully realized at the Second Coming of Jesus Christ. We have victory over death because we have the eternal life in Christ dwelling in us. Right now we can say: "Death where is your sting? Death is swallowed up in victory!" In future, this corruptible nature will put on the incorruptible, and this mortal will put on immortality.

****

When you go after God, the devil will go after you!

****

"We are all like trees marked for the axe, and the fall of one should remind us that for every one, whether as great as the cedar or as humble as the cypress, the appointed hour is fast approaching" ~ Alistair Begg

****

The final product of our devotions (praying / bible study) is obedience. The greatest test of obedience is when God asks us to do something that doesn't make sense to us. Just go ahead and obey because God will never ask us to do something that does not make sense. Leave the consequence of your obedience to God rather than suffering from the consequences of disobedience.

****

The greatest threat to Christianity is secularism. Christians are stereotyped as backward, ignorant and bigotry. Whereas every genuine thing has a counterfeit, fake Christians who have distorted characters have been used to represent authentic Christianity. Hollywood has been influential in marginalizing Christians through movies. Family values have been the obvious target because an attack on families is an attack to the morality of God. We can fight stereotypes by just being what we are called to be. I mean radical biblical living. Let the world see us in the prism of our authenticity. This is recommendable persecution.

****

God knew that in your Christian walk you will stumble. That is why He prepaid for your future failures. The issue is not to fail but to acknowledge that you have failed and seek His restoration. Jesus said to Peter that Satan: "Simon, Simon, Satan has asked to sift each of you like wheat. But I have prayed for you, Simon that your faith will not fail. And when you have turned back, strengthen your brothers" (Luke 22:31). It is a calling of acknowledging your own wrongdoings and flaws, and denying yourself by walking in the righteousness of Christ.

****

Luke 7:47 – "Therefore I tell you, because her many sins have been forgiven, she has loved much. But he who has been forgiven little loves little." Satan uses our past to condemn us. That is why most people struggle to see you in your current new nature. God doesn't make you forget your past; He turns it into raw material for your spiritual growth. Your past is a testimony for your triumph. The more you remember where God delivered you from, the more you love Him. It is for the same reason Paul confessed that "Christ Jesus came into the world to save sinners--of whom I am the worst" (1 Timothy 1:15). Consequently, Paul loved Jesus and suffered for His name more than any other apostle. People will keep on reminding you of your past, partly, because they want you to carry forward the weight of your wounds. Never allow your past to dim your lights.

****

I came across this survey regarding the priorities of the things that most people in America, today, put into consideration when shopping for a good home church. First on the list, is the wellbeing of a pastor; most probably the suit he wears, the car he drives, his fat bank account; and the charisma of the pastor. Third on the list is the prestige and splendor of the church building. Last on the list is the nature of the congregation - in particular, the race of the people and the size of the congregation. Unfortunately, none of these factors constitute to a good church. Finding a good home church should not be taken casually. It is choosing where you and your children will learn the things of God and serve the Lord Jesus Christ; it has eternal ramifications. You must seek God's will and be led by the Holy Spirit when selecting your home church. When investigating a potential church home, pay particular attention to how you can fit in the vision of the pastor. Also, its view of the Bible. Does it hold to the inspiration and inerrancy of the Scriptures? Does it believe the Bible is the only rule for faith and practice (2 Tim. 3:16; 2 Pet. 1:20-21)?

****

Little things matter. "If you are worried about not committing the small sins you are never going to be worried about committing big sins".

****

Matthew 6:14 - "For if you forgive other people when they sin against you, your heavenly Father will also forgive you." Forgiving in this scripture is not a prerequisite for your salvation but a requisite for your sanctification. Perhaps forgiveness is the greatest manifestation of the character of Christ. In the natural world, it is unnatural to forgive the intruder; revenge is considered to be a heroic act.

****

Religiosity is religiousness. It is confessing Jesus but denying the power of salvation. That is when you go church every Sunday when sin is normal to you and is your daily routine, and you don't see it necessary to repent. That is when you are committed to the dogma of your pastor as opposed to the true doctrine as presented by the Scriptures. You claim to have faith but without virtues. You end up living by preference instead of conviction by the Holy Spirit. Without awareness, you find comfort and relaxation in darkness.

****

Billy Gram said that if he was given another chance to do it over again, he would study the Bible more and talk less. Serving God begins by knowing His will. God's will is plainly written on the pages of the Bible. If you have thirty minutes to serve God, use twenty minutes studying (reading the Scriptures), then ten minutes implementing what you studied. We can effectively change the physical world when we have confidence in our spiritual nature. The Word cannot be separated from the Holy Spirit. The sanctified minds, saturated with the truth, and flowing with practical implementation, is our legitimate access to the power and authority in the spiritual realm. Jesus gave us the power in His name to overcome the world. The name of Jesus working for us is the renewed minds of Christ in us. It is His character as projected by the Word.

****

Philippians 3:19 - "Their destiny is destruction, their god is their stomach, and their glory is in their shame. Their mind is set on earthly things." These are sensual believers who are driven by their appetites as opposed to their faith. They soothe themselves with the salve of the false pattern set up by the corrupt world system. We are not supposed to elevate our theology, religions, politics, and economics above the Word. Never compromise to temporarily satisfy your instinct and desires. "The accomplice to the malevolent of corruption is frequently our own indifference."

****

At times the people who claim to be the victims of abuse are not sincere regarding their claims. To be sincere is to take responsibility for your mistakes. When you are the trigger of your own deeds, you should acknowledge it instead of blaming others for your mistakes! "Manipulators like to play like the victims. If they truly want deliverance and help, believe me, they will get it because God doesn't hold back when it comes to this, He wants everyone to be free, but He will never go against our will either, so use discernment before giving anything to them."

****

Romans 12:1 - "I beseech you therefore, brethren, by the mercies of God, that you present your bodies a living sacrifice, holy, acceptable unto God, which is your reasonable service." Our bodies become acceptable sacrifices to God when we live a life pleasing to God. We are perfected by Christ. It is a continual process of transformation into what God wants us to be. The lost people of the world put God out of the equation of their lives. "There are consequences for a secular worldview that sees bodies as something we "own," something external to who we are, something we use (or abuse) depending on our desires, our will, or our "identity."

****

April – Resurrection

John 17:5 – "And now, Father, glorify me in your presence with the glory I had with you before the world began." When Jesus came to the earth, He did not give up His deity but He gave up His glory. The resurrection is intended to restore His lost glory.

****

The Romans didn't invent crucifixion. That probably happened in the Medes and the Persians era. The Romans actually got it from the Phoenicians but they perfected it. Several hundred years even before the Romans and their culture existed, the Bible predicted that the Messiah would be crucified. Christ upon the cross is foreshadowed in the Old Testament, as far back as Genesis 22 when Abraham offered his only son, Isaac, as a sacrifice upon the altar atop Mount Moriah. King David a millennium before Christ, gives us the very perspective of the Lord hanging on the cross. It describes how the people mocked Christ (Psalm 22:7-8; Mat 27:41-43), how they cast lots to divide up his clothes (Psalm 22:18;Mat 27:35), how his bones were out of joint (Psalm 22:14), how the wicked had surrounded him and pierced his hands and feet (Psalm 22:16) – the scars of which Thomas later got to touch and feel (John 20:27). Psalm 22 ends by saying God's righteousness would be declared to "a people that shall be born" (Psalm 22:31).

****

"And I said unto them, If you think good, give me my hire; and if not, forbear. So they weighed for my hire thirty pieces of silver. And Jehovah said unto me, Cast it unto the potter, the goodly price that I was prized at by them. And I took the thirty pieces of silver, and cast them unto the potter, in the house of Jehovah" (Zechariah 11:12-13). The prophet specified the metallic composition of the coinage by which the transaction would be made. It was neither gold nor copper, but rather, "silver" (Matthew 26:15). The precise number of coins was prophetically declared—"thirty pieces of silver." The amount is not incidental. Thirty pieces of silver, under the Mosaic Law, was the price to be paid to remedy the damage done to a slave that had been gored by a neighbor's ox (Exodus 21:32).

****

Matthew 20:22-23 - "But Jesus answered and said, Ye know not what ye ask. Are ye able to drink of the cup that I shall drink of, and to be baptized with the baptism that I am baptized with? They say unto him, We are able. And he saith unto them, Ye shall drink indeed of my cup, and be baptized with the baptism that I am baptized with: but to sit on my right hand, and on my left, is not mine to give, but it shall be given to them for whom it is prepared of my Father." The Apostle did not understand that the cup and baptism Jesus was talking about was His pending suffering. Soon these men slept in Gethsemane, forsook the Master when He was arrested, and one of them at least failed Him at the cross by denying Him. It is after they were baptized with the Holy Spirit that they endured and persevered even unto death for His name's sake. "We can only follow Christ in his cup and baptism, after we have been endued with the Spirit of Pentecost."

****

Matthew 26:35 - "But Peter declared, "Even if I have to die with you, I will never disown you." And all the other disciples said the same." Peter failed miserably because he ended up denying knowing Jesus three times as predicted by Jesus. Peter's weakness depended on trusting in his own abilities. God wants us to trust in His ability to sustain us from falling. The Bible says that, "Now unto him that is able to keep you from falling, and to present you faultless before the presence of his glory with exceeding joy" (Jude 1:24).

****

Job asked that "When a man dies shall he live again? (Job 14:14). The question of immortality has been the most troubling way back since ancient times. The truth is connected to immortality. Pilate asked Jesus. "What is truth?" (John 18:37- 38). Jesus said, "For this reason I was born and have come into the world, to testify to the truth. Everyone who belongs to the truth listens to My voice." Jesus came from eternity to testify to the truth. He is the truth because He is the source of eternal life. Any valid information is judged by its source. God is the source of truth. Therefore, rejecting Jesus Christ is the ultimate rejection of God, and hence the rejection of eternal life. Think about it!

****

John 20:17 - Jesus said, "Do not hold on to me, for I have not yet ascended to the Father. Go instead to my brothers and tell them, 'I am ascending to my Father and your Father, to my God and your God.'" Some teach that Jesus did not allow Mary Magdalene to touch Him because He had not presented Himself as the sacrifice to His father. But we know that after that He let Thomas touch him. Certainly Jesus was not objecting to Mary Magdalene's merely touching him, because she was a woman since he allowed other women who were at the grave to 'catch him by his feet.'— Matthew 28:9. The King James Version renders Jesus' words: "Touch me not; for I am not yet ascended to my Father." (John 20:17) However, the original Greek verb, which is usually, translated "touch," means also "to cling to, hang on by, lay hold of, grasp, handle." Reasonably, Mary wanted not to let Jesus go but Jesus restrained her from clinging on Him because He had to go to His Father. Jesus was dealing with a misplaced desire to prevent him from leaving. The Church has an apostolic calling. Like Mary we are sent with instruction to take the Good News of the resurrection to the lost world.

****

The two sides of the cross: When Jesus was crucified for our sins, we were crucified to our sins. When Jesus died we all died. When He was raised, we were raised with Him. We are seated with Him in heavenly places: "And God raised us up with Christ and seated us with him in the heavenly realms in Christ Jesus" (Ephesians 2:6).

****

2 Corinthians 8:9: "You know the generous grace of our Lord Jesus Christ. Though he was rich, yet for your sakes he became poor, so that by his poverty he could make you rich." His heavenly riches are ours at the expense of His sufferings.

****

Resurrection is not just consolation — it is restoration. The resurrected life of Christ is the glory of the Church. The resurrected life of Christ is the only spot on earth that reflects the glory of heaven. Apart from the glory, everything is vanity of vanities.

****

Matthew 27: 46-47 - "My God, My God, Why Have You Forsaken Me?" If there was a time when God was going to be lenient to sin, it would have been when the sins of the world were imputed on His Son. But He did not. Instead of turning to His Son, He turned His face away from His Son. If God did not overlook sin when it was placed on His Son, what makes you think that He will overlook the sins which are on you?

****

Where did the soul of Jesus go after He died? In the Old Testament, Sheol is the place of the souls of the dead, both the righteous (like Jacob, Genesis 37:35, and Samuel, 1 Samuel 28:13–14) and the wicked (Psalm 31:17). In the New Testament, the Hebrew word Sheol is translated as hades. First Peter 3:18–19 says, "Christ also suffered once for sins, the righteous for the unrighteous, that he might bring us to God, being put to death in the flesh but made alive in the spirit, in which he went and proclaimed to the spirits in prison" (ESV). The word spirit refers to Christ's spirit. The contrast is between His flesh and spirit, and not between Christ's flesh and the Holy Spirit. Christ's flesh died, but His spirit remained alive.

Based on Jesus' words to the thief on the cross in Luke 23:43, some Christians believe that after his death, Jesus' soul went to heaven to be in the presence of the Father. But Luke 23:43 doesn't say that Jesus would be in the presence of God; it says he would be in the presence of the thief ("Today you will be with me in Paradise"), and based on the Old Testament and Luke 16, it seems likely that the now-repentant thief would be at Abraham's side, a place of comfort and rest for the righteous dead, which Jesus here calls "Paradise."

Following his death for sin, then, Jesus journeys to Hades, to the City of Death, and rips its gates off the hinges. He liberates Abraham, Isaac, Jacob, David, John the Baptist, and the rest of the Old Testament faithful, ransoming them from the power of Sheol (Psalm 49:15; 86:13; 89:48). They had waited there for so long, not having received what was promised, so that their spirits would be made perfect along with the saints of the new covenant (Hebrews 11:39–40; 12:23).

****

The uniqueness of Christianity is that Jesus Christ Has Risen! For He Is In Heaven Now! All religious leaders are dead except Jesus Christ, He Has Risen! He Is In Heaven Now!

- Charles Taze Russel — founder of Jehovah Witnesses died 1916
- Mary Baker Eddy — founder of Christian Science died 1910
- Joseph Smith — founder of Latter Day Saints (Mormons) died 1844
- Confucius — founder of Confucianism died 479 BC
- Gautama Buddha — founder of Buddhism died 483 BC
- The Patriarchs — Abraham, Isaac and Jacob - all dead and buried with their fathers.
- Muhammad — Prophet of Islam died 632 A.D.
- Abu Bakr and Umar — Two early Caliphates of Islam buried next to Muhammad

- The Garden Tomb — the alleged burial site of Jesus Christ. But he conquered death.

****

Michael Jackson died few years ago they call him late Jackson; Yaradua died few years ago they call him late Yaradua; Mandela died last year they say late Mandela, But since almost 2000 years ago Jesus Christ died and nobody not even the devil called him late Christ. Glory be to God in the highest! He lives! He reigns! He rules! ~ Kasoma Joshua

May - Memorial

Memories are crucial faculty of our social development. "Always carry a notebook. And I mean always. The short-term memory only retains information for three minutes; unless it is committed to paper you can lose an idea for ever." — Will Self

****

Some of the commandments of God begin with the word 'remember' because they were given in the form of remembrance. The Holy Spirit was given to teach and to remind us the words of Jesus.

****

Death is not painful to the body of the deceased but it does not mean nonexistence. Death is painful to the living relatives and friends of the deceased left behind. After losing our beloved ones, we are left with numerous memories of those who departed and left us behind. The weird part is that such memories resemble the dreams, but unlike dreams, they are tormenting, real and long-lasting. They are the reality of the sorrow left with us. Looking at the corpse of your beloved one is like standing face to face with death. At that moment every explanation is treated like a fuzzy logic. Even the fact that those who died in Christ have ascended to eternity where life is boundless in its duration, and love in its sympathy, and joy in its fullness does not count. Sanity is attained by evoking our blessed hope. The resurrection of Jesus is our triumph because it gives us hope. Hope is the wings of faith because hope gives us ability to fly into the future phase of life, where we are heading to, and escape the current abyss. Certainly, the death of Jesus solved the puzzle of death. "Because He lives, I am sure of tomorrow." Because He lives, those who die in Him shall live too! The suffering on this earth is short because life in this world is short. But our eternity is infinitely long. The suffering in this world is the only hell which a believer will ever know. Truly, the heart of God is a deep abyss at the bottom of which we find love, forgiveness, and grace!

****

Jesus called us to die to ourselves so that He might live in us (Luke 9:23). This is a calling to let the flesh be dominated by the spirit. Conversion is a transmission that begins with transformation. Transformation is the change from the old nature to the new nature. Now I know that death is the change of form. Life is progressive and so is death. From the time we are born, we are progressively growing into death until we finally experience the ultimate change by the power of the Holy Spirit. This is called to be born anew or again.

****

All souls are immortal but not infinite because God alone is infinite. But those which are regenerated in the righteous of Christ are both immortal and divine.

****

"Funny how we do not realize the true value and legacy of a living icon until they suddenly pass away. Truth is, there are many living legends among us, we just do not stop and take time to notice their worth until it's too late" ~ Germany Kent

****

According to the news, "Two skydivers dead after tandem chute fails to open." There is a moral lesson in this story. These two young men counted and trusted in the ability of the parachute to bring them down safely but they were let down by the only means they trusted. Who do you trust with your life? Who do you trust to save you from the pending flames of hell? These two skydivers trusted in something that could not save them. Paul said that "But whatever was an asset to me, I count as loss for the sake of Christ. More than that, I count all things as loss compared to the surpassing excellence of knowing Christ Jesus my Lord, for whom I have lost all things. I consider them rubbish, that I may gain Christ" (Philippians 3:8-9). Paul's security is that he lives in Christ. He dies daily to the old nature so that his new nature might reign. Christ came so that we might have life and have it to the fullest (John 10:10). Fullness here, and fullness in the coming life. Christ died so that those who live might no longer live for themselves but for Him. (2 Corinthians 5:15). "Follow Christ for His own sake, if you follow Him at all." It sounds like selfish but it is the only formula that works for the salvation of your soul. Ironically, if you are serving Jesus for your selfish interests, you make God become a slave and you become the master!

****

Somebody asked that "Doesn't God decide the time when we die?" Certainly, if God wants you to be here there is no power that can end your life, and if He wants you to go home there is no viable force that can stop Him. However, God gave us a free will to decide how long to live in this world and where to spend our eternity. Unfortunately, our old nature has a reputation of blaming God for our failures and using Him as a scapegoat. God predetermined the lifespan of mankind: "My Spirit will not contend with humans forever, for they are mortal; their days will be a hundred and twenty years" (Genesis 6:3). But how long we live within the context of the given lifespan depends on us, in particular, our godliness and lifestyle. God instructed us that: "Walk in obedience to all that the LORD your God has commanded you, so that you may live and prosper and prolong your days in the land that you will possess (Deuteronomy 5:33). Also, "Honor your father and your mother, so that you may live long in the land the LORD your God is giving you" (Exodus 20:12). Never blame God for your woes if you decide to live in rebellion to God's Word and recklessly without taking care of yourself. The daily decisions we make and the decisions other people around us make are the major causes of premature death. Watch out how you live, where you live, what you eat, who treats your physical body (doctor), and whom you associate with. Above all, seek the kingdom of God first, then the rest will be added to you (Matthew 6:33). Remember that each day comes with its own problem but when the God of tomorrow is on your side, tomorrow will be in your favor.

****

Somebody asked, "Why do some of the anointed men of God die early when the church still needs them?" Nobody can kill what God has anointed to live. At times, God may call people home for reprimanding but most times it is because their calling is over. I believe that serving God is a guarantee to secure life. You cannot die when God still wants you to continue with His ministry on the earth. Remember that Moses did not enter the Promised Land because he offended God (Deuteronomy 32:48:52). God could have forgiven Moses, like, He did in the past but this time the ministry of Moses to the Israelites was over. Moses represented the Law. The Law prepared the people to enter into the Promised Land but it could not take them there. God anointed Joshua (Savior), representing the grace, to take the Israelites (people) into the Promised Land (salvation). The ushering in of the ministry of Aron put an end to the ministry of Moses.

****

30th May is Memorial Day. Memorial Day, an American holiday observed on the last Monday of May, honors men and women who died while serving in the U.S. military. Originally known as Decoration Day, it originated in the years following the Civil War and became an official federal holiday in 1971. Memorial Day's date has changed over the years, but the very first holiday was planned for April 26, 1866, in the wake of the American Civil War. In January 1866, the Ladies' Memorial Association in Columbus, Georgia, passed a motion agreeing that they would designate a day to throw flowers on the graves of fallen soldiers buried at the cemetery, Gardiner said. However, the ladies didn't want this to be an isolated event, so Mary Ann Williams, the group's secretary, wrote a letter and sent it to newspapers all over the United States. In May 1868, the day became a federal holiday. But there were few, if any, flowers blooming in the North in April. So, the government pushed the date up a month, to May 30, so that people could decorate the graves of fallen soldiers with wildflowers, Gardiner said. Many Americans observe Memorial Day by visiting cemeteries or memorials, holding family gatherings and participating in parades. Unofficially, at least, it marks the beginning of summer.

****

On this Memorial Day, special thanks go to all those who served and who are still serving in our military to protect the country we call home. America is synonymous with liberty, peace, and democracy. Your boots on the ground is an honorable and viable civil act, allying with the oppressed to stand against the oppressors, who contemplate denying freedom to others. You sacrificed your temporary freedom so that others may enjoy the permanent freedom. Indeed, it is better to die fighting for freedom than to be a prisoner of conscience all the days of your life. Partial freedom is no freedom at all. "For to be free is not merely to cast off one's chains, but to live in a way that respects and enhances the freedom of others." ~ Nelson Mandela

****

"They who can give up essential liberty to obtain a little temporary safety deserve neither liberty nor safety" ~ Benjamin Franklin

****

Liberators do not liberate themselves otherwise they cease to be liberators. Self-sacrifice is idiocy to common senses but it is embraced by genuine liberators. They would rather spontaneously bleed to death than abandon the struggle. Every liberation is a book of blood; whatever chapter is opened, it is painted red with the blood of the liberators. Their narrative stories are written with the ink of their own blood. Happy Memorial Day!

****

Our accomplishments in this world matter, because they become our legacies after we are gone. No legacy is as rich as honesty. However, before you are honest to others, it is imperative that you be honest to yourself. It helps to prepare your soul for a soft landing after you shed off this corrupt tent (the body). The truth is that all of us are sinners. The soul that is not sanctified by the Word and the spirit that is not regenerated by the Holy Spirit will surely be separated from God forever.

****

Romans 8:35-39 – "Who shall separate us from the love of Christ? Shall tribulation, or distress, or persecution, or famine, or nakedness, or danger, or sword? As it is written, "For your sake we are being killed all the day long; we are regarded as sheep to be slaughtered." No, in all these things we are more than conquerors through him who loved us. For I am sure that neither death nor life, nor angels nor rulers, nor things present nor things to come, nor powers, nor height nor depth, nor anything else in all creation, will be able to separate us from the love of God in Christ Jesus our Lord." A mature Christian is less afraid of this life and even death. Our security is not in our own capabilities but in Christ. It is not in our love for God but in the steadfast love of God for us. The winning life is that of faith. Faith is trusting and believing in what Jesus has done and can do on our behalf. The saving faith must grow into the sanctifying faith. The lifestyle of obedience is committed to the steadfast love of God. This is the liberating truth.

****

When the anointed person dies, the anointing does not die with them. God anoints others to replace them but it is not like inheriting in the secular world. "When a Christian leader dies, their "mantle" does not mystically pass to another. Sure, someone might come along and walk in their footsteps or even go on to complete their work, but there aren't non-corporeal bits of fabric passing from the shoulders of dead men and women onto those of the young. Some Charismatic leaders like to boast of the mantles they've caught over the years, thinking this adds to their credibility, but a Christian leader ought to be known by their love and passion for the Gospel, not their associations with the dearly departed. Let the dead rest, and don't use them to prop up an empire. Trust the Spirit you've been given, be faithful to your sphere of influence, and love everyone you meet and you'll have done more than most whose ministries sag beneath the weight of mountains of mantles."

Remembering those who passed on to eternity

Dr. Kibirige Lwanga: When I received the bad news of your death, it was like the world had lost its conscience. Several years have passed since your death; our Uganda still cherishes the ideas that you represented: charity, justice, equality and the liberation of the oppressed. I will always recognize your strategic efforts to remove barriers, change attitudes and reinforce the principles of tolerance and respect through reasoning and dialogue. You stood by my side through thick and thin. In my darkest times, you are the one I turned to. You were there for me when everybody forsook me. You will always be greatly missed by your family, my family, relatives, friends and the moral world at large.

****

Israel Kyeyune: Dad, though you disappeared a long time ago from our eyes, your passion and love to serve God and your country still live on. You served in tough times of terror when there were unwarranted killings and unprecedented displacement of people. You stood firmly by your convictions. The guns of Idi Amin could not silence your legacy. You were a beacon of light in much of the world's conflicting darkness. You are an inspiration for all of us. "Those you love don't go away, they always walk beside us". Love you much Muzee Dad.

****

Today August 5th, 2016, is one of my saddest days. My sister, Juliet Nabulime passed away after surgery on her leg. Sister, words cannot express how much I loved you. I will always miss you. RIP

****

"With tears rolling down my eyes, I want to send my sincere condolences to all of the family members of the Kyeyune and Katumba families upon the death of our own daughter, sister, aunt, and wife. Juliet Nabulime had a big heart accommodating all people. She was the light of Nasana. Most of us primarily visited Nasana to see our mother, but Juliet was the light that welcomed us to the place. She always had a wide smile on her face that would revive joy into your heart. Unfortunately, I did not know of her sickness until one day before her death. By the time she died we were making arrangements to pay the hospital bills, in case she was discharged. I will miss her always. Special condolences go to my beloved mother, Mukko Katumba, the children of the deceased, my sisters, my brothers, relatives and friends. I appeal to you to let this tragedy unite us instead of dividing us. United we shall come out this situation strong. May God comfort us in these days of trials. Good bye my sister; see you in eternity."

****

Thanks to all my friends on Facebook who stood with me in this testing time. Special thanks to those who stopped over to comfort me. You're the epitome of compassion and goodness. True love has eyes to see misery and need, and ears to hear the sigh of sorrow. You remembered me in times agony and shared in my tears. The same way I will remember you all. God bless.

****

I don't want to say to you goodbye but that is life. Will miss you always. Love you Juliet. You didn't have to go so early! You are dismissed from our sight but never from our hearts; will love you always.

****

"She has joined my dad, Israel Kyeyune, my aunt Nabulime her namesake, my dear sister Yayeri. May God rest all of them in peace!!! Will never leave my mind; you will always be on my mind! RIP" ~ Mabel Kyeyune

****

Today, we have a visual culture that is obsessed with losing weight. We developed the mentality that every aspect of weight loss is a sign of a healthy person. This year I visited my country for a short time. I was privileged to briefly interact with my sister. She looked good and happy. I complimented her for losing weight. Little did I know that it was an unhealthy weight loss due to sickness. A couple of months later I received the devastating news that she is dead. I learned a lesson in a hard way that observation involves paying attention. Attention is vitality. It is a receptacle for emotions but it revokes ambiguity and invokes articulated feelings. Visioning the invisible amidst the confusion and the turmoil of daily living is an anchor to practicality. It is more than general impressions and excitement, it concentrates upon details.

****

Life is a quilt of puzzles. Lots of questions to which we have no logic answers. "But blessed are they who don't know the why, but trust in the character of the One who is supervising the process."

****

The rain falls because the clouds can no longer hold (handle) its weight. The tears fall because the heart can no longer handle the pain.

****

"Epstein and others may not mention the soul, but it's evident that much more than the material world is at work in what they're observing. We really don't understand the brain, or the mind, or how they relate. And that's okay. But if we want to progress in our understanding, let's drop figurative language that trains us to think of ourselves as things, rather than as persons who bear the divine image."

June – Celebration of Family

The family is the most important institution and place on the earth. Life is within the context of the family. There is the divine family representing God on the universe and also the earthly families representing God on the earth. The marriages we have on earth were God's idea that originated in heaven. Marriage is a covenant relationship whereby God sets up the standard that rules in the relationship. Marriages are the same and married couples, all over the world, face the same hurdles. The reason is because we did not invent marriage but God did.

****

"When God wanted to build civilization, He started with the family" ~ Tony Evans

****

Mark 10:8 –9 - "For this reason a man will leave his father and mother and be united to his wife, and the two will become one flesh.' So they are no longer two, but one flesh. Therefore what God has joined together, let man not separate." God did not use 'oneness' concerning any other relationship in the family apart from the husband and wife. He did not say that a mother and a daughter will become one flesh but He specifically said that a husband and wife become one flesh. Marriage is the most important relationship on the face of the earth; more important than the children and parents relationship. It is because our relationship with Jesus is defined as a union of marriage. (Ephesians 5:22-33; Revelation 19:7).

****

Redefining married is the greatest threat to morality. The Gay rights thing is not a fight for equal rights but a fight against marriage reality. It is a delusion for the activists to think that two people of the same gender can become a husband and a wife.

****

The biblical marriage begins in Eden. God put Adam (man) in the Garden of Eden. Eden was an orderly environment. It means the spot of light on the face of the earth which had an opening to heaven. Compared to a place which Jacob saw in a dream: "And he dreamed, and behold a ladder set up on the earth, and the top of it reached to heaven: and behold the angels of God ascending and descending on it" (Genesis 28:12). In Eden, God moved from heaven to earth in the evening of times. Eden represented the presence of God. The first thing a man needs before he looks for a woman is the presence of God. We are at home whenever we dwell in His presence. We need His presence forever.

****

"So the woman was going to be a helper to the man in cultivating the Garden of Eden. That means if a man is thinking of marriage he must have a God-given task. He must know God's desires for him and must have a well-planned and established purpose for his life and he must work on fulfilling it. And also a woman must look for a man who has a well-established purpose for his life, and a God-given task. And she must be a person who will stand by her husband at all times, praying for him, supporting him, being empathetic and sympathetic towards him so that the purpose of God in their family comes to pass" ~ Brain White Nyika

****

Examine well whom you are going to marry before saying "I do". Search for a good heart. Don't search for a beautiful face because beautiful things from outside are not necessarily good inside. But good hearts make things beautiful all the way.

****

The Marriage Shoe: This is my opinion on marriage, "Marriage is like a shoe. When you wear oversize be ready to drag it along throughout life, and when you marry under-size be ready to feel the pains throughout life." One thing about marriage is that you don't drop your shoe or remove it at any point no matter how painful or how stressful it is, except in the case of battering!"

****

The good marriage involves finding the right person and creating the right environment for peace to flourish in your relationship. It's how we care in the beginning till the very end that constitutes to a lasting relationship.

****

Commitment to a lasting relationship involves embracing the leadership of Jesus Christ and the wisdom of God. Marriage is basically portraying the relationship between Jesus and the Father, and Jesus and the church.

****

The beauty of a woman can take her to a place but her character will determine how long she stays in the place. Beauty attracts men but character keeps them.

****

My aunt lectured to me how to detect an unfaithful woman. She said that I should avoid three kinds of women. The first woman is the one who is very attractive but her age is past due to get married, and she lives alone as a single woman in her own house. She said that ask yourself: "Why it took this very attractive woman a long time to get married?" My aunt compared this woman to a very ripe and attractive mango fruit on a tree situated by a busy street that is ignored by all. Most probably the reason it is ignored is because there might be wasps and snakes scaring people away from that mango tree. The second woman she asked me to avoid is a woman that tries to convince you that she has no female friends because all her friends are male. The third woman is the one who regularly reports to you different men who tried to go with her to bed but she resisted. I am not saying that my aunt is right or wrong. Just want to hear your opinion. What do you say?

****

To cherish your wife is to warm her with your body like a hen hovers over the eggs till they hatch. Nothing will make a hen abandon her eggs.

****

Like shining glass pieces which dazzle and glitter like diamonds, the appearance of men can be greatly misleading.

****

"Every extramarital intimate relationship has a spiritual resonance, the consequences of which can be very severe" ~ Sunday Adelaja

****

"You will reciprocally promise love, loyalty and matrimonial honesty. We only want for you this day that these words constitute the principle of your entire life and that with the help of divine grace you will observe these solemn vows that today, before God, you formulate" ~ Pope John Paul II

Communication

There is no graduation when it comes to learning the principles of communication; you must grow into it by experience. All growth is uncomfortable but it is a good investment in any relationship. Your spouse is like a book, you must read and study them in order to know them. Different people are handled differently. There is no one formula that works for all. Your spouse is not like a button that was designed to fit in just one buttonhole. Try to apply several tactics until you get the one that works.

****

The biggest communication problem is that we don't listen to understand but to reply.

****

"The most important thing in communication is hearing what isn't being said. The art of reading between the lines is a lifelong quest of the wise" ~ Shannon L. Alder

****

Talking and listening are crucial aspects of human communication. People talk with prior intention to be heard. Listening is more difficult than talking. Yet, listening lessens urgings. Always, your reactions should send a message to your spouse that you want to hear what they are saying. Not just to listen but listening with objective to settle the pending disputes.

****

Football players spend more time listening to their instructors than playing football in the field. The reason is because listening is the key to understanding and knowing.

****

Accepting the uniqueness of each other, without compromising on the values is the key to lasting relationship. Don't try to change somebody into the person you want them to be. Accept them the way they are. The goal of marriage is to allow Jesus Christ to transform us into the image of God.

****

There are positives and negatives in any relationship. Please focus on the positives in anticipation of changing the negatives.

****

Love & respect your spouse and he'll reciprocate that back to you in full force.

****

"Love sometimes doesn't need a reason. It speaks from the irrational wisdom of the heart..." ~ Andrew Galiwango

****

You can't love others without loving yourself. Loving yourself begins by knowing who you are. You don't expect to know who you are if you don't know whose you are.

****

Honesty is the key to trusting. A dishonest person cannot be trusted. Dishonest people have the followings characteristics:

Misrepresentation - Distorting facts to consciously mislead or create a false impression. Spinning the truth, presenting opinion as fact, and using revisionist thinking or euphemisms to masquerade the truth are all forms of misrepresentation.

Fabrication - Deliberately inventing an untruth or spreading a falsehood such as gossip or a rumor.

Denial - Refusing to acknowledge the truth or to accept responsibility for a mistake or falsehood that was made.

Hypocrisy - Saying one thing and consciously doing another. When words don't match actions, someone is being dishonest with others or themselves.

****

Humility is the first step towards repentance. Brokenness involves humility and willingness to apologize in case of mistakes. It is important to willingly accept responsibility by admitting a mistake or an error in judgment — in a timely fashion.

****

Romans 12:21 – "Do not be overcome by evil, but overcome evil with good." The only way to overcome evil is not yielding to temptations. Let your faith be the guide to your conscience. Temptation follows us inconsistently but it ceases when there is a consistent focus on the truth.

****

There is a need to be authentic and honest about your struggles and to let down the facade of perfection. Don't be afraid to show others your scars and imperfections because it is one of the ways you can get help.

****

Love is in people (the couple), and people invest it in relationship (marriage). Love is the decision you make even when loving is tough.

****

Our mind and heart often hold us captive, locked up with stuff from past life situations. Avoid bringing into your marriage baggage from the past relationships.

****

Be sensitive when choosing your closest associates. Never compromise your integrity and reputation by associating yourself with people whose standards of integrity you mistrust.

****

Making people of the opposite sex your closest companions is the recipe of future discords. Avoid anything that might incite your spouse into jealous.

****

Never talk to others about the bad things concerning your spouse. If you can't compliment him or her just keep your mouth shut for the benefit of your marriage and integrity. Remember that anything ugly you say about your spouse, in the long run, will make people despise both of you.

****

"Gossip is so dangerous, because it makes you feel like you told the truth. And you did. Just not to the person involved. It scratches the itch, that impulse to tell the truth, but it has no power to transform, and it destroys trust" ~ Shauna Niequist

****

"Think twice before you burden your secrets with your friends." If your secrets are too heavy for your shoulders, your friend won't be able to hold on them either. She will easily pass them on to others.

****

"Be not desirous to know what people say; if they speak well of thee, it will feed thy pride, if ill, it will stir up thy passion" ~ Matthew Henry

****

It is better to be the one who feels the pain than the one who causes the pain. It is better to be gossiped about than to gossip about somebody.

****

Take your conversation to God before you take it to your spouse.

****

Speak only when your words a more beautiful than the silence.

****

Sometimes smiling is the greatest act of defiance. Sometimes just going to bed is the antidote to trials and tribulations.

****

Be ready to handle conflicts. There will be arguments in case of disagreement. Ironically, the absence of arguments means one spouse is dominating the other. Given the fact, avoid the habit of being argumentative for the sake of arguing.

****

"Those who spend time looking for faults in others usually make no time to correct their own mistakes".

****

Nobody has ever gone up by bringing others down, and nobody has every crossed over by cutting others to pieces. Some people are going to try to win your friendship by assassinating other people's character. Always be careful of people who gossip about others in your presence; they gossip about you in other people's presence. They are the source of confusion.

****

Children, as much as adults wherever they are, deserve your love and affection. It is the responsibility of the parents to give fulsomeness love to their children. Also, tough love involving rebukes of wrong doings. However, we should be careful not to overstep. There is this thing called self-esteem. Watch what you say to your kids. Never pull them down by your words, and never spoil them by your words. For example, it is not appropriate to say to your kids that they are better than anybody. Just let them know that they are special to God but they are as good as any other kids. Hope I am helping somebody.

****

Fix your focus. Look for something good in your spouse to cherish. Never focus on the negatives. Never rehearsal on anger because it causes resentment.

****

Give God time to change your spouse. God uses time and pressure. He is working on your spouse as He is working on you.

****

Nobody is perfect. Can't master yourself until you acknowledge your flaws, they are always there, influencing your behaviors and thoughts.

****

Resentment, anger, and fear is the triangle of self-obsession.

****

Anger is a letter short of danger, and always think before you act, even when someone annoys you please don't talk immediately, take your time or leave the spot ~ Ssenyonjo Enock

****

Anger is a letter short of danger, and always think before you act, even when someone annoys you please don't talk immediately, take your time or leave the spot ~ Ssenyonjo Enock

****

Be ready to forgive. God's forgiveness has no expiry date.

****

Don't pay evil for evil. Hate cannot drive out hate. Only love can do that, and God is Love.

****

Loving God means loving people. "The person who looks up to God, rarely looks down on people."

****

Laugh even when you don't want to. A fake smile can turn into a genuine one!

****

Some people can control their tongues but can't control the attitudes on their faces!

****

A Professor was teaching about Proverbs 15:1. He asked his students, 'why do we shout in anger? Why do people shout at each other when they are upset?' The students thought for a while. One said because we lose our calm. But why shout when the other person is just next to you? Asked the professor. Isn't it possible to speak to him or her with a soft voice? Why do you shout at a person when you are angry? The students gave some answers but none satisfied the Professor. Finally, he explained, 'when two people are angry at each other, there is a distance in their hearts psychologically. To cover the distance, they must shout to be able to hear each other. The angrier they are, the stronger they will shout to hear each other through that great distance. Then the Professor asked, 'What happens when two people fall in love? They don't shout at each other but talk softly. Why? Because their hearts are psychologically close. The distance between them is very close. The Professor continued, 'When they love each other even more, what happens? They don't speak, only whisper and they even get closer to each other in their love. Finally, they even need not whisper, they only look at each other and that's all..... So next time you shout to a loved one, know that you are creating distance between your heart and that person's heart. Proverbs 15:1 says; "A gentle answer deflects anger, but harsh words make tempers flare." Love is the greatest of all; keeping on loving draws us closer to our spouses, partners, workmates, employees, children, colleagues, friends, family, and neighbors..... Let us not create these distances amongst our loved ones through shouting at them when angry. (Sam Kyeyune)

****

Withdrawing in case of hostility is healthy. Learn to be alone and to like it; there's nothing more freeing and empowering than learning to like your own company. You are never alone because Jesus is ever with you. You can count on His companion because He knows how to calm and comfort a troubled heart.

****

Ephesians 4:25 – "Therefore each of you must put off falsehood and speak truthfully to your neighbor, for we are all members of one body." Revealing your feeling is the beginning of healing. You can't become all that God wants you to be until you are honest to yourself and to others. You're never going to get healing until you get rid of all that's bugging you and tell your spouse about it!

****

Don't mistake "guarding" your heart with "hardening" your heart.

****

The best moment of your life is when you decide that your problems are your own. You do not blame them on your partner, your parents, the economy, or the president. You realize that you control your own destiny.

****

Integrity is the husband who guards his eyes, shields his heart and protects his marriage.

****

Don't react in anger because the people that anger you control you by controlling your reactions. "Sometimes the best response is no response at all. We usually can tame the tongue when we realize or remember that God can be trusted to work all things for our good and we have no need to defend ourselves. He does that better than we can anyway!"

****

Trust is earned and shared. Trust naturally flourishes, in spite of arbitrary conditions which we create, and which we feel obliged to maintain at any cost. "The best way to find out if you can trust somebody is to trust them." However, some people, in course of asserting their individual autonomy often overstep by demanding for absolute trust from others. Unfortunately, the same people who demand trust are the same people who betray the trust of others ominously. They are the same people in case of inconsistency, who are fond of asking: "Don't you trust me?" This is a smoke covering or a defensive mechanism for them to cover up their breach of trust.

****

We marry for good and bad times but commitment is for bad times. Anybody can be committed in good times but the test for commitment is in times of trials.

****

"For there to be betrayal, there would have to have been trust first" ~ Suzanne Collins, The Hunger Games

****

The only difference between the bad day and the good day is your attitude. A negative mind will never give you a positive life.

****

Don't look for reasons to love; just do it! "Don't rest until love and faith are the master passions of your soul" ~ G H Spurgeon

****

Making mistakes is better than faking perfection.

****

It is easier to fake a smile when you are boiling with anger within. Sometimes pretending that you are okay is easier than explaining to somebody why you are not.

****

"There is nothing covered that won't be uncovered, nothing hidden that won't be made known. Therefore whatever you have said in the dark will be heard in the light, and what you have whispered in an ear in private rooms will be proclaimed on the housetops." (Luke 12:2-3). Jesus is explaining that the reason you don't want to be a hypocrite is because it is actually irrational. You may be able to keep the truth "covered" from others for a period of time, but eventually, the mask will come off and the truth will be revealed. In Numbers 32:23 we read, "Be sure your sin will catch up with you." You may be able to fool people for a while, but not all times. More important is the fact that God always knows the truth. We can't fool Him.

****

Truthfulness is a virtue. Normally, we demand to know the truth from our spouses but the question is, are we ready to handle the truth when it is told. Sometimes people withhold telling the truth because it will do more harm to us than good. Others fear that regardless of what they say nobody will believe them; they hate being called liars even when they are telling the perfect truth. Given the facts, there is no justification for not telling the truth. The Bible tells us the truth and prepares us to handle it because it is a narration of the words of the One whose name is Truth.

****

Responsibility is 'response abilities'. Never respond to your spouse when you are angry. Wait until you calm down. "Pay attention to the things that disrupt your peace. You must quiet your thoughts and emotions in order to be restored. Peace is the platform of the soul from which you can access God's presence. Refuse to allow chaos of any kind to interrupt your ability to stay calm."

****

What you say and when you say it matter. Know when to cover for your spouse's mistakes and when to bring them out to light. Good timing regarding when to talk to your spouse about tormenting issues is paramount.

****

All of good relationship is due to godliness, and all conflicts are due to sin. It might be a sin of self-centeredness, pride and etc. "Let no unwholesome talk come out of your mouths, but only what is helpful for building up the one in need and bringing grace to those who listen. And do not grieve the

Holy Spirit of God, with whom you were sealed for the day of redemption. Get rid of all bitterness, rage and anger, outcry and slander, along with every form of malice" (Ephesians 4:29-31).

****

When you truly care about someone, their mistakes will hurt your feelings but will not change your feelings because it is the minds that get angry but the heart still cares.

****

"An open rebuke is better than hidden love! Wounds from a sincere friend are better than many kisses from an enemy" ~ Sam Kyeyune

****

A bad mood is no excuse for bad manners.

****

Family conflicts cannot be evaded. But let yesterday's conflicts vanish with the day. In case trouble ambushed your life yesterday, don't start tomorrow with the broken pieces of yesterday. Every day is a brand new start.....

****

Self-Control has to do with having power over yourself! Having self-control doesn't mean you will express complete control in all situations. Self-control comes with maturity, self-respect, maturity, practice and prayer! It's learned on a daily basis through trial & error. It's worth having.... if you don't have it, ask God for it and begin trusting. Trust in His power today for self-control! ~ Noemi Negron

****

They only thing that should come between you and your man is the Bible. Keep your friends and family out of your love life. They don't need to know your man as you do. It makes your toe wiggle

****

"Sometimes we concentrate on what the enemy is doing behind our back then we develop a defense mechanism and struggle so much to be on track. In spite of defending ourselves, we cannot win!" Instead, we should "Let God arise, let His enemies be scattered: let them also that hate Him flee before Him. But let the righteous be glad; let them rejoice before God: yea, let them exceedingly rejoice" (Psalm 68:1,3). When God arises our battles are won. Let God fight for you.

****

If people can't control their own emotions, they start trying to control other people's behavior. The only person you can control is You.

****

"There will always be people in your life who treat you wrong. Be sure to thank them for making you strong." ~ (Zig Ziglar)

****

Never be upset when people reveal to you their true colors. "When people shows you who they are, thank them and thank God." The reason is because an enemy that disguises as a friend is very deadly.

****

When you learn to master your own emotions you can respond to others with more emotional intelligence! Never allow your mood to dictate to you what to say because you can change your mood but you can never change the words spoken.

****

Tension is a more dangerous force than any feud known to man. "Unexpressed emotions will never die. They are buried alive and will come forth later in uglier ways" ~ Sigmund Freud

****

Too much talking often creates more problems than solving them. Watch your mouth in particular when you are angry. The tongue has no bones but it is strong enough to break a heart. Therefore, think twice before you say something.

****

The people who are close to you are most likely to hurt you most because they are acquainted with your weaknesses. They can inflict the worst damage by using your weaknesses against you. This is a sacrilegious breach of trust and is offensive in the sight of God as it is derogatory from your own honor or interest of happiness. "Don't be afraid of enemies who attack you. Be afraid of the friends who flatter you." ~ Dale Carnegie

****

The true friends never breach the trust of their companion. They are trustworthy and reliable. They help you recover the lost smile, courage, and hope. They encourage you to stand behind your beliefs. They don't judge you. They let you be you!

****

"Be careful whom you vent to. A listening ear is also a running mouth".

****

Gossip dies when it hits a wise person's ears.

****

If you spend time praying for people instead of talking about them, you'll get better results.

****

Words hurt compared to stones thrown at you. However, normally, we focus on what people say and forget that at times they are merely blowing hot air in order for the smoke to hide their real motives. In actuality, nobody really stresses what one says so much as the motive behind what one says. The height of your maturity and sagacity depends on your ability to ignore the spoken words and dig deep into the people's conscience to discern what they don't say. Remember that non-spoken motives are shattering when they become actions.

****

Forgiving is the greatest power at our fingertips that we often ignore. The grace of God is the unconditional love of God revealed to us in His forgiveness. Real freedom is when we forgive and let go. That is when we plead to God and allow Him to take care of the situation to our advantage. Don't ever allow the mistakes of others to drain your life. "Never regret or apologize for having the sense to let go of the nonsense that causes you stress negativity or drama"

****

Three things control the world;

1. I am sorry
2. Please
3. Thank you

With these, the world will be a better place.

****

Four of the most encouraging words you can hear from or tell someone are..."I'm proud of you."

****

1 Corinthians 13:4-5 – "Love is patient, love is kind. It does not envy, it does not boast, it is not proud. It is not rude, it is not self-seeking, is not easily angered, it keeps no account of wrongs." Ladies are weak vessels and are victimized by grudges more than men. A woman divorces way back, months before, the divorce papers are signed. Paul advises that true love keeps no records of wrongs but forgives and moves on with life.

****

Brokenness is the key to humility and hence lasting relationship: It takes broken soil to grow the crop ---- Broken cloud to give the rain ----- A broken seed to grow the plant ------ Broken grain to make the bread ---- -- Broken bread to nourish & give strength ---- A broken alabaster bottle to release the perfume.

****

The priceless perfume falls to the floor, scattered in brokenness. In disbelief we face two choices: wasted or restored. When facing our personal brokenness, any hope of restoration often eludes us. It is as if we are accepting a loss -- unaware of God's hand in brokenness. "Sometimes you have to break down in order to break through!"

****

The rule of making marriage exciting is don't be boring. Mix humor with your conversations. Life is too short to blend in. There is this prescription about laughter for psychological healing: "Laughter like water ripples down the jagged rocks at the foundation of our lives and seeps into the soil of our roots drowning our eternal sorrow continually with momentary floods" ~ Evelyn Michon

****

"Every sunrise is a second chance.... Remember laughter is an instant vacation and a smile is free..... A smile reciprocated is priceless!" ~ Kereena Maria Cox

****

Successful people have two things on their lips "Smile and Silence" Smile can solve problems while silence can avoid problems.

****

Be selective when fighting your wars. Remember, don't ever wrestle with a pig, you'll both get dirty but the pig will enjoy it.

****

"The most beautiful things in the world cannot be seen or touched, they are felt with the heart!"

****

You don't have to respond to everything. Ignore some of the things that are offensive to you. "Those who leave everything in God's hand will eventually see the hand of God in everything."

****

"Like wildflowers; you must allow yourself to grow in all the places people thought you never would."

****

The Bible says, 'It is better to trust in the Lord than to put confidence in man' (Psalm 118:8). Mary, unlike her sister Martha, held on to the Lord firmly. Likewise, hold on to the Lord firmly and He will be your very present help. The more we trust Him, the more He will help us.

****

Marriage is not about the right people meeting marriage, it is two people becoming the two right people for one another to glorify God! ~ Bobby Bonnet

****

Some of the biggest challenges in relationships come from the fact that most people enter a relationship in order to get something: they're trying to find someone who's going to make them feel good. In reality, the only way a relationship will last is when you see your relationship as a place that you go to give, and not a place that you go to take ~ Anthony Robbins

****

Marriage is exchanging your selfishness with selflessness. It is abandoning the consumer mentality in exchanging to service delivery.

****

According to Joweria Nakyeyune, today, our precious daughters are pampered through the nursery and primary schools. They speak the English we want and know all the cartoon slangs by heart. We beat the maids blue black if they ever ask our girls to help out in domestic duties. They see kitchen things as maids' things. We overwork the maids and they adjust with equanimity because they need us to survive. The maids turn out to manage the indignation and insolence we and our children subject them to. All these make the maids better wives who can manage even the angriest of men. In practice, love can't cover the stench of bad; this being the early formation of our daughters. Like a perfume, good guys perceive well-trained wife materials from afar and dump the daughters of the bourgeois like hot iron. At time, they opt to promote the well-trained maids to be housewives.

****

"Don't allow someone else's choices cause you to violate the core values you've chosen for your life. Make the decision that you will remain committed to a standard of honor, integrity, and love even in the midst of temptation, opposition, or pressure." ~ Jesika Tate

****

Withdrawing from conflict is good but never let it escalate into prolonged ignoring of your spouse. "Some people are hurt by words. Some are hurt by action. But the biggest hurt is when someone ignores you when you value them more than anything else!" ~ Tasha Marylin Kasey

****

You can be a straight forward person and still do it in love. Face issues with intention of finding a permanent solution. Exchange monologue with dialogue in order to solve the pending conflicts. Find the root cause of the problem. At times you are the problem and you can't run away from yourself. In this case, reallocating won't solve your problems because you move with yourself wherever you go.

****

The Lord corrects those people whom He loves. Unfortunately, most people detest being reprimanded. They are not ready to receive anything less than a compliment and an encouragement.

****

"The depth and strength of a human character are defined by its moral reserves. People reveal themselves completely only when they are thrown out of the customary conditions of their life, for only then do they have to fall back on their reserves." ~ Leonardo ad Vinci

****

"You get to know people better by their reactions rather than their actions. Reactions are spontaneous and reveal who really they are while actions can be intentional, premeditated and deceiving." ~ Sam Kyeyune

****

"Feelings of inadequacy and shame are part of the fallen nature. But it's also our souls searching and seeking for our purpose in this, often mundane, lives we are living. When we have friends who love and accept all of us, including our brokenness and imperfection – our ability to feel worthy of love is rebuilt."

****

Universalism labels all people bad depending on the evils of a handful of corrupted people within the same sector. For example, a woman that was abused by a man, and concludes that all men are bad. I heard somebody saying that all Black people are lazy! What about this common saying: "All cops are racists." Don't judge all of them by the mistakes of a few.

****

If you have a strong purpose in life, you don't have to be pushed. Your passion will drive you there! ~ Roy T. Bennett

****

The gift of physical intimacy is received from your spouse but it is supposed to be developed by both of you progressively.

****

Review your relationship regularly. Ask your spouse what you should do better or improve on to be a better spouse.

****

Learn to love yourself in order to love your spouse. Be gentle to yourself. The way you treat yourself is the way you are likely to treat others. The way you talk to yourself is the way you are likely to talk to others.

****

Strong-willed heart attracts applauds. Never settle down without a fight. Fight a good fight with the right cause to the end but not for the end of you.

****

Starting marriage in the wrong place involves going into marriage in search for happiness. Happiness should be the benefit of marriage as opposed to the cause.

****

People change for two main reasons - When their minds have been opened to new ideas or when their hearts have been broken.

****

You can't change a passive aggressive person - you can only control how you react to their behavior.

Mother's Day

She gave me her world, ever since I was in her womb: She implanted values in me from the moment I started reasoning, and she keeps injecting into me wisdom and inspired instructions whenever there is a need. She disciplined me to respect my parents and the elders but the toughest discipline was to respect God my creator. Mom, it is because of you, that I am the voice of honesty and the echo of integrity. I need you now as much as I needed you when I was a toddler. You are the jewelry of value that fits me regardless of my size. I will cherish every moment at every stage of your life's journey. May God bless you with many more years to nurture your children, grandchildren, and great-grandchildren? Happy Mother's Day to you.

****

The role of the parents to the stability of the nation cannot be underestimated. When parents play their role effectively they help to obliterate the future crime and hence misery from the society. Parenting never expires. Certainly, there is a boy inside every mature man and a girl inside every mature woman desiring to be parented. Thank God for the persistent efforts of our parents. They rarely leave us. There is a popular saying: "Children are made readers on the laps of their parents."

****

Superheroes are real people faced with real problems but who strategically overcome. My mother is my superhero. I can't relate to any other superhero, but I can identify with a real woman who in times of crisis draws forth some extraordinary quality from within herself and triumphs, not for her own sake, but for the sake of her children.

****

Life is compared to the weather. It is composed of all seasons (sun shine and rain fall). Mom, you are the shadow where I take shelter from the beam of the sunburn, and you are the umbrella that shields me from the heavy rainfall. You make me dance in the favorable and the hostile seasons of life, at the edge of time without fear and worry. Happy Mother's Day to you.

****

"Among other traits, a woman manifests the qualities of beauty, compassion, sensitivity, and intuitiveness. She possesses these attributes to accomplish her role of influencing the actions of others for good. Influence involves the ability to produce an effect without apparent exertion of force or direct exercise of command. Just about every woman in the Bible was an influencer to a leader; Eve to Adam, Ruth to Boaz, Esther to King

Ahasuerus, Sarah to Abraham, Herodias to Herod, Rebecca to Jacob, Rachel to Jacob, Delilah and Samson, and Pilate's wife to Pilate. These women modeled both the negative and positive outcomes of this role." Behind a successful man there is always a good woman; she might be a mother, a wife or a sister.

****

"Even in high school, I'd tell my mom I was sick of swimming and wanted to try to play golf. She wasn't too happy. She'd say, 'Think about this.' And I'd always end up getting back in the pool" ~ Michael Phelps

****

The most precious jewels, you'll ever have around your neck, are the arms of your children.

****

A mother's love is constant, no matter how far or near her kids are!

****

A mother is always a mother, there is no duplicate!

****

"To be in your children's memories tomorrow, You have to be in their lives today." ~ Barbara Johnson

****

My job as a parent is to parent my boys not to be their "friend". They are loaned to us by God and it is our responsibility to raise them according to God's Word and not according to the world's standards.

****

2 Timothy 1:5 - "When I call to remembrance the unfeigned faith that is in thee, which dwelt first in thy grandmother Lois, and thy mother Eunice; and I am persuaded that in thee also." The word "unfeigned" means genuine (not fake). Paul discerned the character of Timothy by looking at the character of his mother. The faith of his mother was not in form of pretense. Parents do not live their own private lives because the children wear the fragrances of the characters of their parents.

****

Then Jesus said to John, "Behold, your mother!" (John 19:26-27). At this crucial moment of crucifixion, John, the disciple whom Jesus loved needed the comfort of a caring mother. Also Mary, the earthly mother of Jesus needed a son to comfort her. Beyond doubt, there is no role in life more essential and more eternal than that of motherhood. If your mother is not around, please listen to the words of Jesus: "Behold, your mother!" Go ahead and hug all the mothers around you, and wish them a good Mothers' Day.

****

The beauty of a woman can take her to a place but her character will determine how long she stays in the place. Beauty attracts men but character keeps them.

****

The woman who respects her husband is the best wife anyone would ever have. There is nothing wrong in accepting that you are wrong when you are wrong. Be ready to forgive when he admits that he is wrong. Don't compete with your husband; compliment him.

****

"A woman's heart should be so hidden in God that a man has to seek Him just to find her!" ~ Max Lucado

****

Life is composed of lights and shadows, and we would be untruthful, insincere, and saccharine if we tried to pretend there were no shadows. "A Mother's shadow is a place you'll always feel welcome and like family to learn to better yourself, practice life skills and become more perfect."

****

Train your children to love themselves and take pride in their melanin-filled skin tones! It's who God created them to be! Inferiority complex kills creativity, innovation, originality, culture and self-confidence! It makes people prefer being copycats!

****

Parents raise their children in anticipation of the children to take care of their parents when they grow up. This is the primary responsibility of all of us. Responsibility is about looking inside yourself and doing all you can to do what you are expected to do. It is putting others' needs above yours; and knowing what to do and when to do it. In short, when you practice responsibility, you're on your way to be a person of value with moral integrity. "The price of greatness is responsibility."

****

Jonathan Zake's posting: The worst disease on the Planet is Unattached Child Syndrome. The child either does not know where he belongs, or has no caring relatives and friends, or is hated by his parents and relatives. He never grows from the REPTILIAN mentality. So, he always behaves as the reptiles do: selfish and destructive. Those who have some parental care but no morality, manifest the MAMMALIAN mentality. Always moving in mob cycles, the herd mentality of gangsters. Only those with Parental Guidance and Care, ever develop the Neomammalian mentality. These can reason and make proper decisions. Isaiah 1:1-27.

****

Our parents gave us this earthly life, then they strategically plan that their children outlive and outlearn them. Children come from parents and so do the promises of the blessings. Children need to brace themselves up and to realize that they have the keys to unlock their future blessings by their thoughts, attitudes, and actions towards their parents. If you are a rebellious knucklehead with a habit of bad mouthing your parents, you cripple your real you. You automatically choke your blessing and hence unlock the curse to direct your future life (Exodus 20:12). Never let your parents live in agony because of your actions; the end of your life will be devoid of peace, joy, and hope. The Bible projects that obedience to parents is a virtue and disobedience is a vice. Jesus specifically quoted this commandment: "For God said: 'Honor your father and mother' and 'anyone who curses his father or mother must be put to death.'" (Matthew 15:4). Isn't it scaring to you? Save yourself a great deal of pain in life and the pending judgment from God – hearken unto your mother and father.

****

Father's Day

Today is Father's day! Thank God for all fathers. How can I forget a great man, my father: Israeli Kyeyune! He was everything you would like a father to be. Daddy you loved us, you cared for us, you shaped us into the human beings we are today, and we thank you very much. So sorry we did not get a chance to care for you, not even to give you a decent burial! But we know that you are where your passion is. You are in the Lord's arms up in heaven. We know you are up there smiling at us with love. You left us the legacy of faith because you died for your faith. Rest in peace Daddy, our love for you will never end. (Posted by Mabel Kyeyune)

****

Malachi 4:6 - "And he shall turn the heart of the fathers to the children, and the heart of the children to their fathers, lest I come and smite the earth with a curse." Elijah is the announced prophet to turn the hearts of the children to the fathers. The prophecy was intended to prepare the people to be on the right side of God on the Day of the Lord. It is a great folly to stay on the other side. John the Baptist came as the first fulfillment of this prophecy. He came in the spirit and power of Elijah preaching repentance and reformation (Luke 1:17). He prepared the people to receive the Savior, who saves us from the consequences of the broken laws of God. When God wanted to save us, He did not send to us a text or a messenger but He stepped out of eternity and put on humanity to save us. Jesus turns the hearts of all men to the Father. We know the Father by our intimate relationship with Son.

Since God is the only all-loving & all-perfect One, He must have a worthy projection for His love and holiness. The Son (Jesus) is the perfect recipient of God's love. God restored us unto himself through His grace. That very moment when we accept Jesus as our Savior, we become His, we are adopted into the divine family; His Father becomes our Father. We are not left as orphans without the father (John 14:18). The earthly fathers are supposed to stand in the shoes of the heavenly Father. Their spiritual integrity is crucial to engage their children into knowing the heavenly Father. Happy Father's Day to you all.

****

The Bible says, "For the husband is the head of the wife, even as Christ is the head of the church: and he is the savior of the body" (Ephesians 5:23). Our earthly fathers are the recipient of the divine mandate to portray the characters of the heavenly Father to their children, mainly by their spiritual integrity. Obedient is always the preface to blessing. In order for us to love God with sincerity, there must be obedience in all joints of the society beginning with the families. An obedient attitude is when the parents raise their children in godliness, and when the children submit to their parents. This is the expression of a genuine and honest love of God - the Father. Happy Father's Day to you all.

****

Regardless of how you feel, your last name changes based on marriage. The majority of the cultures are in favor of the children taking on their father's last name, and the wife taking on her husband's last name. A father gives a baby the last name for various reasons. It is a requisite in order for a man to be certain that the child is his since his paternity is not certain like that of a mother who carries and births the baby. Russians take it one step further, by giving their children – both their sons and daughters – middle and last names after the father. Spiritually, taking on the name of somebody means sharing their values. A father gives the name and at the same time donates the character to his children. That is why it is important to discern with certainty that the man you want to marry will be a real model for your children. Happy Father's Day!

****

Before she got married to you, it was her father's name that was wrapping and protecting her, but as soon she got married to you, she changed from bearing her father's name to your name. Which means, it's no longer her father's name that is wrapping and protecting her, but your name. In the book of Matthew: 19-5, Jesus say's, then shall a man leave his father and mother, and shall cleave to his wife.

****

When there is no father figure in the house the children suffer from various issues in particular depression. Boys who grow up without fathers are more likely to get involved in criminal activities. Girls who grow up without fathers are most likely to become pregnant before marriages and raise their children as single parents.

****

John 13:33-35 - "My children, I will be with you only a little longer. You will look for me, and just as I told the Jews, so I tell you now: Where I am going, you cannot come." Jesus thinks of His disciples as His children whom He is leaving in the world, but He will not leave them destitute and bereaved. He will send to them the Comforter (Holy Spirit), that cannot be seen by natural eyes but His impact will be seen. He instructed the children that "A new command I give you: Love one another. As I have loved you, so you must love one another. By this everyone will know that you are my disciples, if you love one another."

****

There's a big difference between what makes a 'father' and a 'dad'. A father is someone who believes that by donating his sperm for your creation, he has done his duty in life. A dad is someone who gets up every day and does whatever he can to put a roof over your head, clothes on your back and food on your table. Anybody can be a father but it takes commitment for a father to be a dad.

****

A tribute to my husband: "You're My Best Friend". You placed gold on my finger. You brought love like I've never known. You gave life to our children, and to me a reason to go on. You're my shelter from troubled winds. You're my anchor in life's ocean. But most of all you're my best friend."

****

The best men are those who are best to their wives.

****

"Some women fail to realize that men have feelings too, they were just taught not to show them."

****

Men are supposed to lead. "If a girl is talking to your man, she's not the problem, he is. The fact that a woman feels so welcomed reflects how your man acts behind your back. You can't get mad at a female for not staying in her lane if your man hasn't defined a lane for her to stay in." ~ Ssenyonjo Enock

****

"In spite of the situation; no matter how much you grow up, you will always be the apple of your father's eye, the reigning queen of your dad's heart and daddy's little girl forever."

****

"Happy Blessed Father's Day to Abba Father the GREATEST FATHER of all, thank you, Father, for all of the great fathers you have placed here for your children, thank you for the standard you set for us in your Word. Thank you, thank you, thank you."

****

Father's Day is dad's care giving day to the children, and to the wives; it is husband's care giving day. Make it a special day for them please.

****

My dad used to tell me that relationship alone does not qualify me to get what he has. He said that, I must add friendship to the relationship in place because I did not choose to be his son but I can choose to be his friend.

****

To know what it means to be truly man, we look at the man who is truly God.

****

Mankind is supposed to be physically fit, mentally fit and morally fit. "Popular Christian notions of manhood shame, repel, and ruin too many young boys and men who fail to meet those standards" and who don't gravitate toward "'typical' masculine behaviors. We must recover the idea that the marker of a true man is his moral strength, not his muscular fitness."

Life after Divorce

Death in the family also means other losses in all areas of life including finances. Also, it affects relationship in the family. Likewise, death of marriage (divorce) affects all areas of life in the family. Be prepared to handle the consequences of divorce in a reasonable manner.

****

Love is a small four letter word with complex meaning. At times the people whom we love most hurt us most.

****

Sometimes you have just to step forward and move on. No questions, no doubts, no looking back. Just move on.

****

Sometimes burning the bridges is good because it prevents you from going to the places you should have never been in the first place.

****

"Sometimes when a door closes, you have to nail a board over it". Sometimes you have to move on without certain people. It's better to start your own journey alone. If they are meant to be in your life, they'll catch up.

****

"The past should be left in the past, or else it can steal your future." Don't allow guilty to steal your future blessings. Guilt is an odd spirit that should be resisted at any cost. Step forward to the high ground in your calling, please.

****

I do not support divorce but in case it happens, never allow to be held a hostage to the circumstances. Repent and ask God to forgive you. The blood of Jesus is thicker than all of our sins including divorce. Don't let divorce define you, confine you and outshine you. Choose to move on and leave the past behind you.

****

The divorced people fill shame and rejected horizontally and vertically. Always turn to God for comfort. God hates divorce but He loves repented sinners including the divorced.

****

You can't force someone to love you. Sometimes you have to let go for your benefit. At times the person you want most is the person you are best without.

****

Cry. Forgive. Learn. Move on. Let your tears water the seeds of your future happiness!

****

"Relationships are like glass. Sometimes it's better to leave them broken than hurt yourself trying to put it back together."

****

Losing somebody is a hard thing and especially if you were close. We need to understand that everything has its time and sometimes God puts certain people in your life for a short time. It does not mean it is the end of time; life goes on.

****

Don't rush into a new relationship unless you are sure that you are led by God to that person. When the time comes to be in love, never be afraid to love. Often, when people feel betrayed and hurt by love, they fear to be in love again. They feel they have to guard themselves against the words 'I love you' and from any commitment to love. Such words remind them of their EXs. Remember that you are not alone. Most people have been brokenhearted at some time or another, either by breakups, betrayal, death or some other form of losses. You have God, you have love because God is Love and He is the source of love. When you know what love truly is and where love really comes from, your perspective on the subject will change. Knowing Jesus Christ brings the TRUTH of LOVE right into your heart. Love becomes more personal to you than ever before.

****

I have always been afraid of losing people I love, but sometimes I keep asking myself, is there anyone who is afraid of losing me too?

****

"Learn to be alone, and like it. There is nothing more freeing and empowering than learning to like your own company".

****

July: Our Liberty in Christ

1 Timothy 2:5 – "For there is one God and one mediator between God and mankind, the man Christ Jesus". This scripture rules out the possibility of the authenticity of other false prophets who claim to be our guidance to heaven. The mediator mediates the relationship between the fallen man and God. Therefore, a mediator must be as perfect as God. He must need no savior in order to save others from their sins. Otherwise, in case he has sins he must save himself first before saving others. Apart from Adam (before his fall) Jesus is the only perfect human being who has ever walked on the universe. Intriguingly, all of these false prophets claiming to be sent by God to guide people to heaven cannot amend their own faults. They cannot save themselves; they need a Savior too! Why follow them blindly?

****

Hebrews 7:22 depicted the economy of our redemption. Sin is the debt. Man is the debtor. God is the creditor. Christ is the surety. With this language, the Bible tells us that Christ is the One who co-signs the note. He is the One who stands there, backing up our indebtedness, taking on the requirement of what must be paid. Christ stands in as the mediator that reconciles God and man. Paul wrote that, at the cross, God was in Christ reconciling the world to Himself (2 Cor. 5:19).

****

John 6:53 – "Then Jesus said unto them, Verily, verily, I say unto you, Except ye eat the flesh of the Son of man, and drink his blood, ye have no life in you." The physical is symbolic of the spiritual. The food is for the physical body as the Word is for the spiritual body. Jesus is the Word. He gave His life by His blood. Life is in the blood. The blood of Jesus is the saving blood as it is the shared blood. We are saved by His blood, and we share in His life because of His blood. Jesus gave Himself for us so that he might be available to us.

****

The Feast of harvests was celebrated by the Israelites way back in the Old Testament. This festival is known by several names that derive from its meaning and timing. It is known as the Feast of Harvest (Exodus 23:16), it represents the firstfruits (Numbers 28:26) gathered as the result of the labor of those who completed the spring grain harvests in ancient Israel (Exodus 23:16). God established His annual Holy Days around the harvest seasons in the Middle East (Leviticus 23:9-16; Exodus 23:14-16). Just as His people harvested their crops around these three festival seasons, God's Holy Days show us how He is harvesting people for eternal life in His Kingdom. The Feast of Harvests follows the Passover symbolizing Christ's giving of Himself for us so our sins could be forgiven and we could be redeemed from death. It is the abundance grace that saves the chief of sinners. The Feast of Harvests became the birthday of the Church (Pentecost). It could not become Pentecost until the death, resurrection and ascension of Jesus. The Lord continues to harvest when we preach the gospel: "And the Lord added to their number daily those who were being saved." (Acts 2:47).

****

Facing the trials of life without Christ is devastating. In Christ, we have everything we need spiritually. Therefore, in this world, losing for the sake of Christ is gaining. A Christian has no reason to be despaired. We are trekkers on an expedition built on faith and hope. We encounter trials in course of our cosmic journey but despair is not for us. Faith is looking beyond this world and beholding our destiny. We may lose everything this world has to offer but we retain our reason for living. The good news is that we are not indebted to this world. We are all debtors to our Savior's infinite grace—a debt we can never repay. In fact, He died for us because we couldn't pay our debt. "The borrower is a slave to the lender." This world owes us nothing. In Jesus Christ, we are debt free, and in Him, we find an antidote for emptiness.

****

We are sinners but dressed in the robes of righteousness. The only way a sinner can be certainly sure of the forgiveness of sins is to stand before God in His imputed righteousness.

****

"All my hopes and comforts may be summed up by saying I have a rich and gracious Savior!" ~ John Newton

****

"There is no man so good that if he places all his actions and thoughts under the scrutiny of the laws, he would not deserve hanging ten times in his life" ~ Michel de Montaigne

****

Somebody asked, "Did God terminate the old covenant in order to establish the new covenant?" The word 'covenant' means contract. The people of the world make legal contracts signed by witnesses because we are vulnerable to the deceitfulness of mankind. God is a faithful partner that never breaks His contract or covenant. God never broke the old covenant but Israel broke the covenant with God over and over by disobeying God's commandments. Jesus did not come to abolish the old covenant but to fulfill it (Matthew 5:17-18). He fulfilled the Law by rightly interpreting it; by living under the Law without breaking it; by paying the wages of the broken laws (death). Remember that God promised to bless Abraham through his seed (singular): "And in thy seed shall all the nations of the earth be blessed" (Genesis 22:18). That is, in His one and principal seed, the Messiah, that should spring from him, Galatians 3:16, in whom all the elects of God, of all nations under the heavens, are blessed with all spiritual blessings - with peace, pardon, righteousness, and eternal life, with grace here and glory hereafter.

****

Romans 8:3 – "For what the law was powerless to do because it was weakened by the flesh, God did by sending his own Son in the likeness of sinful flesh to be a sin offering. And so he condemned sin in the flesh". The Law (Word) is powerless to save, not because there is something wrong with the Law but because there is everything wrong with mankind. Jesus is the Word (Law) that put on the perfect human flesh in order to defeat the curse brought on us as a result of breaking the Law. He lived under the Law without breaking it. He rightly demonstrated and explained the Word (Law) for us.

The life of Jesus Christ is the perfect example for us to follow in all respects. It is from the same perspective Peter writes, "For to this you were called, because Christ also suffered for us, leaving us an example, that you should follow His steps" (I Peter 2:21). The above scripture means that "The perfect God came in the likeness of the sinful flesh to be a sin offering." Life is in the blood. Jesus' blood is perfect because He is the begotten Son of God. His conception was activated by the Holy Spirit. He was born of a virgin without the corrupt seed of Adam. His perfect blood became the only acceptable offering to God. He condemned sin in His flesh by paying the penalties (wages) for our sins. The wages of sin is death. Sin is the transgression of the law (1 John 3:4). A born again believer does not trace his ancestry to the first Adam but to the Second Adam (Jesus). He or she walks in obedience to the Word as Jesus did. Walking by the Spirit is walking in obedience to God. The Spirit led life is even (the same) with the perfection as projected by the Moral Law.

****

James 2:14-17: "Thus also faith by itself, if it does not have works, is dead." Faith alone saves but the faith that saves is not alone. The saving faith must produce good works of obedience. Works do not save but they follow salvation. James says that show me the faith that works, and I will show the faith proven by good works.

****

Without the temple, there cannot be an accepted sacrifice. Jesus doubles as the true temple and the ultimate sacrifice. The image of the blood in the Old Testament is that another innocent life died in the place of the guilty party, temporarily taking away the sins of the people. But the animal sacrifice had to be repeated over and over because a person sinned over and over. The blood of Jesus was sacrificed once and forever and presented to the throne of heaven to atone for our past, present and future sins (Hebrews 10:12).

****

The blood of Jesus is the blood of God. The Bible says that: "Keep watch over yourselves and all the flock of which the Holy Spirit has made you overseers. Be shepherds of the church of God, which he bought with his own blood" (Acts 20:28). Peter wrote that, "For you know that it was not with perishable things such as silver or gold that you were redeemed from the empty way of life handed down to you from your ancestors, 19 but with the precious blood of Christ, a lamb without blemish or defect. 20 He was chosen before the creation of the world, but was revealed in these last times for your sake." (1 Peter 1:18-20).

****

"Cancer is not one single disease, but a whole group of conditions, which are caused by the abnormal growth of the body's cells." Doctors say that there are cancer cells in every person. Cancer stem cells have the same ability of normal cells (to reproduce and reach for immortality.) Except, unlike normal stem cells, they cannot be lulled back to sleep. People develop cancer when the cancer cells overpower their immune system and become tumors. The corruption of the body is the reality of the curse of sin, which is death. Our liberty is in Christ who overcame death on our behalf. We were redeemed spiritually but our physical bodies are subjected to the curse of the physical death because we are sinners by nature. Death is the means of putting off this tent: "I declare to you, brothers and sisters, that flesh and blood cannot inherit the kingdom of God, nor does the perishable inherit the imperishable" (1 Corinthians 15:50). We shall put on the incorruptible bodies which can see God. Currently, the grace allows God to dwell in our hearts (not bodies) to prepare us for glorification. As per now, we know God by our intimate relationship with Christ but we shall see Him as He is.

****

John 1:4-5 -"In him was life; and the life was the light of men. And the light shineth in darkness; and the darkness comprehended it not." Jesus is God wrapped in human flesh. He removes the veil of the corrupt nature from His chosen ones so that they can see Him in His divine attributes. When we marry the couples, the bridegroom removes the veil of the bride symbolically so that they stand face to face as one! The unveiling of the face of the bride to the bridegroom means complete oneness. The same thing happens when we are married to Jesus. He removes the veil so that we can see Him, know Him intimately and become one with Him! In His light, we have the concept of the world view that is proportional to God's view. In Him we have prominence because He is our righteousness. His life became ours to manifest so that others might see Him in us!

****

John 3:16 - "For God so loved the world, that he gave his only begotten Son, that whosoever believeth in him should not perish, but have everlasting life." The word "so" is attached to the word "loved" to designate God's overwhelming passionate love. His unconditional love is beyond natural. The name Jesus (Yeshua) conveys the idea that God (YHVH יְהֹוָה.) delivers or saves His people. We will never understand the greatness of our salvation unless we understand the greatness of our Savior (God). Our salvation is great because our Savior is infinitely great. We need a greater deliverer because our sins are great. It means that our depravity is beyond repair by any natural means. We were doomed but God stepped in (intervened) to save the unsavable! The indwelling Spirit of God is the assurance of our salvation. Our salvation is not based on any formula but on our faith in Christ. Salvation is for a repentant heart that has sincerely placed its trust (faith) in Christ to save. It is not just answering an altar call and repeating a prayer of confession. It's repenting and sincerely confessing of our sin to Christ that lay hold of salvation.

****

Somebody asked: "What do you say about the generation curse?" The doctrine of the generation curse suggests that the sins of the parents are passed on to the children and grandchildren. However, the prophetic message says: "In those days they shall say no more, The fathers have eaten a sour grape, and the children's teeth are set on edge." (Jeremiah 31:29). The days talked about in this scripture is the time of the new covenant and grace. Jesus is our Savior. He, alone, was sent to die for the sins of others (the world). No more shall a soul that is not in some sense worthy of death for his own sins, perish for the sins of another. Jesus is a personal Savior, and He deals with individual sins.

The children are not guilty of their parents' sins. Given the fact, the sins of the parents can have consequential impacts on the children. For example, children can pick up the bad habits like drugs, alcohol, and abuse from their parents. Also, they can inherit infectious diseases from their parents. We know that when Jesus saves us, we are forgiven but we are not exempted from the consequences of our sins. For example, if a convict that is sentenced to serve a jail time gets saved while still in jail, he still has to serve his jail time. Also, when you lose your leg during vicious activities and you become saved afterward, you will be a child of God but it will not replace your lost leg. Suffering from the consequences of your sins does not mean that God still holds you accountable for the same sins. A saved person takes on the holiness of Jesus Christ. It is the imputed righteous of God. It is unmerited favor bestowed on us. "Therefore if any man be in Christ, he is a new creature: old things are passed away; behold, all things are become new" (2 Corinthians 5:17).

****

"When we really understand how at enmity we are with God when we are outside of Christ, it makes His sovereign grace more amazing!"

****

2 Corinthians 11:14 - "And no wonder, for Satan himself masquerades as an angel of light." Satan's character is revealed in deception. Deception is a creative art for communicating of nonfactual ideas. It is a trap that permits all kinds of misrepresentation and inconspicuousness. Satan's primary objective is to disrepute the identity of the person of Jesus and His character (Word). No wonder some confessing believers still question the deity of Jesus. Jesus is God by nature and the Father made Him the Lord (Isaiah 43:10,11; Acts 2:36; Revelation 1:17; 2:8). Nobody has a right to make Jesus the Lord. Our assigned duty is to accept His Lordship over us. Satan messes not only with the identity of Jesus but with our identity as well. Satan knows your name and he calls you by your sin. But Jesus knows your name and He calls you the righteous of God. Jesus covers (atone) your sins for His glory so that you might be called the redeemed of the Lord. Faith is allowing Jesus to do what He came to do. If all believers understood their identity as Jesus does, then our spirituality wouldn't be the futile muddle which it is.

****

Hebrews 11:6 - "But without faith it is impossible to please him: for he that cometh to God must believe that he is, and that he is a rewarder of them that diligently seek him." The minds can't love God as the heart. Faith defies logic. Faith begins in the minds and is settled in the heart. What we know is meaningless unless it is translated into believing. The word 'translation' comes, etymologically, from the Latin for 'bearing across'." In the process of translation, there is something lost and something gained. I cling, obstinately to the notion that true believing involves giving up something in exchange for something of the greater value. Faith is exchanging the lies of Satan for the truth of God. The price of anything depends on the value of life you exchange for it. Believing is exchanging your corrupted life for His everlasting life. Jesus is the timeless truth personified.

****

Real faith is believing that God will do what He promised to do even if it will happen after you have expired.

****

2 Peter 3:18 - "But grow in the grace and knowledge of our Lord and Savior Jesus Christ. To him be glory both now and forever! Amen." Our salvation includes justification, sanctification, and glorification. Justification is by grace alone. The effect of justification is transformation, and it is a one-time event. But the whole of Christian life is conversion. It is a process of sanctification involving repentance, obedience, and faith. After we are saved, we are called to grow into grace, meaning a process of growing into obedience to the statutes or ordinances of God (sanctification). Constantly growing into the grace is moving forward and following Christ by walking as He walked.

****

Jesus prayed for the oneness of the glory. The first time oneness was mentioned, it is related to the Father's name and the Father's life—the eternal life (John 17:2, 6, 11b). Hence, this oneness is in the Father's name and in His life. This is the first level. When 'oneness' is mentioned the second time, it is related to the Father's Word (John 17:14-21). When the Father's Word with the Father's reality is applied to us, it produces an effect, which is to sanctify us from the Satan-ensnared world and to separate us unto God. This is the second level of the oneness, the oneness in the Father's Word, that is, in the Father's reality. When oneness is mentioned the third time, it is related to the Father's glory (John 17:22-23). In the Father's glory, we are one. This is the third level of the oneness. When these three levels of oneness are fulfilled, the Lord Jesus' prayer for the oneness of the believers is accomplished. The oneness the Lord wants is one in which we have the same source and the same life, taking the Father as the source and living by His life. When the Father's life with His nature becomes the element of oneness in us, we will spontaneously be one.

****

God didn't promise us a trouble-free-world but He promised that He will keep us from evil in this troubled world.

****

Romans 8:39 - "Neither height nor depth, nor anything else in all creation, will be able to separate us from the love of God that is in Christ Jesus our Lord." Paul meant that all dimensions of life are set to work in our favor. All things including the manifested miracles and angels must add rather than subtract the glory from Christ. The Universal Law is that "Take Christ out of life and everything falls apart." We are complete in Christ, without Christ we are nothing compared to the vapor that disappears in a moment of time.

****

1 Corinthians 13:4-7 - "Love suffers long and is kind; love does not envy; love does not parade itself, is not puffed up; does not behave rudely, does not seek its own, is not provoked, thinks no evil; does not rejoice in iniquity, but rejoices in the truth; bears all things, believes all things, hopes all things, endures all things". Put the name 'Jesus' in place of the word 'love' in the above scripture, and He will be everything demanded by love in the above scripture. But when you put your name in place of the word 'love' in the above scripture, you will fail miserably. It means that loving God's way is manifesting the life of Jesus in your life. It is allowing Jesus to love others through you.

****

Blessed are the meek, for they will inherit the earth. This world is not what we are fighting for but what we are fighting against. God is in the process of redeeming this world for our inheritance. If all people knew this truth, nobody would kill another person for this world which is passing away!

****

The world has only one direction which the people of the world take when running away from God. When Adam sinned he ran into hiding from God. The people of the world are running as fast as possible to hide from God. The Church has two directions: You are either moving closer to God or away from God.

****

John 5:24 - "Verily, verily, I say unto you, He that heareth my word, and believeth on him that sent me, hath everlasting life, and shall not come into condemnation; but is passed from death unto life." There is no drop of grace outside Jesus. Jesus has the monopoly access to God. Patent truth justifies His monopoly and rules out the possibility of any other means of salvation outside Him. There are many ways to hell but there is one way to heaven.

****

Jesus is the objective truth. The truth is personal. Jesus is not just the mere source of life but He is the embodiment of it – He is the life. He doesn't give love apart from Himself – He is Love; He doesn't give peace apart from Himself - He is the Prince of peace; He doesn't give grace apart from Himself – He is all gracious. Need eternal life? Receive Jesus today!

****

Just a reminder: When you reject Jesus, you decide to manage your own sins. The grace influences obedience. Obedience is surrendered will. It is His will at the expense of your will. Allow Jesus to clean your conscience and to be the sole proprietor controlling your will. Observe and absorb the truth.

****

Marriage is the two becoming one physically and spiritually. When you marry a heathen Satan becomes your father in law, and he moves in with your spouse.

****

Somebody asked "I consider myself to be a child of God and a prince. Why did Paul call himself a bond-slave? The scripture is, "Paul, a bond-servant of Christ Jesus, called as an apostle, set apart for the gospel of God" (Romans 1:1). The word 'slave' also means servant. *Doulos* is a Greek word meaning bondservant. "Bond-slave" arises from the same origin and is a direct (albeit emphatic) synonym to "slave," again meaning an owned or purchased slave, one bound to a master. A bond-slave is the one who has surrendered his will to his master. He is the one who is committed to the cause of his master. Paul merely uses the basic word for a person who is permanently owned by another person.

James, the brother of Jesus also out of humility introduced himself as a servant of Christ (James 1:1). Paul compared himself to a bond-slave in accordance to the Mosaic Law: "But if the slave plainly says, 'I love my master, my wife, and my children; I will not go out as a free man,' then his master shall bring him to God, then he shall bring him to the door or the doorpost. And his master shall pierce his ear with an awl; and he shall serve him permanently" (Exodus 21:5). The Hebrew slave was supposed to get his freedom in the seventh year and in the year of Jubilee. In case, for some reasons, he did not want to leave the house of his master, he was taken at the door of the temple and his ear was pierced as a mark of a voluntary act to stay loyal to his master. Paul sees himself as a bond-slave who voluntarily became a slave of Christ by his choice, after being liberated from sin.

****

When the grace impacts your heart, you purposely choose and desire holiness. Obedience to the commandments of God becomes your priority.

Every aspect of your life must draw attention to your faith. "What we think about heaven affects how we live for God today."

****

God's laws without the existence of the relationship become distressing decrees. But when the laws are given within the context of relationship they are precepts or principles we love to implement. The person you love does not have to force you doing the things they like. You just feel privileged to do them!

****

"God gave 10 commandments because man asked for it, man took the 10 they asked for and turned them into 613 laws, then Jesus under the law, before his death and resurrection broke them down to only two which is really only one commandment of "Love""

****

James 2:18 - "But someone will say, "You have faith; I have deeds." Show me your faith without deeds, and I will show you my faith by my deeds." We have no evidence that we are saved apart from our obedience to the commandments of God.

****

John 14:15 - "If you love me, keep my commands." If you truly have a new relationship with God, you must have a new relationship with sin. You can't have the same old feelings for sin and claim to be in love with Jesus. Sin is the transgression of the Law (1 John 3:4). A new relationship with God loves obeying God. The Holy Spirit changed the commandments of God from a burden to our object of affection and pride. After we are born again, we are supposed to share a passionate commitment to holiness as Jesus did. The requisite to obey the commandments of God aligns with the desires of your new nature. For example, the commandment instructs us not commit adultery, and our new nature already hates adultery because God wrote

His commandments on our hearts (Hebrews 8:10). When you are in a relationship with somebody, you will voluntarily do certain things for them without being pressured. But when you are not in a relationship you do the same things out of obligation, contrary to your desire. Therefore, obeying the commandments without having a relationship with Jesus Christ equals to death. And having a relationship with Jesus Christ without obeying His commandments equals to death. "We are not saved by faith plus works but we are saved by the faith that works". I mean the faith that has evidence of a sanctified soul.

****

Jesus said to them, "Truly, I say to you, the tax collectors and the harlots go into the kingdom of God before you" (Matthew 21:31). Jesus insinuated that it will be easier for the prostitutes to go into the kingdom because nobody has gone too far beyond the reach of the grace. On the contrary, the Jewish religious leaders rejected the Savior and trusted in their personal capability to go to heaven by keeping the Law. Nobody can work hard enough to earn the grace. The acceptable righteousness to God cannot be merited, it is imputed to us: The Bible says that "For he hath made him to be sin for us, who knew no sin; that we might be made the righteousness of God in him" (2 Corinthians 5:21).

Also, "And be found in him, not having mine own righteousness, which is of the law, but that which is through the faith of Christ, the righteousness which is of God by faith" (Philippians 3:9). The Bible says that "For he chose us in him before the creation of the world to be holy and blameless in his sight. In love" (Ephesians 1:4). It means that your righteousness preceded your existence.

****

There are Ten Commandments (Moral law) representing the character of God. The Sabbath is the fourth commandment, and it is valid to us as the rest of the nine commandments. The word sabbath is the Hebrew word SHABÀT, meaning 'cessation,' or 'time of rest. The word Sabbath in Greek is *sabbaton*: i.e. the seventh day. As such it was a cherished gift of God, to

His people: "a sign between me and you for generations to come" (Exodus 31:12-17), testifying of God's faithfulness to his covenant throughout the generations. The covenant relationship demands Israel's sanctification, and by keeping the Sabbath holy Israel is reminded continually that the God who sanctified the seventh day also sanctifies her. Adam represented the entire human race. Likewise, Israel represented all of the ethnic groups. When God made a covenant with Israel, He made it with mankind. God chose Israel in order to bless the entire human race. The promised Savior came from Israel and was born under the Law. He came to show us how to walk rightly. We are His followers.

****

Somebody asked that. "Did God do away with the Sabbath?" The word 'sabbath simply means resting. There are multiple Jewish sabbaths in the Bible being holidays to honor Jewish festivals. For example the Sabbath of the Passover that preceded the crucifixion of Jesus. Our salvation does not depend on observing the Jewish festivals and holidays but it depends on Jesus Christ who became our Sabbath. The Sabbath given in the Ten Commandments started with creation to honor God that created the universe by resting. That is why the fourth commandment was given in form of remembrance. The fourth commandment of observing the Sabbath is as valid as any other nine commandments. The Ten Commandments are called Moral Law because they represent the holiness of God. The Moral Law cannot change because the holiness of God does not change.

According to historical fact, it is the Catholic Pope that changed the Sabbath from Saturday to Sunday. Given the fact, the early church observed the Sabbath as a day of resting (Luke 4:16) and the first day of the week (Sunday) as a day of communion to commemorate the resurrection of Jesus (Acts 20:7; 1 Cor. 16:1-2). Jesus said He did not come to destroy the Moral Law but to fulfill it (Matthew 5:17). He fulfilled it to us by living after the Law without breaking it, as an example. He fulfilled it by paying the penalties of the broken laws on our behalf. He fulfilled it by rightly interpreting it for us. He did not break any of the ten moral laws. He discredited the tradition way of the Pharisees regarding observing the

Sabbath, and He showed us the right way to observe the Sabbath: "Then Jesus asked them, "Which is lawful on the Sabbath: to do good or to do evil, to save life or to kill?" But they remained silent" (Mark 3:4). I want to say that there is no conflict between the Word and the Law because the Law is part of the Word. Also, there is no contradiction between the Law and the Spirit because the Spirit is as holy as the Law.

****

The Law is divided into three categories: The ceremonial laws involving worshiping God. These were shadows of Christ, and we do not need to observe them. The civil laws involved the practical aspects of citizenship, its rights and duties; the duties of citizens to each other as members of a community which was ruled by God (theocracy). These were replaced by the sermon on the mountain teachings of Jesus. The diet laws involved what to eat. These are still good for our health but they are not applicable to our spirituality. The Moral Law (Ten Commandments) represents the holiness of God. These are still applicable. We are not saved by keeping them but we keep them because we are saved. They are God's commandments given for our own benefit. The traffic laws do not benefit the government and the law enforcement officers but they are for our own safety as we travel on the streets. Likewise, the commandments of God are for our own good so that we might reach our destiny safely without dents. Jesus is coming for a bride without wrinkles or blemish (Ephesians 5:27). He is coming for a bride that loves Him. He said that, ""If you love Me, you will keep My commandments" (John 14:15).

****

Somebody asked that "In Galatians 4:30, why did God reject Ishmael. Yet, He accepted all of the sons of Jacob from different women?" The Scripture says, "Get rid of the slave woman and her son, for the slave woman's son will never share in the inheritance with the free woman's son." True, Jacob had twelve sons and at least one daughter, by his two wives, Leah and Rachel, and by their handmaidens Bilhah and Zilpah. The reason God rejected Ishmael to share in the inheritance of Abraham is because the promise was made to Abraham and Sarah. It is from these two people that the promise is extended to Israel. The illegitimate union between Abraham and Hagar was not approved by God and was outside of the divine plan. The allegory of Hagar and Sarah is written to persuade us (along with the Galatians) not to follow the Judaizers into slavery with Hagar and Ishmael, but to follow Sarah and Isaac into freedom. The Judaizers rejected the idea that salvation is by faith in the finished works of Jesus Christ at the cross alone.

****

Can a man lose everything and still serve God? Can a man be ready to lose himself to serve God? Our contentment does not depend on circumstances but on God. It is not what you have or who you are or where you are or what you are doing that fulfills you. Our faith in Christ is the direct route to serenity and contentment. We are called to define our circumstances in terms of our faith as opposed to our faith in terms of our circumstances.

****

Olympic 2018 news: As you probably know, Phelps carried the American flag during the opening ceremonies on Friday, August 5. Then, as of this recording, he's added three more gold medals to his impressive lifetime total, now numbering 21. To put it mildly, both of these were unlikely less than two years ago. As Phelps told ESPN, following his announced retirement in 2012, he struggled to "figure out who he was outside the pool." In his words, "I was a train wreck. I was like a time bomb, waiting to go off. I had no self-esteem, no self-worth. There were times where I didn't want to be here. It was not good. I felt lost." Like a lot of people struggling with similar feelings, he self-medicated. In the immediate aftermath of that DWI arrest, he cut himself off from family and other loved ones and "thought the world would just be better off without me . . . I figured that was the best thing to do — just end my life." That's when a friend came to his rescue: former All Pro linebacker Ray Lewis, whom Phelps considers a kind of "older brother." Seeing the hopelessness and despair in his young friend, Lewis, an outspoken Christian, told him, "This is when we fight . . .

This is when the real character shows up. Don't shut down. If you shut down we all lose." Lewis convinced Phelps to enter rehab and gave him a book to read while he was there: "The Purpose-Driven Life" by my friend Rick Warren. The book changed Phelps' life. Within a few days, Phelps called Lewis and told him "'Man this book is crazy . . . The thing that's going on . . . oh my gosh . . . my brain, I can't thank you . . . enough, man. You saved my life.'" As Phelps told ESPN, Rick Warren's book "turned me into believing there is a power greater than myself and there is a purpose for me on this planet." The book, which tells readers that "relationships are always worth restoring," also convinced Phelps to reconcile with his father from whom he had been estranged for more than two decades. Upon seeing each other, they embraced. As I record this commentary, Phelps still has two more chances to medal, but his story of hope and restoration doesn't really need any further embellishments—to use one of my favorite words, it's miraculous enough. Michael Phelps' story is a reminder that joy cannot be attained by prestige, fame and money. Also, no matter how big a mess your life may be, and no matter how dim the last embers of hope may glow, God is still there. It's also a reminder of the role that God's people are called to play as bringers of hope and agents of restoration:

****

One of the greatest tragedies in life is to lose your own sense of self. But it comes to our salvation, it is not so. Jesus gives you a sense of Himself and makes you lose a sense of yourself. He liberates you from self-sufficient to God-sufficient. It thus follows, the sense of 'self' disintegrates whenever the Spirit of God is in charge. Therefore, receiving Jesus is accepting the new version of you in the divine. It is allowing God's will to be done on earth as it is done in heaven.

****

1 Corinthians 12:24-25 - "But God has put the body together, giving greater honor to the parts that lacked it, so that there should be no division in the body, but that its parts should have equal concern for each other." Your soul is desperately in search of the real you. Without finding it, life

is essentially nothing but a mystery. We have multiple personalities. Your life cannot be separated from the mundane lives you are living. We were created in God's image to manifest God's life. Such life is restored to us by Jesus and is explicitly revealed in His sacrificial selflessness love. Agape love is, therefore, more than emotional compatibility; it is spiritual and supernatural. It is the kind of love that puts God and neighbor above 'self', and can only be afforded by a regenerated soul. Our new nature is the nature of Christ. It is supernaturally revealed to us, and evidently manifested by the way we live, in particular how we relate to others. His nature in you must be noticeable by His character in you. Your life cannot be lived in secrecy. Your new nature is automatically attracted to the new nature in others. We are one body of Christ (church), and we are intuitively connected. The new nature makes us compatible and helps us to deal with incompatibility. Discover yourself by being other-centered. Have a great week!

****

2 Samuel 6:16 – "As the ark of the LORD was entering the City of David, Michal daughter of Saul watched from a window. And when she saw King David leaping and dancing before the LORD, she despised him in her heart." God judged Michal, the daughter of Saul, she had no children to the day of her death (verse 23). By despising David's rejoicing, she basically despised the victory of God that David was celebrating. Mocking the ministry of the people whom God called to serve is akin to mocking God. Sin in all its forms mocks the holiness of God. On the contrary, righteousness is a mockery to evil. Righteousness exalts God and strengthens our defenses against the powers of darkness. This is the recommended lifestyle of a believer. Keep on pursuing it, advancing it and consolidating it.

****

Ecclesiastes 4:12 - "A cord of three strands is not quickly broken." This metaphor should communicate strongly to anyone familiar with a rope (or, interestingly, in our own day, cable). A cord of three strands is not quickly broken. The triple-braided cord model reflects the central image of the Trinity in, at least, a couple of ways. God gave to us His Word, His son, and His Spirit. When Adam was in the Garden (before falling), he had the company of God because his spirit actively communicated with God, and he obeyed God's Word. God abandoned Adam when Adam desecrated himself by disobeying the Word of God. Ungodly means without God. Without God, man finds himself alone and deserted. Sin isolated man from inside to outside. God reaches out to us from inside (heart) to outside (good works). We are given a three cord strength to witness on our behalf that we are children of God, saved from His wrath. 1) The affirming Word of the Father - The Word eternally settled in heaven, and manifested to us in the Son. 2) The saving grace of Jesus - The surety of our life because of His blood. 3) The atoning power of the Holy Spirit – Jesus working in us and through us. "His name, Emmanuel, which being interpreted - God with us" (Matthew 1:23). He is with us, never to forsake us; He checked in, never to check out. Want to know the address of God? We are the divine residence on the earth (temple).

****

Psalm 145:8 – "The LORD is gracious and full of compassion; slow to anger, and of great mercy." God chooses mercy over judgment. He chooses to judge only when there is no any other option left.

****

The spiritual realm is as real as the natural realm. In fact, the spiritual realm determines what takes places in the natural realm. Whenever something happens in the physical realm, there is a similar thing happening in the spiritual realm. The heavenly (spiritual) realm is where God has His provision for us. When the things you see are falling apart, the things you don't see are holding together. "The spiritual realm is a real world, invisible to the natural eye but visible to the eye of faith" Faith is believing without seeing (Hebrews11:1-2). Go deeper in your faith with life in the Spirit and change the perspective of your life in the natural. Remember that what you get in the spiritual depends on what you do in the physical.

****

God is using your circumstances to change you. So, instead of asking God to take away the bad circumstances, ask Him to use your circumstances to teach you.

****

Saul of Tarsus, a Jewish scholar and zealous persecutor of Christians, who famously converted on the road to Damascus and became the apostle Paul. His original Hebrew name was Saul (the name Saul sticks until Acts 13). The name Saul in Greek is written as Σαυλος, Saulos. The root-verb שאל (sha'al) means to ask, inquire, borrow, beg. This verb occurs all over the Bible, in all expectable ways. Most notably is the usage in entreaty for God's guidance or salvation (1 Samuel 23:2, Joshua 9:14). From the Roman family name Paulus, which meant "small" or "humble" in Latin. Paul was an important leader of the early Christian church. According to Acts in the New Testament, he was a Jewish Roman citizen who converted to Christianity after the resurrected Jesus appeared to him. After this, he traveled the eastern Mediterranean as a missionary. Many of the epistles in the New Testament were authored by him.

****

Luke 24:49 - "And, behold, I send the promise of my Father upon you: but tarry you in the city of Jerusalem, until you be endued with power from on high." To be endued is to be clothed with the power of the Holy Spirit. The Holy Spirit is not an idea or a force; He is an entity that labors with us. I am a debtor client in perpetuity to the Holy Spirit. He has empowered me, guided me, taught me, defended me, and comforted me endlessly. To pay back is to voluntarily become a bondservant of Christ. Any life without Christ is out of control. Spiritual freedom is self-control. It means you are obstructed in living a life that is out of the control of the Holy Spirit. It is deciding to live passionately the life of Christ by surrendering your will.

****

The stiff-necked people are full of pride. They do themselves injury. They would never turn to Jesus for salvation, but the battle to mortify the lusts of the old nature is real in them. It is a constant reminder that they, like all men, are of dust and vulnerable. They too need the true grace that saves to the uttermost, because they have a struggle against the flesh. "Humility is not thinking less of yourself but thinking of yourself less!"

****

Prejudice is a sin of ignorance. Prejudice begins with our biases against some scriptures. Often, some Church goers go to the Scriptures to justify their wrong doings. You can make the Bible say what you want when you pick a verse and you interpret it out of its context (chapter and Bible). We are called to rightly divide the Word of the truth (2 Timothy 2:15). Prejudice is prematurely coming to a conclusion without having all the necessary information at your fingertips. Ignorance is prejudice made plausible. All of us are technically ignorant until we immerse ourselves in the ink of the Scriptures. "We all decry prejudice, yet are all prejudiced."

****

We are called to be merciful all people. Mercy should be extended to the people who offended us and to those whom we owe nothing. A calling to be plenteous in mercy is a mandatory to all believers who experienced mercy from God. Through Jesus Christ, God put on display His attributes of mercy and justice. He saved us from eternal damnation, and preordained us to eternal salvation without any merit of our own. "Where mercy, and love, dwell, there God is dwelling too.

****

If our being in Christ is anchored in eternity, then we have every reason to be confident that He will bring us back into His eternal presence. He will see us safely passing through time to timeless. Our position in Christ is our security.

****

I have a friend in overalls whose friendship I would not swap for the favor of the kings of the world. His name is Jesus.

****

Somebody asked, "Can you explain John 20:22?" This is the scripture: "And with that, he breathed on them and said, "Receive the Holy Spirit." Jesus demonstrated what He came to do. The Bible says that "So it is written: "The first man Adam became a living being"; the last Adam, a life-giving spirit" (1 Corinthians 15:45). Breathing on them was an act of creation. Let us look at the parallel scripture: "And the Lord God formed man of the dust of the ground, and breathed into his nostrils the breath of life; and man became a living soul" (Genesis 2:7). The Hebrew word for God's breathe is typically translated as "spirit" in English is רוּחַ (ruach). This is the image of God in which God created man. Also, man became a living soul. So there is a physical breath as well, which Adam shares with the animals (Genesis 1). But the animals do not have a spiritual breathe because they were not created in the image of God. The animals are not moral creatures, and they are not called to obey any of God's Law. Adam was created moral and incorruptible but he became corrupt and immoral after he violated God's rules. Regeneration is the recreation of man to reverse the corruption, this being the curse of sin. Jesus told Nicodemus that "Flesh gives birth to flesh, but the Spirit gives birth to spirit. You should not be surprised at my saying, 'You must be born again.'" (John 3:6-7). So we see Jesus breathing in man the spiritual life as God did to Adam at creation. Regeneration is instant but transformation is a process of conversion that begins with justification, continues in sanctification and ends in glorification. The grace cannot work without the truth. After regeneration, the Holy Spirit uses the Word of God to renew our minds till we shall be fully restored to the glory of the image of the Son of God (Romans 12:1-2).

July: Political Liberty

4<u>th</u> July is our Independence Day. America is synonymous to liberty.

4th July is our Independence Day. What does it mean to be an American? According to E. Metaxas, unlike other countries, America is not defined by a particular ethnic or religious group. Instead, our country was formed around an idea: liberty. But what does it take to maintain liberty? Now, in order to find the answer to this question, we have to go back 229 years, to 1787. Having won the American Revolution, our founders went about creating a new form of government—one that would be strong, but not too strong; one that relied on self-government. The result, of course, was the U.S. Constitution—a marvel.

After their summer-long convention finished, a woman asked Benjamin Franklin, "Well, Doctor, what have we got, a republic or a monarchy?" He famously replied: "A republic, madam—if you can keep it!" And what could cause us to lose the republic? Well, that's simple: the loss of virtue. Benjamin Franklin, like the other founders, understood that freedom and self-government absolutely depend on the practice of virtue. Have you heard that lately? Me neither. John Adams wrote that "the only foundation of a free Constitution is a pure virtue."

Now I'll bet you didn't learn about this link between liberty and virtue in high school civics class. I know I did not. But it was a deeply familiar and necessary concept to all our founders—one that we have largely forgotten—or even worse, dismissed. What Franklin understood—and what modern crime statistics tragically bear out—is that if citizens do not voluntarily practice virtue, the authorities have no choice but to attempt to enforce it.

As Franklin explains, "As nations become more corrupt and vicious, they have more need of masters." In other words, if we don't govern ourselves, we have no choice but to be governed from above. And what do we need in order to buttress the practice of virtue and morality? We need religious faith. George Washington put it bluntly: Laws by themselves are insufficient. "Reason and experience both forbid us to expect that national morality can prevail in exclusion of religious principles," he wrote.

My friend Os Guinness has resurrected the founders' vision for America in his wonderful book, "A Free People's Suicide." He names this vision the Golden Triangle of Freedom. His argument boils down to this: Freedom requires virtue; virtue requires faith; and faith in turn requires freedom. Remove any one of the triangle's sides, and the whole structure collapses.

So how is it that this concept is so seldom mentioned today? Franklin's warning echoes down to us from more than two centuries ago, from that sweltering summer when he helped create the Constitution. When he told the woman "if you can keep it," he meant that if Americans lost the understanding of the link between virtue and citizenship, we would cease being Americans in any real sense of the word.

Today is a great day to start teaching this all-but-forgotten concept to our children, not to mention ourselves. Re-learning these vital ideas, and living by them, is nothing less than a duty because our first and foremost duty as Americans is to know what it means to be an American.

****

The statue of liberty stands for freedom of all people regardless of their race, gender and religious background. We are a Christian nation but we are called to embrace diversity. The stacks of our politics include conservatism as a political and social philosophy promoting and retaining the traditional social institutions in the context of culture and civilization. Then the liberals who are open to new behaviors or opinions and are willing to discard the traditional values on which this country was founded. Of course, we cannot ignore the challenge of secularism, a belief that religion should not play a role in government.

Yes, Christians have the mandate to preach the gospel but we have no mandate to impose our values on others. Likewise, the liberals should stick to their guns of freedom for all but they should practice what they preach. They should shun the temptation of targeting the conservatives with tendencies of clipping their wings, in the name of tolerance. This is true in particular when it comes to the blatant favoritism and biases on the part of the liberal judges. Unless we practice tolerance in its purity, the liberty we yearn for will be history. This country was founded on the Judeo-Christian values, therefore, it is appropriate to stick to the common ethical values based on the Scriptures, regardless of our political views. This is one way we can put the genie back in the bottle. Jesus alone is the antidote to sin. Happy Independence Day; happy 240th birthday America!

****

America is respected for the pursuit of liberty and observing of the human rights. Liberty is not a blank check to do as you will. If every person enjoys their liberty according to their own terms then every person loses liberty. That is why it is important to have a sense of morality and accountability to someone who is beyond humanity and in this case the Moral God. We are called 'a nation under God' because our individual rights assume the moral responsibility to God. Our practical lives must be the manifested characters of Christ, this being the greatest power that can change the world. Democracy is the hub of our political strength, nevertheless, our hope is not in politicians. Given the fact, we are political animals, and it is our right to vote. Since we share the same values, we must be united as a Voting bloc to vote for moral values. Every vote counts but vote wisely without violating your conscience. Your vote can assist good or evil to flourish. It is a vote of approval or disapproval of the status quo of wickedness.

****

It is independence season, and our yards are littered and decorated with flags with 'God bless America' plea. The same message is flashing on the screens of our computers on advertisements and Facebook postings. It is goodwill in the spirit of patriotism but in reality the blessings of God do not come our way by just posting "God bless America" flags. God does not bless pride and insubordination to His Statutes. These are the very things that made Lucifer ("shining one, light-bearer") to become the devil. We have turned our backs on God and wandered away from God, hence, wandering away from His blessings. The God news is that God is angry but He is still loving. Anger is a separation emotion but it can be unifying too. In fact, it is His holy anger towards sin that makes Him loving. He takes no delight when a sinner dies in his sins. Our prayer is therefore not for God to return to America but America to return to God. There is hope; we haven't reached a point of no-return. As you enjoy the fireworks get ready to return to the fire that works. I mean to be on fire for God, and save our country from joining the rest of the nations that are lingering in Limbo or graveyard!

****

Somebody asked that, "Do you believe in capital punishment?" I believe in forgiveness but also the respect of the laws of the country. Capital punishment is not necessarily a punishment but a means of teaching the masses that there is a consequence for every single action and decision we make. Unfortunately, the justice department is at times unfair ending up killing innocent people. There are multiple cases when innocent people were convicted but later on they were exonerated after they were incarcerated for decades. Laws were made for the safety of the masses. A decree is a law which has been promulgated (or "enacted") by a legislature or other Governing Body. God instructed us to obey the laws of the governments because the ethics are regulated by the Civil laws. Given the fact, civil laws do not necessarily make people civil. The law cannot transform the conscience; it simply tells you how low you can go.

****

It is sad that the same people who are screaming against injustices are the same people perpetuating lawlessness. Justice and order cannot exist without strictly observing the laws governing our countries.

****

A generation without fear of God worships the creatures instead of the creator. No wonder we have children who have no respect for authorities inside and outside the house.

****

"The wounded shadow of a wounded leader imposes itself upon all who are subject to the leader's authority".

****

Somebody made this comment: "Worldly politics business is not a Christian business. Let us be more about God's business." My answer in response to his comment: The word "politics" originates from the Greek word from which the title of Aristotle's books. Politics (politika) derives: "affairs of the cities", a dissertation on governing and governments, which was rendered in English in the mid-15th century as Latinized "Polettiques". Christians are not exempted from influencing the way their cities or countries are run. I believe a pastor should not run for an elected office in partisan politics but we have the mandate to intercede and to advise the people how to vote in order to uphold the moral principles glorifying God.

****

Communism: You have two cows. You have to take care of them, but the government takes all the milk. Socialism: You have two cows. The government takes one of your cows and gives it to your neighbor. You're both forced to join a cooperative where you have to teach your neighbor how to take care of his cow.

****

"If democracy ever dies; it won't be the Red Army; it will be the media that destroys democracy: by denying people the voice so that they can tell the government what they want" ~ Tonny Ben

****

"So, if we lie to the government it is a felony. But if they lie to us it is politics" ~ Bill Murray

****

"In all barracks we won. I thank you we won the votes. It's now a coup. This time they stole an elephant and they have failed to hide it because of its size" ~ Kizza Besigye

****

"You can't get rich in politics unless you are a crook" ~ Harry S. Truman

****

The "freedom" the world offers is just a disguised form of bondage ~ Frank Hammond

****

When exposing a crime is treated as committing a crime, you are ruled by criminals ~ Achile Agabile

****

"Terrorism will never cease in a country where the so-called leaders are criminals and terrorists in disguise" ~ Michael Bassey Johnson

****

"This is not a God-forsaken world – It is a world that has forsaken God"
~ Ray Comfort

****

When a man is denied the right to live the life he believes in, he has no choice but to become an outlaw ~ Mandela.

****

""Yes, I was dead. It's true I was dead. I resurrected as I always do. Once I get back to my country I am real," 92-year-old President Robert Mugabe joked about online reports of his imminent demise. He told reporters at Harare airport."

****

When the only 3-tier leg of the State, the Judiciary, loses its independence, mashes with the Executive, and performs the duties of the Executive, then the State/Country is a non-entity.

****

"Sometimes people lose their right to remain silent when pressured to remain silent" ~ Criss Jami

****

Somebody asked that "Why in America the word racism is not commonly used in reference to black folks?" Racism is the poor treatment of or violence against people because of their race. It is the belief that some races of people are better than others. Racism is prejudice, and it is a sin that affects all people regardless of their races. The reason why the term racism is not commonly used against black people is because racism has to do with power. The black people who harbor the racist views lack the power to enforce their ideologies.

****

"Withholding information is the essence of tyranny. Control of the flow of Information is the tool of the dictatorship" ~ Bruce Coville

****

"Some men change their party for the sake of their principles; others their principles for the sake of their party" ~Winston Churchill

****

"The most difficult thing is the decision to act, the rest is merely tenacity. The fears are paper tigers. You can do anything you decide to do. You can act to change and control your life; and the procedure, the process is its own reward" ~ Amelia Earhart

****

"For to be free is not merely to cast off one's chains, but to live in a way that respects and enhances the freedom of others" ~ Nelson Mandela

****

"I am better off dying doing something to change the situation than dying at the whims of some few people who monopolize power in this country" ~ Besigye

****

Everybody is going to die. The issue is not whether you will die but how you will die. "It's honorable to die for your country" ~ Winnie Byanyima

****

"M7 is a malignant cancer to the region. He creates conflict and instability, and comes in as the only one who can solve it" ~ Dr. Kizza Besigye

****

"You Christians value life, we Muslims value death. I delight to die as martyr" ~ Yasser Arafat

****

The opposition in Uganda appears to be holding the moral upper hand, turning to protest repertoires like prayer, something that is so basic and inalienable a right as to be trampled by any government, however autocratic. Yet, in a most astounding move, the government secured a dubious court order that, among others, banned protest prayers! It has got to be the first of its kind anywhere in the world, that a government explicitly prohibits prayer because it's being endowed with political subversion. If something as inviolable as prayer can be banned, what else can citizens do?

****

Justice Kavuma banned FDC defiance prayers. "Banning our prayers? Compatriots, we should not let any dictators walk through our minds with their dirty feet. Our mind is the only thing God gave us over which we have full control." Remarked Wafula Oguttu

****

"When I set to challenge the dictatorship, I knew I'll have two homes: One I built myself and prison." ~ Dr. Kizza Besigye.

****

"Either the dogs came to us, or we went to them but somehow this country is in dog territory" ~ Tom Okwalinga

****

"What would be best is that the government resolves issues before Besigye brings them up. That would lead to a better Uganda for all. But to attack the man who puts a mirror in your face does not change the way you look."

****

"Demons have taken over Kadaga and are now in Parliament. It was wrong for her to visit the Shrine in her capacity as Speaker," said Miria Matembe, the former minister of ethics and integrity. "Kadaga is a parishioner at All Saints Cathedral. Visiting a shrine is a total mockery of our faith. I was shocked given Speaker Kadaga's decision to visit a shrine and worship the dead despite her education level."

****

"Mr. Museveni killed all State institutions. All and sundry have to go through him if anything is to be accomplished. Then he becomes the "savior"!" ~ E Mpayippayi

****

Idi Amin declared an economic war that resulted in expelling Asians from the country. The economic liberty did not benefit the natives but altercation lead to entrenching his ego and self-aggrandized endeavors. It was African imperialism at its best because all of the businesses were turned over to foreigners, in particular, the Nubians and the Anyanyas from Sudan.

****

"During the tyrannical rule of Idi Amin, living in Uganda was so intense and risky, compared to sitting in a snake pit, swirling with thousands of venomous snakes: Any careless movement and you are dead."

****

Moses Ali protests the visit of Israeli Prime Minister Benjamin Netanyahu to Uganda and the government's celebration of Israel's raid on Entebbe to flee the hostages. This is my response to his protest: "This is a macabre protest. Amin's soldiers never protected Ugandans at any time. Actually, they bore the worst atrocities ever melted on Ugandans. They wiped out families, and worst, the people who were murdered, up to today, their families don't know the whereabouts of their remains. The raid on Entebbe by Israel showed the world that Amin was not as sophisticated as he portrayed himself to be, and hence galvanized Uganda and the peace loving world to throw him out. For that, it's in order to celebrate Israel's raid. In fact, it should be declared to be a public holiday because the event marked the beginning of the end of the most brutal dictator of the century and his henchmen like Moses Ali."

****

In Haifa, 60,000 people evacuated, two prisons evacuated; thousands without power, airport closed. "Every fire that was caused by arson, or incitement to arson, is terrorism by all accounts — and we will treat it as such," said Prime Minister Benjamin. For years I have been expressing my concern about these foreigners, most notably Muslims owning almost every gas station in America. I wondered in case they use fire as terrorism weapon, then America will be on fire.

****

And a saying goes; "A hungry man is a hungry man". But the largest part of Amin's regime made Ugandans not just hungry but angry and desperate.

****

"Unnecessary exhibition of power is an indicator of an empty soul. A soul that overflows with God's knowledge never parades exhibition of power and authority. It operates within the realm of God's graciousness, patience, and humility. Self-motivated exhibitors are never part of the Kingdom!"
~ Godfrey Nsubuga

****

"Aspire to inspire before you expire or retire... Everything is a building block; everything that comes in your life, including serving time is a building block and time does not become still when you are imprisoned. Grab every opportunity you get" - Justice Julia Ssebutinde

****

As the expression "Christian Europe" suggests, over time Europeans came to see themselves as part of a larger entity that was, like the Islamic world, defined in religious terms. Kaplan quotes the 1957 book, "Europe: The Emergence of an Idea," which tells readers that "European unity began with the concept . . . of a Christendom in 'inevitable opposition' to Islam."

The most famous example of this "inevitable opposition" is, of course, the Crusades. While the Crusades are endlessly debated, one thing about them isn't: The European forces saw themselves primarily as a force of Christians, which was their shared identity and basis for unity. Christianity was the source of the "cultural and political" elements that make Europe a continent and not simply a glorified peninsula at the end of the Eurasian landmass.

If so, the current moral decay in Europe is a self-inflicted wound. European elites have long worked overtime to downplay their Christian heritage, and have "used idealistic rhetoric to deny the forces of religion and ethnicity." The most famous example of this was the preamble to the EU's constitution, which omitted any mention of Christianity as a source of Europe's "values."

This is, historically-speaking, nonsense. It's also self-destructive since, because, as Kaplan tells us, Christianity is one of the forces "that provided European states with their own internal cohesion." Without Christianity, Europe is hobbled in its attempts to resist the "reassertion of classical geography." In other words, if Europe is eventually "Islamized," as many predict, it will only be because it was first "de-Christianized."

****

"I am not African because I was born in Africa, but because Africa was born in me" ~ Kwame Nkrumah

****

There is a reason why Mandela did not amend the constitution to seek re-election. He knew that by amending the constitution he would invite a Strong Man (dictator) to succeed him and the cycle of self-destruction would start in South Africa. Imagine Zuma without term limits.

****

There is a stubbornness about me that can never bear to be frightened at the will of others. My courage always rises at every attempt to intimidate me ~ Jane Austen

****

According to Vicent Magombe, one of the core and distinguishing characteristics of these African despots and tin pot dictators is their shameless determination to transform the whole nations and governments into personal fiefdoms and mini-empires, where the ruler's main pre-occupation is to loot the state to crumbs, and, accordingly, apply all manner of subjugation and coercion to subdue the masses in order to keep and preserve the loot.

****

How do we solve the puzzle and the darkness eclipsing our politics? History is important in order for us to know how we got where we are today. "Study the past if you would define the future." We can't find a solution if we don't diagnose the problem correctly, not only will we fail to fix it—we'll create even more turmoil.

****

The most difficult thing is to be in the position of authority and not use it selfishly on yourself. "Nearly all men can stand adversity, but if you want to test a man's character, give him power." ~ Abraham Lincoln

****

Aged politicians should pave way for young folks to serve. They should turn down any offer of sensitive political posts. It is not as if the entire country is so bereft of any other suitable promising youth to serve. No disrespect intended: I am also an old age sage at death's door!!

****

"It is unfortunate that in Africa we don't value great people. In European countries like the UK, people who have done good things are treasured. Books are written about them and the musician sing about them. But in Africa, we talk about people when they die. I wish we could have more birthdays than death days" ~ Gen. Kale Kayihura

****

The recent shootings in Texas are symptoms of a nation preoccupied and dominated by racial tension. It is a social issue that demands a spiritual solution. I appeal to all pastors to break the silence and address it. We tried in vain to solve it politically. In the past two elections, people from different racial backgrounds united and elected a president of color, in anticipation of uniting the nation, but the situation has escalated from bad to worse. It is not appropriate to point fingers. There is an urgent need to act now in order to avert the eruption of a civil war. Racism applies to all ethnic groups: There are white racists and black racists too. We must resist the evil of racism at any cost. This should be a concern of each of us individually. Let us win by that Old Rugged Cross and everything it stands for. "A nation is what individuals make it. For a nation to be reborn, its people must be born again." (John 3, 7) ~ Reinhard Bonnke

****

The past week has been full of drama. Four black Chicago teens are currently in custody after broadcasting the torture of a mentally challenged white teenager on Facebook Live. The four teenagers could be seen kicking the bound and gagged victim and burning him with cigarettes while at various points shouting the "F' word to Mr. Trump" and the white people! CNN blamed the behaviors to bad parenting. Then the recent alleged shooting in Florida. It has been said that the suspect in the Fort Lauderdale shooting who killed at least five people on Friday was a U.S. military veteran who "lost his mind" after a tour of duty in Iraq. It is true that wars can cause trauma and psychological disorder. But not all of the mental disorders have to occur by abuse. There are entities in the spiritual world of darkness called demons that can cause mental disorder by exposure. Unfortunately, the psychologists of today readily admit the existence of evil but deny the influence of the demons. Ignoring something is the deadliest form of denial. Demons have ranks conferring to power and privileges, and we are most probably confronted by the highest ranking entities baptized in the art of spiritual warfare, which can only go by fasting and praying. (Matthew 17:21)

****

Racism and tribalism are not due to not liking people of different color and tribe but denying them equal opportunities to prosper.

****

"Black, white or other, we are all people with lives that matter and count. We all deserve a life of peace and love and freedom from any form of bigotry, from prejudice, from discrimination or antagonism. Racial prejudice is a hate crime that deserves to be abolished and should not be tolerated. It is based on an ignorant belief that one race is superior to another" ~ Kareena Maria Cox

****

Renewed fierce fighting in Southern Sudan has killed an estimated 272, as an increasingly tense security situation threatened to send the young country back to all-out civil war. This is a clear indication that African leaders, who are addicted to power will do anything to rule even at the expense of the lives of the people whom they desperately want to rule. Their motto is that "The cost of accessing and clinging to power is measured in terms of accumulated counts of dead bodies, and the cost must be paid regardless of the magnitude of the price involved." Tyranny is cruel and oppressive, and it is usually the rule by persons who lack legitimacy, whether they be malign or benevolent. Our people should be aware that tyranny is an important phenomenon that operates by principles by which it can be recognized in its early emerging stages, and, if the people are vigilant, prepared, and committed to liberty, countered before it becomes entrenched.

****

In this corrupt world, when you are not corrupt, you are vulnerable!

****

"Helping with the liberation of the oppressed should never be for economic gain, but only to gain in conscience" ~ Fidel Castro

****

You cannot speak of change when you have no mandate to do so. God gave to the Church the mandate to change the world, but not to the politicians. That is why He did not give the keys of the kingdom to Caesar but to Peter.

****

We are always on the move in search for perfect places to belong - like a perfect family or a perfect church. Yet, in this world, there is no such a thing as a perfect place because there is no perfect person. We find our perfection in our Savior. He is ruling from the highest throne and His reign stretches from coast to coast. The corruption of sin that dwells in us repels the holiness of God but the Agape Love turned the eternal throne of God into the throne of grace accessible to all repented sinners without guilt. A sinner is safe and secure before the highest throne of God. We are not guilty because positionally we are as holy as Christ. Christ is for us, for we are for Christ. Salvation is being catapulted into a whole new life. I mean a life that is in contradiction to our human nature and instincts. Jesus came in human form to bring to us the consciousness of the spiritual dimension. The very reason for our existence in human form is to bring the consciousness of the spiritual dimension into this world.

****

"Those ignorant of history are prisoners of the latest cliché, for they have nothing against which to test it" ~ Dr. Robert Francis Taft

****

On a visit to Germany, Mr. Buhari said that: "I don't know which party my wife belongs to, but she belongs to my kitchen and my living room and the other room." The Nigerian President Muhammadu Buhari was responding to criticism from his wife. Mr. Buhari was standing next to Chancellor Angela Merkel, who seemed to glare at him.

****

January 16, 2017 is Martin Luther King's Day. More than forty years ago, on August 28, 1963, a quarter million people gathered in front of the Lincoln Memorial. They marched here for the cause of civil rights. And that day they heard Martin Luther King Jr. deliver his famous "I Have a Dream" speech, a speech in which he challenged America to fulfill her promise. "I have a dream," he said, "that one day this nation will rise up and live out the true meaning of its creed. 'We hold these truths to be self-evident that all men are created equal.'"

Many think of King as a liberal firebrand, waging war on traditional values. Nothing could be further from the truth. King was a great conservative on this central issue, and he stood on the shoulders of Augustine and Aquinas, striving to restore our heritage of justice rooted in the law of God.

Election year postings:

The Liberals believe in big governments but the Conservatives believe in small government. The Liberals want big governments because they want the people to depend on government's handouts instead of God.

****

Have you wondered why most politicians are lawyers? Democratic Party has increasingly become detached from ordinary Americans and attached to the upper-middle-class professional elite and lawyers. Somebody compared lawyers to rhinoceroses: thick-skinned, short-sighted, and always ready to charge. Lawyers have a reputation of screwing everything up. We have Liberal lawyers that will sue you for even mentioning the name of Jesus Christ in any public forum!

****

Hallucinations of polls: I am not one of many people obsessed with likeability polls. When we talk about candidate likability, we use sample polls of favorability ratings, among likely voters from different political parties. The question is 'who likes who and why?' Certainly, moral people will not favor an immoral candidate. Likewise, immoral people will not favor a moral candidate. It is, therefore, impossible to determine the integrity of a candidate by using favorability rating. There is no uniformity regarding the standard used by the people to like or dislike a particular candidate. We might as well be promoting relativism. Relativism is the philosophical position that all points of view are equally valid, and that all truth is relative to the individual. Relativism maintains that morality is like beauty, it is in the eye of the beholder. On the contrary, God's truth is absolute and is applicable to all people at all times - it is perennial and immutable.

****

"Unlike George W. Bush he (Trump) is not an idiot, he says things that are bigger than him. No-one knows what he's capable of" - Depardieu told the Journal du Dimanche newspaper.

****

Trump's tape that was recorded a decade ago has recently been the main topic of discussion by the media. The unfolding of the trajectory of the saga and the drama caused by the tape is an eye-opener to all of us. Politics is like a game of chess whereby in order to win you have to make a move. But a wise move comes with insight, awareness, information, and by learning the lessons that are accumulated along the way. Without doubt, Trump used vulgar language. Nobody including Trump is proud of it. Thanks to God that he looked behind regretfully and apologized. My main concern is that the people who claim to be mostly hurt by the vulgar language are the Liberals. Since when did morality become an important issue for the liberal? I remember when Bill Clinton had an affair in the White House, his performance approval rate went up! Aren't the people screaming foul, the same people that regularly applaud the rappers whose music are composed of vulgar language? Aren't they the same people who occasionally cheer the movie stars of XXX-Rated movies when they are walking on the red carpets to be crowned with Grammy Awards?

The tape that is causing commotion was recorded some ten years ago, and it was not a problem as long as Trump was within their circles. There was no hallucination because it fitted admirably within the perimeters of their characters. It only became a problem after Trump crossed over to the other side of the fence. Common sense suggests that a person without morals cannot prescribe morality. As much as I disagree with the vulgar language, I strongly believe that the tears of the Liberals concerning the vulgar language are crocodile tears. The crying we see is fake. It is not because they are hurt, it is deliberately staged to hurt the Conservatives. When they sneeze, it is the conservatives that catch a cold.

During the second presidential debate, the most important words were spoken by Hillary. She insinuated that this is the most important election in the history of our nation. The reason is because the elected president is going to appoint the Supreme Court Justice. She is right. The Liberals need just one more judge on the benches of Supreme Court in order to push through their liberal agendas. It means that this election is not about Trump or Clinton; it is about America. You have the right to fight for our conservative values by voting. In case out of the two candidates, you don't see any you can relate to, definitely, you cannot fail to see who is against us. Jesus said that "He who is for us is not against us" (Luke 9:50). Use your vote in form of defiance to resist that candidate that is against God ordained family and pro-life. I pray that your ego will die so that you put your faith and America above your personal wishes.

****

It has been almost a week since Trump's tape with the vulgar language that was recorded some eleven years ago surfaced on the media. His polls have gone all the way below. Hillary is surging and she is predicted by all polls to win even the red states. The Republican Party establishment is calling Trump to step down. We are losing enthusiasm and hope. Then today, very early in the morning when I woke up to do my routine morning praying, I had a mini-vision when Trump had won the election, and there were riots by frustrated supporters of Hillary. This rejuvenated my strength in spite of the practicality of the events in reality.

****

Liberal theology is antichristian. Liberalism is the religion of Romans 1:25: "They exchanged the truth of God for a lie, and worshiped and served something created instead of the Creator, who is praised forever. Amen." Liberalism puts the liberty of the flesh above the liberty of the spirit. According to the Christian values, ending life prematurely, at all stages of life is a sin; it is a crime as well in accordance with the civil laws. Liberal theology elevates the liberty of a person above the truth as portrayed by the Scriptures. For example, they believe that the world is overpopulated and we should find a way to reduce the population of the world. Same-sex marriage and abortion are some of the conspiracies intended to reduce the world population. Also, a sacrilegious belief that killing the unborn babies is right as long as a woman carrying a baby wants to do it. According to the Liberals, the rights of a woman to choose what she likes transcend the prescribed standards of the Scriptures prohibiting any person to take a life of the innocent ones. During the last presidential debate, Hillary Clinton chanted that women should be able to end the lives of their preborn babies, right up to nine months, just weeks before a child is viable outside the womb. Legalizing abortion contradicts our laws. Ironically when you murder a pregnant woman you are charged with double homicide.

This is a critical season of electing our leaders. Go to vote with such awareness that your vote is the voice of your conscience. A vote for the Liberals is an approval to abortion and same-sex marriages. These values are vice to our morality, and are unacceptable in our highest offices of honor! Did I hear that a vote against Hillary is a vote against the liberal media who are scandalizing our country? Indeed, this is a desperate situation involving desperate people fighting for a desperate cause. We have good reasons to fight. The venue is politics but the ultimate cause is morality. And we shall prevail because God is on our side.

****

Why is America's election a concern of the whole world? The main reason is spiritual. It is estimated that about 85% of the resources of evangelism come from America. In spite of adversity, we must secure this divinely assigned obligation. We have God-given right to preach the gospel but we need to secure a favorable political environment to effectively evangelize the world. America is a great nation because it is a nation whose foundation is God. The solid foundation has helped the superstructure of the nation to stand the test of time. Unfortunately, we are slowly losing our divine purpose, and hence our greatness. America is a country primarily made up of foreigners. All of the people who choose to settle in America are attracted to the stability of this great country. Unfortunately, there are many people who admire the greatness of this country without necessarily admiring the values which made this country great! Americans, are called to welcome strangers but without a possibility of forsaking the values that make this nation great. Without true values, civilization will soon descend into revolution and anarchy. The strangers must be ready to be assimilated instead of them assimilating us into their values. As one statesman said, "The mission of the United States is one of benevolent assimilation". Without assimilation, any culture will cease to exist.

****

The social media is saturated with alarming images projecting voting malpractices. A decade ago, such things were unthinkable in the USA. This country was considered to be the cream of democracy for the rest of the world to imitate. Democracy was upheld to a maximum standard of satisfaction in the federal elections in spite of highly decentralized and variable fashions of individual states. The corrupt establishment system supported by the corrupt media is the impediments eclipsing the quality of the quantity of our ethics. Their goal is to impose on us the corrupt leaders in order to sustain the status quo. The ambiguity and the surging malpractices are not accidental; they are typical of a society that is racing down towards a severe moral decay. The flawed voting is parallel to the skyrocketing immorality. It is reported that cheating in classrooms, during examinations, is at a record increase. Cheating in relationships has been normalized and reduced to a simple manageable affair. We have activists fracturing our communities instead of building them. They are frequently paraded on our streets in demonstration against lawfulness and advocating vicious unlawful activities. The more people rationalize cheating, the more our culture evolves into a culture of dishonesty. And that can become a vicious, downward cycle. Because suddenly, if everyone else is cheating, you feel a need to cheat, too. The current odor of malpractices could have been avoided if we did not remove God from our institutions, in particular, the schools. It is time to reclaim our country by electing honest leaders into our high offices. Vote wisely by standing up for our traditional ethics on which this country was founded.

****

"Salvation will never come in Air Force One" There is no presidential candidate that is a human Savior. Given the fact, we (Christians) must exercise our right to vote. Vote carefully with such awareness that you are neither voting for a Sunday school teacher or a pastor. Put into consideration the values that make this nation a great Christian nation. Remember that the strength of a country is determined by the strength of the families. God created the family values involving a man and a woman in a marital relationship. We have no mandate to declare something unnatural to be natural because God alone can define nature. Don't forget to be the voice to the voiceless babies who are murdered before they are born. Do what is right. Don't violate your conscience because of politics.

****

This is the timely message for the Church in the USA: "For if you remain silent at this time, liberation and rescue will arise for the Jews from another place, and you and your father's house will perish [since you did not help when you had the chance]. And who knows whether you have attained royalty for such a time as this [and for this very purpose]?" (Esther 4:14). Mordecai was inspired by God to give this message to Esther, and she responded accordingly. Consequently, God used her obedience to save the Jewish people from genocide. God is giving the same message to the Church during this election season. He has given the Church the mandate to change the direction of this country. Your vote is your voice. If you do not keep quiet and vote for the Christian values, God is going to use your vote to save the Church from the pending catastrophe planned by the leftists.

****

Somebody asked that "Why do you brag about the Christian values? Doesn't the Bible support slavery in 1 Corinthians 7:21-22?" I want to say that slavery is bad regardless of how it is packed. Slaves were treated as second class citizens. However, the slaves mentioned within the context of the scripture were different from the slaves of our generation. The slaves of the biblical times were economically oriented. For example, most

Roman slave masters owned the Roman slaves, from within the same social setting. Often people volunteered to be slaves of others whom they owed money, and work for them for a period of time, to settle their debts. On the contrary, the slaves of our generations are racially oriented who were forced into slavery contrary to their will.

God is the greatest liberator. He rescued the children of Israel from slavery in Egypt. He liberates us from the slavery of our sins. The abolitionists who pioneered to abolish slave trade were Christians. In the same way, today, the activists fighting to end the murdering of the unborn babies (abortion) are Christians. William Wilberforce was a parliamentarian when he became convinced of the truth of Christianity. Upon his conversion, he thought he should withdraw from parliament, but Pastor John Newton, author of the beloved hymn "Amazing Grace" convinced him otherwise. God used him in parliament tremendously. He allied with the evangelical leaders, exerted his influence to end slavery and ameliorate the social ills of England. You can fight with your vote to end abortion by voting for a pro-life candidate or you can promote abortion by voting for a pro-choice candidate. Your vote is the voice of your conscience.

****

This election is the nearest to the Second Coming of Jesus Christ because it will affect the future generations to come. The next president will fill in the empty vacancies on the Supreme Court benches, who have the supreme power to interpret and decree the values of our country. This election is a choice to restore morality to our country or forget America as a nation under one supreme God. Prophetically, the most solemn warning recorded in the Bible for our day is found in the fourteenth chapter of Revelation. Called the mark of the beast, it has generated countless discourses and theories as expositors attempt to explain its execution. This election is a preview of what will happen in future when the mark of the beast is given as the only escape route from the economic repression. This election is a test of loyalty to God. It presents to the Church two choices: Either to bow down and worship the Caesar of this world or to worship the Lord the creator of the universe. It is like being given an opportunity either to accept the mark of the beast or to reject it. The people who choose to worship the Caesar of this world might as well be vulnerable when the mark of the beast is issued as an alternative choice for the comfort of their bodies.

****

Romans 1:25-26 – "They exchanged the truth of God for a lie, and worshiped and served created things rather than the Creator, who is forever worthy of praise! Amen. For this reason, God gave them over to dishonorable passions. Even their women exchanged natural relations for unnatural ones. Likewise, the men abandoned natural relations with women and burned with lust for one another. Men committed indecent acts with other men, and received in themselves the due penalty for their error." According to history, every nation that participated or approved the wicked behaviors mentioned above ended up trashed into the dustbin. The Bible says that "The wrath of God is being revealed from heaven against all the godlessness and wickedness of people, who suppress the truth by their wickedness". (Romans 1:18). The verdict is that God surrendered them to the reprobate minds. It is the mind that cannot be convicted but compromises because it is desensitized. The perpetrator is surrendered to the fate of the corrupt nature absolutely.

This curse is pronounced over those who participate in the wickedness of same-sex relationship and those who approve of it. The Bible pronounces blessings to the upright: "How blessed is the man who does not walk in the counsel of the wicked, Nor stand in the path of sinners, Nor sits in the seat of scoffers!" (Psalm 1:1). Applauding evil often glamorizes the recurrence of vicious behavior. A rebuke wrapped in love in a sensitive, caring way is recommended. I mean boldly standing for sanity without contradicting the Savior's message of loving one another. In this election, we have two political parties from which we are electing our leaders. One party openly promotes the same-sex relationship, whereas the other disapproves of it. Your vote is either an approval or a disapproval of the above wickedness. Whenever you cast your vote, you are either applauding or rebuking the vice behaviors. Vote wisely. Vote your conscience.

****

Somebody asked that "Do you think that the Democratic Party has no elements of virtue in it at all?" All of the political parties are not perfect because they are made up of the imperfect people. Most probably compared to our Christian denominations, there are some things I agree with and disagree with in all denominations. But we have some basic principles (doctrines) which separate the Christian denominations from the cults: For example the doctrine of the deity of Jesus (He is very man and very God); the doctrine of salvation by faith in the finished works of Jesus Christ; the doctrine of the authority and the infallibility of the Scriptures. Any denomination that does not recognize any of the above doctrines is a cult. Likewise, we have some values which must be embraced by any God fearing political party in order for it to be pro-Christian: The supremacy of God (God is the standard and measure to our values as opposed to man); the sanctity of life (pro-life); the sanctity of family (marriage between a man and a woman). God is pro-family and He created for us a model of the family in the Garden of Eden. It is not a coincidence that the first miracle of Jesus was performed at a wedding involving a man and a woman. Any political party that ignores the above values is considered to be anti-Christianity. Pastors are supposed to be non-partisan but there are values which we cannot embrace. Although 81% of evangelicals voted for the Republican presidential candidate, there is still an urgent need for the pastors to educate these things to the members of their congregations.

****

Tomorrow is our long awaited election day. Nothing quite focuses the mind like discordant details awaiting harmonious resolution. The chapter of the tantalizing discomfort of the Liberals is finally going to be closed. For a decade, liberalism has antagonized and crippled our social structures without serious repercussion. Our moral values have been trodden on the floor and degraded. Liberal theology is a spiritually moribund religion awaiting burial. Tomorrow, it will be uprooted and the obituaries will be read loud for everyone to hear. "To live defeated and inglorious is to die daily."

****

The United States marks 42 years of legalized abortion in all fifty states at any time for any reason throughout pregnancy on January 22ⁿᵈ, the anniversary of the Roe v. Wade Supreme Court decision. Since then, millions of the unborn babies have been murdered before they celebrated their first birthday. There have been approximately 57,762,169 abortions that have destroyed the lives of unborn children. As for the liberals, millions of babies dying in abortions is a cause for celebration rather than lamenting.

Tomorrow is the D-day. The babies who were murdered before they celebrated their first birthday will be vindicated. The lives of the aborted babies are placed in the memories of the living as they walk to the polling stations to cast their votes. The power of the ballot will turn into the power of change. For the first time, we shall have leaders in the highest offices that respect the sanctity of life and marriage. Go and vote and be part of history in the making. Remember that history is kind to those who intend to write it.

****

Finally, the Election Day is here. All polls are predicting a landslide victory for Hillary. I woke up very early to go to vote because I expected a long line. When I turned on my radio, the news media gave Hillary 90% chances of winning. In fact, they were discussing how to persuade Trump to concede defeat. I was frustrated and I decided to go back to bed. While in bed, God spoke to me in a powerful way that, "The situation is unpredictable. The reason is because when it happens, the world will know that God did it". When I woke up, I received the same message again. There was that compelling conviction inside my heart to post it on my Facebook page to restore hope to many people who were facing uncertainty. At the same time, there was a counter thought within me saying "What if it is not from God? You are a pastor, you don't want to dent your reputation." I decided to obey God and I posted it early in the morning. I thank God that I did.

****

Polls are true when they stop you from voting. Most people went to vote when frustrated because of the massive polls which predicted a landslide win for Hillary. As for me, I decided to stick with my faith. This has been my motto always: "When God speaks; polls don't matter. The will of God cannot be swatted". This election is kind of a glass ceiling breaking. As for a glass ceiling, the best way to do it is to give it your absolute best with whatever gifts and talents that God has given you. Not when armed with a hammer like that one in Hillary's hands. The devastating hammer is liberalism. And what is at stake is our fragile moral ceiling.

We had two candidates with contradictory values and professionalism. Trump is an outsider and unpredictable. But God gave him a mantle to steer this country away from its current mess. Hillary is an insider of the establishment with a display of multiple tags projecting her past failures hanging on her collar. For a decade, the Liberals under their Messiah Barack Obama have shoved their liberal filthiness down our throats. Most prominent is the rainbow flag of the homosexuals flying over the white house. If you are truly a Christian and you voted for Hillary, you really need to repent. Today, people have spoken with their votes. Together we have said that 'It is enough". We badly wanted to change the status quo, and God has answered our prayers. The real winners are the unborn babies. Praises be to Jehovah Nissi - The Lord is my banner ... God who fight our battles.

****

Daniel 2:45 - "This is the meaning of the vision of the rock cut out of a mountain, but not by human hands--a rock that broke the iron, the bronze, the clay, the silver and the gold to pieces." No earthly kingdom is indispensable. Kings and kingdoms come and go. All of the earthly kingdoms we fear will fail and fall until the kingdoms of this world become the kingdom of our Lord (Revelation 11:15). God's kingdom will be forever and ever. We shall rule with Christ: "And You have made them a kingdom (royal race) and priests to our God, and they shall reign on the earth!" (Revelation 5:10, 11:15). The First Coming of Jesus was intended to preach "the gospel of the kingdom of God" (Mark 1:14-15) and to pay the penalty for mankind's sins. Responding to a question from the Pharisees about when the Kingdom of God would come, Jesus said, "The kingdom of God does not come with observation; nor will they say, 'See here!' or 'See there!' For indeed, the kingdom of God is within you" (Luke 17:20-21). The Second Coming is for the King to rule over the earth. We are sent to preach the gospel of the kingdom and prepare the people to receive the coming King of kings. We are not sent to make this world a comfortable place for sinners but to open their eyes to focus on the coming kingdom of God. The kingdom of God is for those who have overcome this world (John 17:16). They are absolutely ecstatic about His coming, and standing ajar, in anticipation.

****

Post-election postings

This election defied rational logic. The media is still in a dilemma, puzzled, asking themselves how they missed it in their polling. Even the Trump campaign said that though they were optimistic, they were out-polled. Mr. Trump said that her daughter, Ivanka, called him very early in the morning of the Election Day saying, "It doesn't look good". Senate Republican leader Mitch McConnell, R-Ky., admitted he never thought Donald Trump would win the presidential election. In an interview on Kentucky Education Television's "One to One," McConnell confessed: "It never occurred to me that he might be able to win." And McConnell said he thought the GOP "would come up short" in trying to hold the Senate majority.

Meanwhile, most Liberals are going nuts over the election results. Gabriel Sherman — best known for being Roger Ailes' worst nightmare — reports that a group of computer security experts believe that "they've found persuasive evidence that results in Wisconsin, Michigan, and Pennsylvania may have been manipulated or hacked" and they're urging Hillary Clinton to contest the election results in those states.

The media is now face to face with the surprise of the irrefutable Trump effect but they are still in denial of the cause. They are not ready to acknowledge the divine factor as the primary cause of Trump's triumph.

Very early in the morning of Election Day when almost all polls gave Hillary 90% chances of winning, and some talk shows were discussing how to persuade Trump to concede defeat, amidst frustration, God gave me the following message twice: "The situation is unpredictable. The reason is because when it happens, the world will know that God did it". I posted it in the morning on my Facebook page for everyone to read. This was a confirmation of something that was revealed to me in the past. But our culture is obsessed into believing in what they can see, and we risk degenerating into the same obsession. The popular saying is that "I will believe when I see it". God shows no favoritism (Acts 10:34), He can reveal His knowledge to anybody but the world would not hear from God because they are driven by their darkened minds. "The greatest deception men suffer is from their own opinions". I suggest that any search for knowledge should begin with God. We are the lights sent to light up this darkened world; it is our born again birthright privilege. God used a donkey to speak to a prophet (Numbers 22:28). What if Trump is God-sent as some of us are aware and believe? Fighting him would mean resisting God's will to be established on the earth.

****

Luke 19:8 - "And Zacchaeus stood, and said unto the Lord; Behold, Lord, the half of my goods I give to the poor; and if I have taken anything from any man by false accusation, I restore him fourfold." America is a melting pot. The challenges of living in a diverse and free society are real. The Bible encourages us to love our enemies and to welcome strangers. There is a need to take self-inventory and say "If I had taken anything from any man I will restore him fourfold". Restitution is an attitude of the remorseful heart. Forgiveness is created by restitution. Forgiveness is not something to be forcefully squeezed out of us; it is a voluntary act of conscience-cleansing and favor restored. The indisputable fact is that we are one nation under God. Reconciliation is the Christian way of capsizing radical antagonism and division. We owe each other a debt that could only be paid if we seek the salve of reconciliation. There is a need to take self-inventory and say "If I had taken anything from any man I will restore him fourfold". This is how we ought to love. Our culture encourages all of us to always put our best foot forward. Let us do it by being considerate of others. "The world is the difficult realization that something other than oneself is real."

****

Trump's slogan has been "I am not politically correct." Political correctness is married to inconsistency. When people are politically correct they don't say the truth out of fear to offend others. Like in case the leader in the high office is of a different race or gender, any criticism against Him or her might be viewed either as a racist or anti-women slang. The language of political correctness, in all its myriad manifestations, is a thesaurus of illogic and inconsistency. Intriguingly, political correctness infiltrated the church institution already. Relativism is akin to political correctness. It is the mindset believing that everyone is true depending on what they deem to be true. Therefore, no one has a right to tell others that they are wrong or to criticize the opinions of others. It is true in particular in a chaotic situation where principles and ethics are regarded as applicable in only limited context. We (Christians) believe that there is an absolute truth that is revealed to us in the Scriptures, which must be embraced by all sane humanity regardless of our opinions. If the Bible says it is wrong, there is no earthly right that can make it right.

****

It is another day of God's sovereignty on the earth. No matter how disappointed you are, get over it because God is ever on the throne. The incontrovertible fact is that heaven rules this world forever. It is for the same reason that every day I bow down to Him in adoration. And I am passionately waiting for that day when the whole world will bow down to Him (Romans 14:11). This is the recommendable prescription and painkiller for a hurting soul. It works for me, and it can work for you. Love you all.

****

"The Clinton campaign had hoped that the glass ceiling of the Javits Center would become the night's enduring symbol. But instead, its basement cafeteria became a microcosm of the Clinton campaign."

****

My response to organized riots by the Leftists as a counter reaction to Trump's victory: God created mankind and gave us dominion over all creations. I think the term "all creations" includes other human beings as well. Although we have God-given dominion over all creation, nature resists being dominated by man. For example, we have to subdue animals in order to bring them into subjection. The situation is not different regarding humanity. We naturally resist being dominated by others. Resisting oppression is a positive reaction which is an emanation from our own nature and faculties. But there is a negative way of resisting democratically elected leaders. Democracy is not perfect and it is not supposed to make everyone happy. But it is a fair political system that secures the happiness of the greatest number. The riots we see and the existing hysteria are inflamed by opportunists who believe that there should be no ultimate winner unless they are the winners. We should shun the notion that human beings are naturally competitive, rather than cooperative.

****

"The world as we have created it is a process of our thinking. It cannot be changed without changing our thinking" ~ Albert Einstein

****

Democrat Pollster Pat Caddell said the Obama's are lacking "grace" in the final weeks of their presidency. Snarky Obama and his rude wife are angry that the leftist mumbo-jumbo they've been peddling for eight years was soundly rejected. The Obamas could have gracefully exited the scene – but no.

Reviewing the Triumph of Trump

2016 has been a thrilling year because of the election. Mr. Trump entertained us throughout his campaign. He occupied the front pages of most of the newspapers even those belonging to the haters (Liberals). No matter how much you hate the man, you cannot ignore talking about him. No wonder his favorability grew every day.

Tracking our election year 2016, you cannot fail to trace an irresistible hand of God that helped Mr. Trump to prevail. Hillary had an upper hand as a very experienced politician compared to Trump. Hillary, who had been in Washington for 30 years, as First Lady, Senator and later Secretary of State– had a résumé unmatched by any of the candidates of the 2016 U.S Presidential elections and had become the heir apparent for the Democratic National Committee, after her loss to Barack Obama in the 2008 Democratic primary race. As one news reporter said jokingly "Hillary has an experience of 423 years compared to 46 weeks experience of Trump".

Mr. Trump was very competent. He amazingly deployed his business skills and comedy in the field of politics. The Republican candidate and his backers spent only half that of Democratic presidential candidate Hillary Clinton and her supporters on the way to his Nov. 8 victory, according to media reports on campaign spending released Friday. The Clinton campaign, Democratic Party and pro-Clinton expenditure committees and PACs spent a record $1.2 million, twice as much as the $600 million laid out by the Trump camp, Republicans and pro-Trump groups, the New York Post reported. He may be a billionaire, but President Donald Trump showed during the presidential race that he knows how to stretch a buck.

Right from the primaries, I saw the hand of God paving way for Mr. Trump to prevail. Bernie Sender's defeat was good for Mr. Trump. He could have been a tougher nut to crack than Hillary. Partly because Bernie Sender appealed to the independents who formed the base of Mr. Trump's supporters.

Morality is the trademark of the Republican Party. Hillary used the moral card to isolate Mr. Trump from his home base conservatives. But it was a mistake and a miscalculation. Remember that in the primaries, Mr. Trump run against fourteen very moral candidates and he prevailed.

The greatest obstruction in the presidential campaign was the surfacing of Trump's tape with the vulgar language, recorded some ten years ago. The Hillary campaign had the same tape during the primaries but saved it as the last minute game changer during the presidential debates. Ironically, this tape could have had a devastating impact on Trump if it was produced during the primaries. It is believed that Hillary did not want to end Trump's victory in the primaries because she thought Trump was the soft target and easier to defeat than other Republican candidates. But Mr. Trump turned out to be the nightmare!

Hillary's vice president choice was a liability. Hillary is best described as experienced and boring. Tim Kaine is more boring. Tim Kaine himself jokes about how boring he is. Adding Kaine on the ticket didn't make Hillary surge in polls. As one reporter commented: "Hillary's vice president pick didn't move the meter. It was met with deafening silence. If a tree fell in the forest, but no one saw it, did it really fall? Was Tim Kaine really announced as Hillary's vice president? No one saw it … no one heard it … no one in Hillary's core voter demographic has ever heard of him."

Was Kaine pick similar to Trump's pick of Mike Pence? Yes, on the surface, they are similar. Both Pence and Kaine are experienced, credible and boring middle-aged white men. In short, "safe" traditional politicians. "But no one noticed the Grand Canyon-sized difference between the two picks. Trump is wild, exciting and high energy. The last thing Trump needed was more energy on his ticket. He needed stable, credible and experienced." Gov. Mike is the only brick that missed on the foundation of Trump's building. He is strong born again Christian and very conservative as well. He appealed to the home base of GOP conservatives and Christians.

Hillary took advantage of the privileges provided by her ruling party and the incumbent. In past elections, sitting presidents haven't often stuck their neck out for the next in line, but President Obama has been a valuable player in Hillary's campaign. Also, the former president, Bill Clinton campaigned heavily for his wife. Both Obama and Clinton enjoy high favorable rates among minority voters. Hillary Clinton used both of them, deploying them in states where they are popular, using them to help mobilize minority voters and young voters who have supported Obama and Clinton in the past. Regardless of the maneuver, Mr. Trump ironically won the Black American voters. He won them not because they voted for him but by convincing the majority of them to stay home instead of voting for Hillary. Clinton's real weakness was her inability to motivate the Democratic base like her predecessor. Although Trump's Republican votes aren't significantly less or more than Mitt Romney's in 2012 and John McCain's in 2008, Clinton is far behind Obama's 2008 and 2012 levels.

Hillary's campaign claimed to have the majority of the minority voters. She had the majority of the women voters as well. Trump had over fifty percent of men. Over 231 million Americans are eligible to vote. However, based on early results from the 2016 Presidential election, just over 130 million of them voted for either Hillary Clinton or Donald Trump. Projections from the United States Elections Project show that there were 231,556,622 Americans eligible to vote, but 134,765,650 voted. That means that 41.8 percent didn't vote, while 58.2 percent did. Although Clinton did receive more votes overall, Trump's razor-thin victories in Michigan, Wisconsin, Florida and Pennsylvania gave him the electoral vote lead needed to win the presidency. The Trump campaign will be remembered for breaking the blue wall and turning most of the blue states red.

In politics, like any other game, there are rules set to restrain foul praying but rules do not necessarily eradicate rough playing. There were reported malpractices in the election, in particular, the early voting in Florida State. Some people voted multiple times. Fox news reported eighteen million invalid voters registered. Other sources reported an estimate of three million illegals voting for Hillary, four million dead people voted. Somebody made this humor: "Hillary has millions of dead people voting for her! She has a chance to become the 1st President of the Dead." Then there are reports of the tempered voting machines sponsored by George Soros.

We cannot ignore the intriguing factor of Soros' sponsored professional protestors at Trump's political rallies. He has been in the spotlight for financing the riots and protests around the Trump rallies, even bussing in rioters to certain places and now it appears that he is ready to commit even more money to the post-election chaos to finish the mission he started.

The effect of Brexit cannot be overlooked. Bill Clinton talked about Brexit all the time. Hillary Clinton was concerned about it but they underestimated its impact on American politics. According to Allen, populism was a concept Clinton could not adjust to. The co-author said former President Bill Clinton frequently talked about the Brexit vote, Britain's decision to leave the European Union, which many observers said was bolstered by a populist movement. Populism in Great Britain could have been a major concern for Hillary Clinton. "She really never had the feel for what was going on in this country and how to adjust for it in the right way. It was like standing on a beach and seeing a slow-moving tsunami from the middle of the ocean moving towards you, and you never move," Jonathan Allen

The radically simple reason Hillary Clinton didn't run a different campaign is that she thought she was winning. The Clintons were optimistic of the victory. They prematurely signed a contract with the Trump campaign stating that fifteen minutes after the winner is declared, the defeated candidate must concede defeat in fifteen minutes. Of course, they thought that the defeated candidate was definitely Trump. Unfortunately, the hunter became the victim of his own snares. The contract favored Mr. Trump and worked against Hillary. Later on after conceding defeat she sought for a recount in three battle states.

The obvious rigging of the election begun with the biased media which reported only the negatives and fake news against Mr. Trump. "One of the mainstream media reporters made the following comment on the morning of the Election Day: "History in the making; America is excited to receive her first Woman President!" But he had to eat his words soon or later. The next day after the results of the presidential election was known, the same reporter said that "America is mourning!"

The Clintons came prepared for nothing less than victory. It is evidently seen in the purple colors they dressed in. Purple is a kingly color. They came with such enthusiasm to embrace victory as opposed to defeat but their hopes were dashed by the Trumps. "On Election Day, Hillary Clinton's campaign was confident she would win. The party was planned: She would stand on a blue stage shaped like the United States in the Javits Center, a glass building — a not-so-subtle nod to the glass ceiling Clinton would be shattering. Donald Trump shattered her seemingly unbreakable electoral firewall in three crucial states: Michigan, Wisconsin, and Pennsylvania."

All of these factors did not deter the Trump triumph. Mr. Trump ran a good campaign that kept his supporters on their toes with enthusiasm. The momentum did not cease until the last vote was cast.

Trump ran a campaign projecting Hillary as anti-African Americans. For example, the movie called Hillary's America: The Secret History of the Democratic Party. Also, broadcasting numerous interviews with William Clinton (the presumed son of Bill Clinton) who was rejected by Hillary because he was half-African American.

On the other hand, Obama's failures haunted Hillary. The significant ones are the Obama health care and the unpopular program of resettling tens of thousands of refugees from Syria without proper screening.

WikiLeaks exposed the corruption and dishonesty of Hillary Clinton and her campaign chairman John Podesta. The emails exposed her weaknesses when she was in the office of the Secretary of State. Every day there were more revelations of wrongdoing, so much so, it was hard to keep up with. During this campaign, we had a situation whereby the hawkers became the news reporters, and the news reporters became the hawkers.

Certainly, Mr. Trump ran a relatively very good campaign. He focused on winning the "battleground states", where the outcome was unclear according to the opinion polls, along with some states considered to be the firewall for either candidate. When Trump breached the Rust Belt states that border on the Great Lakes it became clear that a Clinton win had evaporated, leaving many shell-shocked. With Pennsylvania, Wisconsin, Michigan and Ohio voting Trump it was clear that Obama's eight years had not impacted this region that had seen many factory jobs move overseas. Adding to the uncertainty came the fall of Florida, New Hampshire and North Carolina, states Obama had won comfortably in his previous elections, and it became clear that Hillary could not count on a majority of women or the minorities to vote for her consistently.

During campaign, Mr. Trump violated all of the traditional rules a candidate requires to be elected as a president but he prevailed. But the Leftists still bamboozled by Trump's landslide win are still searching for various people to blame for their loss. Recently, President Obama authorized CIA to investigate if Russia influenced USA elections.

Inauguration: The public inauguration of our new political leaders is tomorrow, January, 20th 2017. It will be accompanied by prayers. This is in line with our pledge of allegiance: "One Nation Under God". It is a commitment to fight for justice that is "rooted in the eternal law." The Bible instructs us to obey the commandments of God and the laws of our countries. The commandments make us accountable to the higher authorities. At no point of time was mankind created to be autonomous. God created a perfect man (Adam) and put him in a perfect environment (Garden) but still, He gave him a law regarding which tree to touch and not to touch. Any law demands submission. Jesus was truly God and truly man but He submitted to the Father. At every stage of life, there are rules demanding submission: Family rules in accordance to Ephesians 5:22-23. Civil rules: "Let everyone be subject to the governing authorities, for there is no authority except that which God has established. The authorities that exist have been established by God." (Romans 13:1). We are a divided nation bleeding to death because of the irrational quantum disputes. Homicide, drugs, violence, racism are no longer a whisper but a shouted calumny. Now that we have a legitimate government in place, the partisan election politics should be put to rest. Let us consecrate this country to

God through prayers. This is the loudest calling to duty: Put your finger on the Biblical passage 2 Chronicles, 7:14, believing God for the healing of our country. Let us rally behind our new leaders and allow the long arms of the law to creep the long fingers of lawlessness. Again, our hope does not come to us by Air Force One; but by the grace of God.

****

President Donald Trump boasted his inauguration would have an "unbelievable, perhaps record-setting turnout but it was far less than Obama's first inauguration." Here's the reason: Obama's election was historic because he was the first African-American to become president. It is not a surprise for the massive people who showed up at his inauguration. Remember that six million African-American who voted for Obama never voted for either Trump or Hillary. They simply stayed home. No wonder they didn't even show up for the inauguration. They are simply not interested. The good news is that God is interested and that is how Mr. Trump won the election. God made them stay home!

August – Evangelism

There is no swag when it comes to the salvation of the soul. We come to Christ as dirty as we are, and He takes care of our mess. Most probably compared to a mother that cleans behind her baby by changing the diapers! Have a great week.

****

Your hope is outside you; it is in Christ. Jesus Christ did not come to win the love of the Father for us. It is the love of the Father that sent Jesus to die for us. In Jesus Christ is the fullness of grace. There is no faith outside Christ.

****

Sin is the only problem and the cause of all problems in this world. Some acknowledge it, others don't, and others even do not know that it is the problem. God provided to us the way to deal with it: It is by the life, death, and resurrection of Jesus Christ. Some choose to accept God's offer, some don't.

****

Matthew 3-2 – "Repent you: for the kingdom of heaven is at hand." There cannot be a kingdom without a king. The coming of the heavenly kingdom on earth is the ushering in the reign of God on earth. In order for God to be your King, you must accept Jesus as your Lord and Savior. You must deny (repent) this kingdom so that His kingdom becomes your kingdom.

****

Matthew 28:20 – "Therefore go and make disciples of all nations, baptizing them in the name of the Father, and of the Son, and of the Holy Spirit, and teaching them to obey all that I have commanded you. And surely I am with you always, to the very end of the world." It is a calling to preach the gospel of the kingdom of God as we go about our daily businesses. Jesus sends us to go, but not without Him. To go ahead of Him is as dangerous as to go behind Him. This is an invitation to come and partake of His life and His Spirit in order to be effective in our ministry. Without the anointing, there is a subtle shift in our motivation to serve God, whether in the Church or elsewhere. Then we are no longer motivated by passion but we serve out of obligation. That is when the atmosphere of heaven— righteousness, peace, and joy—seems to evade us.

****

The gospel affects every area of human endeavor. The Church is equipped with the Holy Spirit to convict the sinners to repent. The gospel reveals the cross. The cross reveals the grace. The grace reveals God's awesome presence. His presence draws others in by conviction. "As Christians, we are a saved people. But we are also a sent people." We have the belief, the hope, and the conviction that we belong to a better world, beyond the horizon, but we are sent to this world to advance the kingdom of God by the power of the gospel. Jesus specifically said that "I have given them your word, and the world has hated them because they are not of the world, just as I am not of the world" (John 17:16). Being "in" the world but not of the world means using the things of the world which God has given us to foster our divine callings as opposed to immersing ourselves or chasing after worldly pleasures. Pleasure is no longer our calling in life, as it once was, but rather the worship of God.

****

Acts 1:8 - "But you will receive power when the Holy Spirit comes on you; and you will be my witnesses in Jerusalem, and in all Judea and Samaria, and to the ends of the earth." All creation witness to the presence of its

Maker. Jesus saved all varieties of people with a wide variety of abilities and equipped them with His Spirit, and sent them off to be His witnesses. He has called people of every race and color who have been hurt by life in every manner imaginable and adorned them with the perfect beauty of the gospel to proclaim the blessed hope to the lost world. Preaching the gospel begins with a simple testimony of your life experience - how you were delivered. To be a witness for Christ is acknowledging that you are not saved for yourself but for others to be saved too. In the secular world, every revolution for peace and justice has been made possibly by a group of people who chose to bear witness and demanded that others bear witness as well. The kingdom principle is to evangelize them and sending them to evangelize others.

****

Your transformed life will definitely attract the sinners to you but people are not going to be converted until you proclaim the gospel. It is the life, death and resurrection of Jesus preached in the gospel that changes the hearts of the people. Your transformed life is supposed to back up the gospel you preach. Remember that there are nice people like you out there who are not necessarily believers. All people can be good (not perfect) for a moment of time because God created mankind a moral creature in His image. Satan persecutes the believers because he hates the gospel. Nobody will persecute you for living right until you openly confess that you are a Christian. Jesus promised persecution for His name's sake: "Blessed are you when people insult you, persecute you and falsely say all kinds of evil against you because of Me. Rejoice and celebrate, because great is your reward in heaven; for in the same way they persecuted the prophets before you" (Matthew 5:12). Jesus compared our persecution to that of the prophets of the Old Testament. The great men of the Old Testament were not the kings or the priests, but the prophets because they were always calling the people to repentance and revealing God's will to man.

****

We are called to fellowship with other believers then go to reach out to the lost world. "We are sent to the lost world. Unfortunately, many Church members are so cocooned in the Church world that they couldn't list several names of non-believers they know well. If our whole world revolves around hanging out with Christians, we're not likely to do evangelism."

****

"If we had more hell fire preaching in the pulpit then we would have less hell bound people in the pew".

****

Every time I meet a person, I ask God the reason why He brought us together, and I start from there to minister to him. Use every opportunity you get to talk to somebody to minister to them the saving grace of the Lord. God is willing to use us more than we are willing to be used.

****

Isaiah 60:15 – "Although you have been forsaken and hated, I will make you the everlasting pride and joy of all generations, says the LORD" I can't express God's love in words but I can express it emotionally in attitudes and smiles. Flash that smile, not a fake one but a real one because Jesus loves you! When people ask you why you are happy all of the times, tell them about Jesus!

****

There is a need to be compassionate but compassion truth and principled as opposed to people-pleaser. "A man-pleaser cannot be true to God because he is a servant to the enemies of his service; the wind of a man's mouth will drive him about as the chaff, from any duty, and to any sin." You can't serve God and always be a people-pleaser. We are called to preach the gospel in season and out of season. The true gospel offends and convicts rather than causing emotional excitement as we see today. Like Leonard Raven Hill said, "If Jesus had preached the same message that ministers preach today, He would never have been crucified."

****

What is the motivation and purpose for your life? The motivation and purpose of my life is to go to heaven and take with me as many souls as possible. We are debtors to Jesus Christ that died for our sins, and debtors to the saints that suffered so that the gospel must come to us.

****

We are given this life to live with a purpose... To determine how we spend our afterlife. I pray we all come to know this abstemious truth: "We have got one change to make – to leave our mark on this planet: To cause a stir, to change a heart, to live intentional, love intentional and to speak intentional" - Rose Queener

****

It is the expectation of Jesus for people to know what you know. Jesus spent His whole life engaging people but most of us have spent our whole lives trying to disengage and avoid strangers. Witnessing is the greatest manifestation of the true disciples, which is probably the reason why so few engage in it.

****

2 Corinthians 12:10 – "Therefore I take pleasure in infirmities, in reproaches, in necessities, in persecutions, in distresses for Christ's sake: for when I am weak, then am I strong." The word 'pleasure' means thinking positively. It is enduring the sufferings with hope. Paul focused on the good that will come out of the current bad situation of sufferings. Paul's primary concern was to preach the gospel effectively through thick and thin without despair. Genuine faith may be stretched by the trials of life but it will never break. Faith is the thick skin that we develop to keep us on our toes even when the going gets tough.

****

An effective evangelist must be a prayer warrior too. Sometimes God wants us to knock at the doors of heaven before knocking at the doors of men.

****

We are called to intercede for the lost world. "Settle it in your mind today that the friend who labors for your conversion to God is the best friend that you have" ~ J.C. Ryle

****

Your life preaches more than the words of your mouth. "I like your Christ, I do not like your Christians. Your Christians are so unlike your Christ." ~ Mahatma Gandhi

****

Use the Word to edify others instead of breaking them. "Biblical orthodoxy without compassion is surely the ugliest thing in the world" ~ Francis Schaeffer

****

We are sent to win the world. But the world wins us whenever the Church feels that we must become like the world in order to win the world.

****

I treat everyone like a Christian until they prove me wrong.

****

Getting people to Jesus is why believers are here. Start by getting your family to the Church today.

****

Psalm 90:12 – "So teach us to number our days, that we may apply our hearts unto wisdom." It is a calling to be time conscious. Live as if every day is your last day to share the gospel, and as if every day is the last day for people to hear the gospel.

****

John 1:40-41 – "The first thing Andrew did was to find his brother Simon and tell him, "We have found the Messiah. Come and see." The Christian life is about giving invitation to people to come and see the difference Jesus has made in your life.

****

Hebrews 11:24 - "By faith Moses, when he was come to years, refused to be called the son of Pharaoh's daughter". I pity the people who sell out to the worldly life of sin instead of becoming testimonies and witnesses to the life of Christ.

****

Biblical preaching is likely to shake things up, making you uncomfortable. Look at the Old Testament prophets, none of them made people feel good! Often it's the religious mentality that is most hesitant when God starts doing a new thing.

****

Egoism affects sincerity. The more our egoism is satisfied, the more robust is our belief. Selfish Christians are ever learning, but they never grow into the character of their Savior... If your opinion does not agree with the Word of God, then you have no right to your opinion!

****

Spiritual growth is manifesting the character of Christ. The Christ-like character is the ultimate goal of all Christians. To settle for anything less is considered to be backsliding. Your passion for Jesus and your compassion for the lost soul add up to the Christ-like character.

****

God will put into your heart a strong desire for the people and places where He wants to send you. The things you are passionate about are not random, they are your calling.

****

If your path is difficult it is because of your high calling. Your vision should be much bigger than what you can actually see and what people can see. Break down your vision into minor chewable goals to pursue.

****

It is possible for a drowning person to cause the rescuer to drown with him. A rescuer may think his swimming skills are sufficient to allow him to cover the distance to the distressed person in peaceful-looking waters. It's what happens next that causes the problem. For example, the lake is calm, but the distressed person is so panicked that they grab and hold the person trying to help them, and both succumb! Whereas rescuers are celebrated as heroes, it's important for would-be rescuers to understand the risks involved in going after a distressed person drowned (in the water). In the same manner, the Bible warns us to be careful not to be pulled down by those to whom we are sent to minister (1 Corinthians 10:12). Remember that we are up, and the people to whom we preach the saving grace are down (worldly), but they have the advantage of the gravity of the earth (worldliness) to pull us down to their level.

****

Romans 10:14 – "'Whoever calls on the name of the Lord shall be saved.' How then shall they call on him in whom they have not believed? and how shall they believe in him of whom they have not heard? and how shall they hear without a preacher?" Faith is hearing the Word of God. Hearing is responding to the character of God. Believing is receiving Jesus Christ as your personal Savior. Jesus told His disciples "the harvest is plentiful, but the workers are few." Many non-believers are open to listening to the gospel. Evangelism isn't just one part of our calling. It is central to our calling. As John Stonestreet says, "we're all called to be missionaries in our daily lives! Until the Lord returns, we face a task unfinished."

****

Romans 10:3 - "For they being ignorant of God's righteousness, and seeking to establish their own righteousness, have not submitted to the righteousness of God". Paul goes on to say in verse 16: "But they have not all obeyed the gospel." The gospel has to do with believing in the finished works of Jesus to justify you. We are required to receive what Jesus finished rather than adding to it. Jesus is God's righteousness. We submit to God by manifesting the sinless life of Jesus Christ.

****

"I don't want just a revival. I want the true revival. I want to see the prophecy of Azuza Street come to fruition. I want to see the world swept with the Glory of the man Jesus Christ. I want to experience, stewardship and live in the never dying revival. Because of this, I've spent the better part of the last two years in the secret place asking God two questions: Who are you? And who am I to you? The foundation of this revival must absolutely be found in the first question. Who is He? Surely, He is God who desires that we experience the spiritual awakening. Surely, a good Father. A fierce King with a long arm and a forgiving heart; the Father of the prodigals. He is the glorious Savior, a friend, and a guide. He is holy and worthy of our worship. One who desires to give good gifts, and by whose stripes we are healed."

****

1 Corinthians 3:6 – "What then is Apollos? And what is Paul? They are servants through whom you believed, as the Lord has assigned to each his role. I planted the seed and Apollos watered it, but God made it grow. So neither he who plants nor he who waters is anything, but only God, who makes things grow" We are laborers hired to plant and to harvest. But God is the owner of the seed planted, and He causes it to grow. It is not about who plants and who waters but God who causes growth that matters.

****

You hear how Muslims in the Middle East are coming to Christ in numbers after experiencing dreams and visions. God is using a form of communication that is not new but instead echoes through generations. It is not the only way for Him to reach them, but one of the ways. Given the fact, this is not an excuse for the missionaries to throw their minds in neutral and relax. We should not lay down our tools and ask God to invade the Muslim world through dreams and visions as He has done in the lives of countless individuals. We still have the responsibility to vigorously evangelize the world indiscriminately.

****

Somebody asked that "Can God use angels to preach the gospel?" God can use the angels to preach the gospel but He will not. Why? Because the angels have never experienced the joy of salvation. God uses people like you and me who are acquainted with the saving grace and have experienced the joy of salvation to be the witnesses of what we have experienced to the perishing world. The more we grow into the grace, the more we grow into knowing God. The more we know God, the more we want Him to be known. The angels do not know the love of God as we do because they have never been given a second chance. The angels who sinned were banished from heaven without a possibility of reconciliation or returning. But we are given multiple chances to return to God because God reconciled Himself to us through Jesus Christ (2 Corinthians 5:18). We, who have experienced the love of God are in better position to tell those who have not. The angels look into our salvation with awe: "What is man, that You are mindful of him, or the son of man, that You care for him? You made him a little lower than the angels; You crowned him with glory and honor and placed everything under his feet." (Hebrews 2:6-7)

****

As posted by Kasoma Joshua: I went to a king and asked him: Who is Jesus? He said He is the King of Kings. I went to a prince and asked him: Who is Jesus? He said He is the Prince of peace. I went to an electrician and asked him: Who Is Jesus? He replied: Jesus is the light of the World. I went to a plumber and asked him: Who Is Jesus? He replied: Spring of life. I went to a doctor and asked: Who is Jesus? He replied: Jesus is the greatest physician. I went to a hunter and asked: Who is Jesus? He replied: Jesus is the Lion of the tribe of Judah. I went to a psychologist and asked: Who is Jesus? He replied: Jesus is the source of wisdom. I went to a builder and asked: Who is Jesus? He replied: Jesus is a house built on the Rock. I went to a baker and asked: Who is Jesus? He replied: Jesus is the bread of life......... The only person I didn't meet at home was you. Now that I am in touch with you, let me ask you, Who Is Jesus to you?

****

Somebody posted a card on his homepage reading: "I will vote for Jesus". Intriguingly, Jesus is not running to be elected to any political office. If we continue to take the name of the Lord casually, people will not take us seriously, and our evangelism will be less effective. I remember watching on television an advertisement of car sales involving half-naked ladies in bikinis with the name of Jesus branded on their panties. I know at times people do such things without prior ill intentions, but in the long run, it does more harm than good. It is good to be creative when preaching the gospel but let us do it with reverence, care, and precision lest it escalates into an abomination. Remember that not everything that sounds good is godly. Preach the gospel wherever you are and with whatever you have but when you are led by the Spirit. Strive to resist the insidious temptations of emotional excitement and the pleasures of the corrupt world. Remember that hedonism is the highest form of worshiping at the altar of the strange fire, and can jeopardize your effectiveness in the ministry, even in evangelism.

****

Somebody asked, "Don't you think that using the worldly things like musical instruments have been instrumental in winning the youth to Christ?" The musical instruments are not worldly; it is what you do with them that matters. A drum set apart to glorify God is an instrument of honor as a guitar or a piano. God created the emotions in us for the good purpose, if they are submissive to the spirit. True, many young folks can be reached at their level but we must be careful not to overstep our boundaries. We cannot seek help from the devil as if Heaven is depleted of resources. We are not sent to be changed by the world but to change the world. The word 'Church' means called out of the world.

The emotions at their best can be used just to convince somebody to lend to you their ears (listen to you). Regeneration needs no help from man. It is the divine work on the human soul (transformation), and it is only possible by the conviction of the Holy Spirit when the gospel is preached. Regeneration involves a new genesis, a new beginning, a new birth. It is that birth by which we enter into the family of God by adoption. When by faith we are united with Christ, we are adopted into that family of whom Christ is the firstborn.

Again, at times you need a bait to draw their attention to you but know that the same worldly baits of pleasure have worldly hooks beneath them. According to statics, the number of youth leaving our local churches is staggering. It is because many of them joined our churches for wrong reasons. They joined our congregation but they were not added to the Church by the Lord. The Bible says that: "And the Lord added to their number daily those who were being saved (Acts 2:47). The Bible says concerning those who left the Church: "They went out from us, but they did not really belong to us. For if they had belonged to us, they would have remained with us; but their going showed that none of them belonged to us" (1 John 2:19).

If I asked you to name the places where Christianity is growing the fastest, you, would probably respond "Africa" and/or "China." And you'd be correct. The explosion of Christianity south of the Sahara is so great that a colleague of mine is surprised whenever he meets a West African immigrant who's not a believer. And as we previously told you on Breakpoint, Christianity in China is growing so rapidly that, by one scholar's estimate, there will be more Christians in China than in any other country by 2035.

But there are other, less-known places where the Good News is being heard and received.

One of these is Nepal. When Americans think of Nepal—if they ever do—what comes to mind is an exotic blend of the Himalayas, "wind-swept prayer flags," and temples, lots and lots of Hindu temples, with a few Buddhist stupas thrown in for good measure. Until recently, that would have accurately summed up Nepal's religious scene. In 1951, Nepal's census showed no—that would be zero—Christians in the country. Ten years later, it showed just 458.

Forty years later, the number had risen to 102,000 and ten years later, i.e., in 2011, it had risen to 375,000. What's more, according to a report by the International Institute for Religious Freedom, Nepalese Christian leaders believe that this last figure underestimates the number of Christian by a factor of six: instead of 375,000 Christians there are closer to 2.3 million.

While Nepal is officially a secular country, it has an overwhelming Hindu majority that, historically, has tolerated a small Buddhist minority that poses no threat to the country's Hindu identity. By way of protecting this Hindu identity, Nepal's interim constitution states that "no person shall be entitled to convert another person from one religion to another and shall not take actions or behave in a way that would create disturbance in another's religion." This of course effectively outlaws evangelism. Yet Nepalese are converting to Christianity in large numbers. Part of the reason is that the law is difficult to enforce. A larger part is that Christians have stepped into areas of need that neither the government nor the Hindu majority can or even will serve.

As is the case in India, many of the converts to Christianity come from the lower castes. Even though, as in India, discrimination on the basis of caste is illegal, centuries, if not millennia, of custom and practice aren't reversed by the action of a parliament sitting in the capital.

What makes a difference in the lives of these people is other people whose own faith not only reject the idea of caste but also insists that in ministering to the "least of these," they are ministering to God himself.

****

Your life must be relevant to your message. "Show me by virtue of your living that you are redeemed, then I will believe".

****

Eternity is unlimited and timeless. There is a time when time will cease to be but there is no time when life will cease to be. The life you live now will affect your eternity. Don't gamble with your life because you are not the captain of your soul. Put your past and present in the hands of Jesus, and He will put your future into the hands of God.

****

"People don't resist change. They resist being changed!" It is easy for them to change their conducts without changing their character. For example, a gay person that feels comfortable to change his orientation and become straight and anti-homosexual, without becoming a Christian. You have the capacity to change your conducts but it takes the divine intervention to change your character because changing the character isn't just changing the lifestyle, it is changing life. Any change that does not affect the destiny of your soul is no change at all. Jesus institutes the profound change based on the fundamental truth that yields to the fundamental change. He affects our conducts, character, and destiny through transformation.

Genuine change involves a total man, and it is easy if you figure out the worthiness of what you gain. I mean if you realize what you have to gain by giving up what you have. Choose to put His will above your will that gratifies your carnal desires! You want to change the world? Begin with yourself. This is the change that will not fail. Let reality be reality.

****

It is thrilling to hear the testimonies of people saved while in jail. However, you don't have to wait to go to jail or to run into trouble in order to get saved. Every time you hear the gospel, God is extending to you an opportunity to respond. Please respond to the gospel, now rather than later" (Hebrews 3:15). Today, if you hear his voice, do not harden your hearts as you did in the rebellion." Whenever you hear the gospel, you have a divine appointment to meet God and to talk to Him directly. Timing is the key element in life. You are in the right place and at the right time. Don't let this opportunity pass!

****

"Any mission work that doesn't include the proclamation of the gospel is a mission the world can do. We're to go & do everything in His name!" ~ Katheel Peck

****

There is a true story when the inspectors of the airport refused a man to bring fresh cheese into the country. The man insisted that he will bring it in. He ate it in front of the inspectors and walked in. They can restrict you to preach Jesus but they have no power to restrict Jesus in you. Eat Him (John 6:53), and Walk in with Him wherever you go!

****

The Most High God dwells high beyond the sky, beyond the imaginations of the astronomers; where no space shuttle can go; but He revealed His dwelling place to us, and He will return to take us there!

****

Luke 5:4 – "Now when he had left speaking, he said unto Simon, Launch out into the deep, and let down your nets for a draught." Jesus picked the experienced fishermen and taught them how to fish. We are disciples of Jesus because we are students of Jesus. He calls us with different talents and teaches us how to be fishers of men. Our own goodness without Christ isn't good enough. It is when you become uncomfortable with your own goodness that you seek your greatness in Christ.

****

The fact that there are so many troubled people troubling you is the very reason for your very existence. Much trouble from people means much opportunity to express the love of Christ in you to them. Love is like a luxurious perfume in a bottle. The perfume cannot be effective unless the bottle containing it is cracked open. Your love cannot be accessed unless your comfort is cracked. The bottom line is that people are going to be drawn to God when they see the love of Jesus in you (John 13:35). Walking away from them without displaying to them the love of Christ treasured in you, is like walking away from your divine appointment. How we relate to God depends on the grace but our good works depend on how we relate to others. We are not saved by our good works but God is going to reward our good works. This is what is called a good fight of faith that is not void of works (James 2:14-26).

****

John 16:13 - "But when he, the Spirit of truth, comes, he will guide you into all the truth. He will not speak on his own; he will speak only what he hears, and he will tell you what is yet to come". The Holy Spirit guides us into all truth. Half-truth is not all truth; it is deception. Jesus is the absolute truth. The Holy Spirit never guides you to Buddha, Mohammed or any other false prophet. He guides to Jesus because He is the embodiment of all truth.

****

The children of God are children of the light. They are busy minds with urgent tasks lurk inside them, demanding immediate attention. We are busy trying to figure out which one assignment to grab first. The nightmare is ending up doing nothing just because you don't know what and which to do first. God does not release His revelation to the lazy minds. The happiest folks are those who are busy meditating on the truth of the Scriptures, for their minds are starved of time to seek out misery. The most practical way of controlling your thoughts is when you hedge your minds against the destructive vibrations to the minds. How? By tuning your minds to the constructive divine vibrations due to the Inspiration of the Word. In every man's heart, there is a secret nerve that answers to this vibration. This is the recommended positive thinking and the right way of disciplining your body.

****

"It takes more than bread to stay alive. It takes a steady stream of words from God's mouth." (Matthew 4:4).

****

2 Timothy 2:24-25 – "And the Lord's servant must not be quarrelsome but must be kind to everyone, able to teach, not resentful. Opponents must be gently instructed, in the hope that God will grant them repentance leading them to a knowledge of the truth". Humility is the inward feeling of kindness. Gentleness is the natural impulse to express it. Paul uses the term "must be kind" in the imperative form. He appeals to us to do it without hesitation. Give it without measure and without expecting returns. We are children of the day armed with the message of the light (gospel) to pull down the darkness of the world. We are the light to the darkened souls whose light has dimmed. But the integrity of your words depends on your attitude towards others. Need to be heard? Then tune up the volume of your voice by seasoning your words with kindness and gentleness. "Kindness is the language which the deaf can hear and the blind can see."

****

"For anyone who feels like it's too late and they missed God's calling on their lives, be encouraged. Smith Wigglesworth was a plumber well into his 50's before he pursued God's call and became a preacher. He went on to become one of the most influential preachers of the 20th century."

****

Religion is a specific fundamental set of beliefs and practices generally agreed upon by a number of persons or sects: "Just as a candle cannot burn without fire, men cannot live without a spiritual life." Every person is religious in a certain way. Throughout human history, people have developed strong loyalties to traditions, rituals, and symbols. Religiosity is to be bound up with what you worship regardless of its validity. Religious rituals and practices spill out well beyond the sanctuary. Sometimes it is the little things we are accustomed to, and we are not willing to give up unless we are delivered from them. The people of the world sacrifice to their deities in return for provisions and protection. The Christian God is unique from the rest of the gods of the world in such a way that He issued the moral code (Ten Commandments) and demanded that His people live after them in order to maintain the smooth communication with Him. He is deeply involved with their day to day activities.

****

What is the religiosity mentality? Religiosity, in its broadest sense, is a comprehensive sociological term used to refer to the numerous aspects of religious activity, in particular, the traditions of men that are in contradiction to the Scriptures. "Sometimes people hold a core belief that is very strong. When they are presented with evidence that works against that belief, the new evidence cannot be accepted. It would create a feeling that is extremely uncomfortable, called cognitive dissonance. And because it is so important to protect the core belief, they will rationalize, ignore and even deny anything that doesn't fit in with the core belief." Such characters deny the truth as presented to us in the Bible. The Word in us is the light of the world (Matthew 6:22). The word "light" here in the Greek *photeinos* "fo-ti-nos" where we get our English word "photon" which is the fundamental particle of visible light that is capable of removing the dark cloud from the surroundings.

****

There is one way leading to Heaven. Jesus is the way. There are thousands of ways leading to hell, yet not one exit to get out of hell. Think about it.

****

Somebody asked, "Is America already under the judgment of the reprobate minds in accordance to Romans 1:28?" The scripture says: "And even as they did not like to retain God in their knowledge, God surrendered them over to a reprobate mind, to do those things which are not convenient". This judgment is not prophetic and it does not involve the whole nation. The word 'surrendered' is past participle showing something that started in the past but continues until now. Since time past, individual people including some Americans of today have been surrendered to the reprobate minds. Reprobate means condemned and foreordained to damnation; morally abandoned, depraved; condemned strongly as unworthy, unacceptable, or evil; rejected as worthless. Elsewhere, Paul called it "conscience seared with a hot iron" (1 Timothy 4:2). It is a conscience that is void of feelings that can no longer be convicted to repent. To them, listening to the gospel is like listening to one of grand papa's tales which has no spiritual significance at all. They are surrendered to themselves to be absolutely driven by their corrupt desires. Basically, it denotes a voluntary surrender of self to a life of self-indulgence; self-control and a demon-controlled, purely evil, lost soul.

****

Somebody asked, "When we go to heaven, will we feel the pain because of our beloved ones who will be languishing in hell?" We are going to be changed to the glory of God. Our minds will not be in contradiction to the minds of God. We shall like what God likes and hate what God hates. It pleased God to crush His Son (Isaiah 53:10), and it will please Him to destroy the unwanted (polluted souls) from the face of the earth. What pleases God will be automatically pleasing to us. It sounds crazy but we will rejoice with God for purifying the earth. We will be so purified and sanctified by the Holy Spirit such that our obsession will be the glory of God alone. God will wipe away our tears by getting rid of our tear glands; no pain whatsoever! So, the only chance we have to cry for our relatives who are not saved is now. We do it by ministering to them the saving grace and crying to God in prayers for them to be saved.

****

"Five minutes after you die you'll know how you should have lived."

****

September – Labor Day

Colossians 3:23 – "Whatever you do, work at it with all your heart, as working for the Lord, not for human masters". God wants us to represent Him wherever we go, and in whatever we do. Working is part of serving God and serving others. Working constitutes the unbroken fellowship with God from Sunday to Sunday. Laziness is in utter contradiction to the virtues of morality. We must work in order to avoid neglecting our responsibilities, in particular, taking care of our dependents. "To feel much for others and little for ourselves; to restrain our selfishness and exercise our benevolent affections, constitute the perfection of human nature".

****

Christ must be central in everything we do. Our tithes and offerings represent our labor. Therefore, working is worshiping. Our characters at workplaces must be elevated above our jobs. I know working involves competition for better accomplishments. Given the fact, we are called to have the same reputation but different accomplishments. Remember that success in any endeavor depends on the degree to which it is an expression of virtues. Let us endeavor to work with a servanthood attitude. It is an attitude that elevates God and shuns self-aggrandizing and hence self-worshiping. The Bible says that "But he that glorieth, let him glory in the Lord" (2 Corinthians 10:17). Happy Labor Day.

****

Proverbs 20:4 – "The sluggard does not plow after the autumn, So he begs during the harvest and has nothing." Hard working is a virtue. The Bible is against sluggish. Laziness is kind of sickness and is obnoxious. Laziness is a decision; it is fighting against something that God gave you to fight for. It is a lie and a conviction from the devil ingrained in your minds. You have the capacity to get rid of it. "Most of the life's demands are within our reach, but decisions take willpower". Remember that God does not bless idle hands; He works with your availability to increase your capability. Have a blissful Labor Day!

****

October – Halloween

The origins of Halloween are Celtic in tradition and have to do with observing the end of summer sacrifices to gods in Druidic tradition. In what is now Britain and France, it was the beginning of the Celtic year, and they believed Samhain, the lord of death, sent evil spirits abroad to attack humans, who could escape only by assuming disguises and looking like evil spirits themselves. The waning of the sun and the approach of dark winter made the evil spirits rejoice and play nasty tricks. Believe it or not, most of our Halloween practices can be traced back to these old pagan rites and superstitions.

In the fourth century, Christians attempted to co-opt the holiday by celebrating the lives of faithful Christian saints the day before Halloween. This was a conscious attempt to provide an alternative and re-focus the day away from ghouls, goblins, ghosts, witches and other "haunted" experiences. Since that time many Christians have decided to allow their children to dress in more "innocent" costumes of pumpkins, princesses, Superman or as a cowboy. Part of this is due to the simple reality that in today's Western culture it is nearly impossible to "avoid" Halloween.

****

Should the Christians celebrate Halloween? Halloween represents an opportunity to embrace the evil, devilish, dark side of the spiritual world. Christians should avoid participating in Halloween even if it is just for fun. Remember that hedonism (pleasure-seeking) is the highest form of worshipping. "The art of pleasing is the art of deception".

What about Horoscopes/Astrology? A horoscope is an astrological forecast. It can produce superstition-doubt-maybe confusion, false hope. Astrologists claim to predict a person's future through the use of a birth chart. Astrology is considered to be witchcraft. Why do you need astrology and horoscopes when you have a direct line to the throne room of God and can hear from Him for a right direction regarding where you are heading. God also blesses us with messages and confirms his words by the Holy Scriptures. The Holy Spirit telling us what is ahead is the best prediction we can have.

November for Praying

Tomorrow, May 5 is a national Day of Prayer. Praying is our right that precedes the constitution; it is the right granted to man by God that no man should temper with. The National Day is intended to awaken us to pray. We enjoy a rich, dynamic and unbroken relationship with God through Jesus Christ but we must communicate to God in prayers. Whenever Jesus went to a place, He did not look for a motel but for a mountain, a lonely place to talk to the Father in prayers. He taught us how to cultivate and maintain the daily fellowship with our Father. "When we are in Christ, God is on our side. Therefore, prayer is not a means to get God on our side; prayer is a means to align ourselves with God's purposes, plans and will". Praying is not an option. You must pray.

****

Praying is the language that we use to talk to our heavenly Father. Praying is not vain talking or babbling. It is heartfelt sincere communication with God. It is a perpetual expression of our intimate relationship with the divine: Not any other gods but the God of the Bible whom we access through Jesus Christ.

****

Prayerless means graceless. Praying is what you have to do in order to get what you want.

****

"Prayer is not asking. Prayer is putting oneself in the hands of God, at His disposition, and listening to His voice in the depth of our hearts" ~ Saint Teresa of Calcutta

****

The word prayer comes from a Greek word *proseuche* actually, the word *proseuche* is a compound of the words pros and *euche*. The word pros is a preposition that means toward, and it can denote a sense of closeness, Prayer goes beyond asking but it is a way of having a personal intimate relationship with God. "Just imagine you have your daddy at home whenever you see him you are just asking, this does not draw any closeness at all but just imagine that you have that closeness with your daddy, you enjoy each other's company, you listen to each other, talk to each other in between that you tell him your need" ~ Brain White Nyika

****

Romans 8:34 - "Christ Jesus died for us, but that is not all. He was also raised from death. And now he is at God's right side, speaking to Him for us." Jesus finished all His earthly works of reconciling us to God on the cross except for this one work: He is a living, exalted, and triumphant Redeemer, raised to life and interceding on our behalf before the heavenly throne. The fact that Jesus is sitting implies that His work of redemption is finished, however, He is still very active on our behalf in heaven. Finding out what Jesus is doing now is more than satisfying my curiosity. It has a tremendous impact on my spirituality. I have discovered that to be like Jesus is to pray radically.

****

Psalm 100:4 – "Enter his gates with thanksgiving and his courts with praise. Thank him and bless his name." We go to Churches with praises on our lips. During the exodus, the tribe of Judah went ahead of the twelve tribes. The word 'Judah' means praising. An effective praying begins with praising God. Praising takes our focus from 'self' to God. Jesus taught His disciples, in the Lord's Prayer, how to pray: The Lord's Prayer begins with "Our Father" because praying begins with our Father. His concerns precede our petitions. "Whenever you put your petitions ahead of God, you are going for pennies instead of the whole treasure." We praise God in times of joy and sorrow. Certainly, we go through trials but we don't weep as the world weeps; their tears run through the darkness of pain, and can only offer temporary relief at best—that will end in death eventually. God turns our tears into rivers of joy through the light of Christ.

****

When you kneel down before God, He stands up for you. When God stands up for you there is no man that can stand against you.

****

We are the living stones that make up the true temple. We are living because we were regenerated. "One hundred religious persons knit into a unity by careful organizations do not constitute a church any more than eleven dead men make a football team." ~ Aiden Wilson Tozer

****

Never forget to pray when you wake up because God never forgot to wake you up.

****

Praying and sinning will never live together in the same heart. Prayer will consume sin or, sin will choke prayer ~ J. C. Ryle

****

The devil can't knock you down when you are already on your knees.

****

Deuteronomy 32:30 - "One shall chase a thousand, and two put ten thousand to flight" The impact of being in agreement is measured in multiplication as opposed to addition. By the mighty power of God, one person can chase a thousand demons, two people do not chase two thousand but ten thousand. There is such a thing as agreement even in prayers. If you are great in prayer alone, you can be greater with someone (when someone joins you). It is called the prayer of agreement. The power of cooperative praying cannot be underestimated. Pray together in your house with your family, and fellowship with other believers at your local churches. Today, we have chains of prayer warriors hooked up on social media. In the Book of Revelation, the Bible describes the golden bowls full of incense, which are the prayers of the saints (Revelation 5:8). In other words, the prayers of God's people collectively fill heavenly bowls with the sweet aroma much like the burnt offerings did in the tabernacle.

****

"Lord teach me how to pray". This prayer of dependence is the most significant prayer because it depicts our deficiency and accentuates our completeness in God. The disciples of Jesus asked Him to teach them how to pray (Luke 11:1-13). This is the most humble act of the disciples during the earthly ministry of Jesus. Jesus was ready and willing to teach on this subject of praying, but only when His disciples were eager to learn. The motivation for learning is at its highest peak when the student asks the teacher to teach.

****

The greatest prayer is saying to God: "You promised". This is not intended to remind Him because God never forgets. Real praying is holding God accountable for His Word. He likes it because it is proof that we are standing on His promises.

****

John 11:42 – "I knew that you always hear me, but I said this for the benefit of the people standing here, that they may believe that you sent me." Jesus taught us that when we pray we must believe that God always hears our prayers. Harmony is the essence of praying. There is perfect harmony between the Father and the Son because the Spirit of God is the Spirit of Christ. An effective prayer begins in the Spirit. God hears every word of our conscience because the conscience is the voice of the spirit. In the conscience, there is no idle word. An effective prayer is like a beautiful melody, the lyrics of which are composed in heaven. Praying is simply singing the melody of your spirit. The prayer that goes to heaven begins in heaven, not the contrary.

****

Sometimes God answers our prayers but he creates gaps before the manifestation. He stretches time, purposely to strengthen our faith. Never take the initiative to fill in the gap or to help God out by manipulating the situation as Abraham and Sarah did to have the promised son. God tactically delays delivering in order to build your faith. Remember that, God reserves His best for those who are willing to wait.

****

If God answers your prayers, He is increasing your faith. If he delays, He is increasing your patience. If He doesn't answer, He has a better plan or something better for you.

****

God is in the business of answering prayers. What we call unanswered prayer is our inability to accept 'No' from God. Yet, God's 'No' is as good as His 'Yes' to us. Whenever God says 'No' to the child of God, it is because your petition had repercussions which you can't see at this moment.

****

Sometimes unanswered prayer is the answer. God delays to answer prayers when He is preparing the answer for us, and preparing us for the answer.

****

In John 15:7, Jesus says, "If ye abide in Me, and My Words abide in you, ye shall ask what ye will and it shall be done unto you." Taking these Words of our Lord seriously transforms our prayer life from a lifeless form to a conversation with our all-powerful Creator. Always align your will with His will. Bring before the Father His promise for explicit requests. Ask for forgiveness, salvation, the Holy Spirit, healing, sin problems and etc. God does not lie. His Word is as much His voice speaking to us verbally if we could hear Him.

****

We are accountable for our personal sins, and we must pray for forgiveness. Also, we depend on other people's prayers. We are called to pray for others and cry out to God to forgive their sins. Ezra prayed a deeply moving prayer of repentance for the nation of Israel. Ezra blushed and was greatly ashamed of the sins of the nation. The nation was all one family. Ezra set up for us an example regarding family repentance. The Prophet Daniel did the same thing in the following prayer: "And I set my face unto the Lord God, to seek by prayer and supplications, with fasting, and sackcloth, and ashes: And I prayed unto the Lord my God, and made my confession, and said, O Lord, the great and dreadful God, keeping the covenant and mercy to them that love him, and to them that keep his commandments; We have sinned, and have committed iniquity, and have done wickedly, and have rebelled, even by departing from thy precepts and from thy judgments" (Daniel 9:3-5). Daniel approached God when using a collective pronoun "We" that is inclusive of others. Although Daniel himself had not forsaken God, he knew his people had done so. Daniel loved his people (family) enough to cry out to God, 'We have sinned.' Such brokenness reflects the depth of the love he had for God and the neighbor (Mark 12:30-31).

****

The Apostle Paul used the word 'Amen' seven times in his epistles at the end of his doxologies and benedictions purposely to engage everybody in His prayers. Praying is a cooperative worshiping of God. In one accord, one will, and one heart we join the heavenly host to honor the One seated on the highest throne. We are supposed to seal our prayers with these words: "In the name of Jesus Christ, Amen" because within the Spirit of Christ we come into permanent accord with the Great Harmony. This is what advances and perseveres our prayers. Taking these Words seriously transforms our prayer life. I want to end by warning that, we should say the word "Amen" quite often, but it should never be spoken casually.

****

Intercessory prayer is the act of praying on behalf of others. It overrides the human will because we can pray for others with or without their permission. Intercessory prayer involves sharing prayer requests whereby there is the temptation of gossiping over the people whom we pray for. Gossiping diminishes the effectiveness of intercessory prayers. God wants us to have peace within ourselves and to be at peace with others.

****

Fasting is disciplining the body into submission. It is training the body to deny what is not essential. Also, saving time to focus on God instead of the stomach.

****

God still talks to His children. He is willing to talk to us than we want to talk to Him. But only those who have their spiritual antennas up can receive the signal of God.

****

Prayer is not about giving an excellent speech before God because God is not looking for excellent speakers! The sweet aroma that ascends to heaven comes from a clean heart. Prayer is a matter of the heart. God listens to the heart even before the words are spoken. Moses was a stammer but his prayers always had access to an open heaven. Sequencing our words properly, coherently and wisely during prayer is good but not good enough to attract God's ears. ~ Godfrey E N Nsubuga

****

Don't wait for the weekend to go to Church and pray. God wants full custody, not just weekend visitations.

****

"Prayer does not fit us for the greater work; prayer is the greater work." ~ Oswald Chambers

****

The Bible recommends praying persistently. Much praying means much faith. When praying becomes your habit, miracles become your lifestyle.

****

To pray is to let go and to let God take over - Philippians 4:6-7

****

We don't pray to get God's attention. We pray to turn our attention towards Him.

****

Pray in spite of your failures. Holiness is not the way to Jesus. Jesus is the way to holiness.

****

"The best place to be is in someone's thought, someone's prayers and someone's heart".

****

Tough times never last but tough people do. Tough people talk to God.

****

According to the Hebrew literature, meditation is not emptying your minds but filling it with the Word of God. Praising is bragging about the goodness of God. Every good thing comes from God the righteous one. He is near to all who call upon His name and fear Him.

****

Psalm 32:7: "You are my hiding place; you will protect me from trouble and surround me with songs of deliverance." Some translations use the words shelter, covering, or dwelling rather than "secret place." In the Old Testament, the term "secret place" comes from the Hebrew root word *cether*, which means "to hide or be concealed." This word is used in Psalm 139:15, "My frame was not hidden from you when I was made in the secret place." God has become a place of safety. He is Spirit, and when we are regenerated into a new nature (spirit) by His grace we can dwell in Him (Psalms 91). Also, a believer must have a secret place where he can have time alone with the Father on a regular basis. I mean a secret place that is chosen and known by you alone where you withdraw from the public and talk to God in prayers. Your companions should know better not to bother you whenever you are in your secret place. When you are frustrated and offended instead of attacking the intruders, raid your secret place to talk to God in prayers. Fight back when you are alone on your knees.

****

If you have time to worry, you have time to pray. "Worry changes nothing, prayer changes everything....... Your prayer might not change the situation or the people involved. But it can help you heal and show you better ways to handle the situation. Your prayer can change you" ~ Ade Dayo

****

Praying is reporting on duty! We report on duty to be given instructions not to instruct.

****

Matthew 6:7 - "And when you pray, do not babble on like pagans, for they think that by their many words they will be heard. Do not be like them, for your Father knows what you need before you ask Him...." The Scribes and Pharisees were guilty of two great faults in prayer, vain-glory and vain repetitions. They repeated themselves because there was no God to hear them and to answer their prayers. Our God has no voice mail and His phone line is never busy.

****

Make it a habit to pray in all seasons. When you pray only when you are in trouble, you are in trouble.

****

Praying is not asking God to do for you what He didn't want to do in the first place. Praying is asking God to deliver into your hands something that is already yours according to His promises. It is compared to using a Credit Card or the ATM machine whereby you withdraw only the money that belongs to you.

****

"When we're praying thy kingdom come, we're ultimately saying 'my kingdom must go. 'When we're praying thy will be done, we're ultimately saying 'my will must be undone" ~ Elizabeth Elliot

****

If our heavenly Father knows what we need why do we pray for them? Because praying is intimate. God is interested in our relationship with

Him: Knowing Him intimately through Jesus Christ and communicating with Him in prayers daily.

****

God is already watching His promises to fulfill His Word. Praying is saying His promises to Him. Praying is not desperately asking for what God did not promise but desperately humbling down in anticipation of seeing His promises fulfilled.

****

Scripture reading is an important portion of praying. When we read the Bible we give back to God the very scriptures He treasured with us. Read the Bible for proper understanding, wisdom and inspiration. You can't shut the Bible and claim to love God. Read the Bible as God's letter of love to you. The written Word is as real as the voice of God verbally speaking to you romantically!

****

Isaiah 40:31 – "But they that wait upon the Lord shall renew their strength; they shall mount up with wings as eagles; they shall run, and not be weary, and they shall walk, and not faint". Eagles fly alone at high altitude and not with sparrows or with other small birds. No other bird can go to the height of the eagle. A few birds like the eagle have the capacity to soar. Birds fly by flapping their wings but soaring through the vast expanse of the sky does not involve the flapping of wings. Waiting in the presence of God is relaxing and shutting down everything around you in order to hear from God. When Moses went to commune with God on the mountain, he left the crowd at the foothills. In the same way, eagles stay away from sparrows and ravens.

****

Isaiah 56:7 - "For my house will be called a house of prayer for all nations." Jesus quoted the same Scripture in Matthew 21:12-13. The Temple at

Jerusalem was for all people (Jews/Gentiles) to pray. The entire Temple compound was considered holy, but it became increasingly more holy as one entered farther in, from east to west. King Herod had enclosed the outer court with colonnades and it was referred to as the Court of the Gentiles because the "gentiles" (non-Jews) were permitted to enter the Temple area. They could walk within it but they were forbidden to go any further than the outer court. The Temple was a symbol to all nations, regarding how God wanted His will to be established on the earth. God is looking for somebody praying for His will to be done on the earth. Tough times should not deter us from praying but should make us desperate to pray.

****

We have a habit of manufacturing the presence of God in particular when we feel that He has withdrawn. But the reality is that God is never absent. He is ever present even when we cannot feel His presence. God uses withdrawing as a catalyst to activate our faith rather than as a hint that He is mad.

****

"It is easy to want things from the Lord and yet not want the Lord Himself, as though the gift could ever be preferable to the Giver." ~ St. Augustine of

****

"The correct concept is to think of prayer as the breath in our lungs and the blood from our hearts. Our blood flows and our breathing continues "without ceasing"; we are not even conscious of it, but it never stops. And we are not always conscious of Jesus keeping us in perfect oneness with God, but if we are obeying Him, He always is."

****

Your life does not get better by chance, it gets better by change. People are going to be attracted to you when they discover that you are on fire for

God. Fire is not a matter but it is the side effect of matter. The natural fire is caused by the reaction of oxygen, fuel, and heat. The spiritual fire is the impact of the Holy Spirit on our lives. To be on fire for God is to be super sensitive to His presence. This is the essence of worshiping. "Worshiping is the provocative response of the human soul towards the saving grace."

****

Fellowshipping is a direct encounter with the presence of God. It is the manifestation of the existing relationship with God and your neighbor. We go to churches at different locations, individually, but in the spiritual realm, we are one body of Christ, and He is the head of the body (Romans 12:1-8). We worship Jesus seated at the heavenly throne. Faith bridges the gap between heaven and earth, and between your heart and your neighbor's heart. We are not individual members of a big organization but we are an entity related and connected to each other (we are part of each other), and we find our unity in Christ. At the end of the day, we will be presented to God in Christ. "This is what life looks like when you know that you have peace with God by faith alone and Christ has become the foundation and summation of all your hopes."

****

Each of us has a special place. A place where the LORD can be blessed. So I lift my hands up and my heart and my voice today to praise His name. It is my ultimate desire to praise Him and to live for Him.

****

"To dance in the rain, you must first learn to praise Him in the storm".

****

"And He hath put a new song in my mouth, even praise unto our God: many shall see it and fear, and shall trust in the Lord." Psalm 40:3

****

There is always a reason to praise God. My first blessing of the day is that I woke up.

****

Today's prayer: "Lord, you are full of life, love and grace. Place in me an unmovable faith and teach me unfathomable love so that I may worship you! Let me not envy what others have but what you have. You have set before me your treasures of heaven for my inheritance. Yet, I am passionate about other illegitimate things. My ambition comes from my passion. Help me to love you with such thriving authenticity and passion."

****

Today's prayer: "Lord, I come before you not just to be blessed but to be a blessing to others; so that by teaching I might learn, and after learning I might teach. Lord, please pull down and shut up all of the obstructions intended to divert my focus from you. In Jesus' name, I pray."

****

Today's prayer: "Lord, you said that "Things that cause people to stumble are bound to come, but woe to anyone through whom they come." (Luke 17:1). Dear Lord, life experience is a toil but can be a snare at times. The surmounting temptation is the crucible that forms the character. The world is more connected than ever, yet falling apart. We are connected to each other in one way or another in particular by Internet and we can impact each other. Help me not to be a hindrance to others instead of a help. Guide my heart so as not to be a snare to somebody, and don't allow others to be a snare to me. Amen."

****

Today's prayer: "On this pilgrimage, there are unlimited numbers of wants that seem to be satisfying but most of them are delusions and snares. I pray for contentment. Lord, you are my portion and providence. If I have you, I have everything. If I have nothing but you, I am fulfilled. Supply my needs as opposed to my wants. Just enough, not too much that might cause me to stumble. Sometimes I am impatient. Guide my heart and steps so that I don't run ahead of you because they stumble that run fast." Amen

****

Today's prayer: "Lord, in the real life, it is when I am honest with myself that I am vulnerable. It is when I decide not to be corrupt that I am vulnerable. Lord, I don't want to be everything for this world but I want you to be everything to me. Give me an audible voice to say constructive words glorifying to you. The Bible says that "The patient in spirit is better than the proud in spirit" (Ecclesiastes 7:8). Teach me to control my tongue so that if I don't have something good to say about someone, I don't say anything. And if I can't say it to their face, I keep it to myself". Amen.

****

Today's prayer: "Lord, Life in this world is akin to traveling a dark journey. Every day is a journey that must be traveled no matter how dark it is. Be with me as I trek on this journey of life, for without you, I cannot see my path, and I can't know where it leads. At times, my wobble feet drag me into a speed wobble cruise and I crash. Then waves of guilt and condemnation come after me until you get hold of me. Lord, guide my steps with certainty, give me firmness with humility, love with passion, and steadfastness without dogmatism. In the name of Jesus, I pray."

****

Today's prayer: "Lord God Almighty, in this tiny world, we live at the bottom of a deep gravity. It is a troubled world where one person's craziness is another person's reality. Quite often, I receive bad reports. This explains how skewed our perspective tends to be. Nevertheless, I am reminded that the majority report is so often based on human sight and earthly resources, and refutes your promises. Whose report should I believe? I choose to embrace your knowledge that surpasses human understanding. I want a perspective that is based upon what You have promised and what You are able to do, so help me God. In Jesus' name, I pray."

****

Today's Prayer: Lord, this life is an arena of battles. There are battles inside my heart and outside me. A person's inner nature or what he possesses in the inner man is his spiritual part of his being and determines what he is tempted by on the outside. The battles on the outside often come with an obvious starting point and finishing point and are often noticeable to all. But the war inside me is tougher, it is often fought for extended periods of time, and sometimes goes on unnoticed by those around me. Lord, life in the natural is a spiritual warfare. I have to master the art of "living" because I am the one involved in the battle. Man's intellect seeks for peace and by nature seeks it apart from the Lord Jesus Christ. But as for me without you, victory is out of my reach. My heart testifies that I am not alone. Your Word says you will be with me all the way to the uttermost ends of the earth (Acts 1:8). Also, "If I can believe, 'all things are possible for one who believes.'" There is no 'if' regarding your power, but my capability is limited by my unwillingness to believe. Increase my faith to believe.

****

Today's prayer: "Lord, You have been good to me. I don't have a right to ask for your goodness but through Jesus, you granted to me the birth rights of your progeny. This one thing I know: "I am safe and secure in your hands." I do not despair even when the tides turn against me. I know beyond doubt that you are in control of the situation. There are tough times when I can't see you in the picture, but you are in the background hidden in the negative, developing it into the visible image where you can be clearly seen. In spite of my wildest experiences, you keep me as the apple of your eye and hide me in the shadow of your wings. Thank You, in Jesus' name I pray."

****

Today's prayer: "Lord we are the people of your pasture. We all, like sheep, have gone astray, each of us has turned to our own way; and You have laid on Jesus the iniquity of us all (Isaiah 53:6). At times, I am selfish, impatient, insecure, stubborn, out of control, and at times I have a tantrum in particular when I can't figure out why you allow certain things to happen. When I am hard to handle, you have the patience to handle me. You handle me in thin and in thickness, even when I am at my worst. You are my righteousness and my defender from the evil one. When my enemies hear the roaring of the lion of Judah, they are scattered in seven ways. Surely, in the days of peace and of trouble, I will call on you because you hear my supplications. I lift up my eyes to the mountains-- where my help come from."

****

Today's prayer: "Lord, you are infinitely superior to any of your creations. Yet of all creations, you placed greater value on mankind and you chose to share your nature with us. Infinity of merit can only result from a nature that is infinitely divine or perfect. You created man in your image and gave him dominion over all the works of your hands and put all things under his feet! Above all, you crowned us with your glory by virtue of your indwelling Spirit, in whom you authentically qualified us to be your children. I am overwhelmed that the Creator of all things would humble Himself to come to us to have intimacy with us when we were yet sinners. I praise you for that."

****

Today's prayer: "Lord, your promise says that "When we get over yonder, we shall see your throne like a sea of glass glowing with fire and, standing beside the sea, those who had been victorious over the beast and its image and over the number of its name. They held harps given to them by God" (Revelation 15:2). The greatest moment will be to see you and to see our departed beloved ones standing beside you. The day is coming closer. What a day it will be! Indeed, the eye has not seen, nor ear heard, the things which You have prepared for those who love you."

****

Today's prayer: "Lord you are the light, this universe is an open book to you. Everything has a shadow except the light; it has no shadow. There is no dark spot hidden to your eyes. Even the little things that I do in darkness are never hidden to your eyes. "If I ascend to heaven, You are there; If I make my bed in Sheol, behold, You are there. If I take the wings of the dawn, If I dwell in the remotest part of the sea, Even there Your hand will lead me, And Your right hand will lay hold of me. Your word says, "Surely the darkness will overwhelm me, And the light around me will be night," Even the darkness is not dark to You, And the night is as bright as the day." (Psalm 139:8-9). Your throne is exalted in the highest of the heights. But your love turned your highest throne of sovereign into the throne of grace, so that in spite of my state of dishonor, I can honor you in the highest of the heights. The highest I can go is when I bow down on my knees, and it suffices to restore hope in a hopeless situation and to make the gloomiest person happy. Just want to say thank you, in Jesus' name. Amen"

****

Today's prayer: "Lord, in the kingdom of God where love is the dominant strategy there is peace and unity. You are the unit of the unity in whom we are united. In all situations, regardless of the diversity of our opinions, when we focus on the truth of the Scriptures we can always find a common place of love and unity. Lord, open our eyes so that the dogma of our denominations and our political allegiances do not demean the loyalty we pledged to you, and cause divisions. Deliver us from cynicism and skepticism. It is by faith that we encounter you. Lord, increase our faith. When we are 'seized with alarm' or 'struck with fear', help us to 'keep on believing'. May your will be done on earth as it is done in heaven. Amen"

****

Today's prayer: "Lord, you instructed me that if I love you, I should obey your commandments (John 14:15). To be sincere, I have not loved you as you said. At times I slip and break your commandments but your grace sustains me. Lord, forgive me because the spirit is willing but the body is at times weak. Help me not to slip into a deep existential crisis to the point of no return. All my desire is to worship you in the beauty of your holiness. My sufficiency is in you alone. Refine me and restore my oneness with you and a sense of self-worth. May your grace continue to help me to do what I can't do. Thank you, Father, for your unfailing love. In Jesus' name Amen.

****

Today's prayer: "Lord, as gold is tried in the fire, in this world we are tested daily in the furnace of adversity and affliction. There are times when I feel like I am facing a superheated furnace in particular when I am betrayed by the very people I trusted. The Psalmist lamented that "Even my close friend, someone I trusted, one who shared my bread, has turned against me." (Psalm 41:9). Often, my life is wrecked by the very people I love. Lord, you instructed us to love our enemies but these are not enemies but friends who happen to turn against me. I am not harboring hatred but hatred is stalking me. Lord, you alone can fix the wreck. I am not asking you to turn off the heat of the furnace because it would mean taking me out of this world, and hence this life. The trials are part of life, and the purest ore is produced from the hottest furnace. I am asking for your comforting presence to walk with me through this heat like you did to Daniel. Counteract the blazing indiscretions of other people with a blazing hearth in my soul and hence a blazing bonfire of a consecrated life. In Jesus' name, Amen".

****

Today's prayer: "Lord, you gave me the power of the tongue to praise you and to change the world but not without limitation. You said that "If I speak in the tongues (languages) of men or of angels, but do not have love, I am only a resounding gong or a clanging cymbal. (1 Corinthians 13:1). I don't want to love blindly because you turn a deaf ear to a dumb heart. Lord, you are my commander in chief. Keep me on my knees until I receive your matching orders. Teach me to control my tongue so that I can talk less and listen more to you. All days belong to you but you gave me the resting day (Saturday) to pause and to rest my body so that I can sit at your feet to learn from you. Then you gave me the resurrection day (Sunday) to sing and to shout in joy your praises. Take away all of the hindrances that make me virtually deaf, dumb, and blind. In the name of Jesus, I pray.

****

Today's prayer: "Lord, in this world, we have some physical and spiritual needs. But you have no needs because you are all sufficient. We find our sufficiency in you. You created all things, and by your grace, you met all of our needs. You said that "My grace is sufficient for you" (2 Corinthians 12:9). Your grace is all I need. At times I gamble with other things forgetting that I could have had all you ever wanted me to have if I had asked for the grace! I came empty handed and I brought nothing to the foot of the cross but by your grace freely I have received. Indeed, heaven is never depleted of supplies. Even when the doors of heaven seem to be closed, it is because I am depleted of the viable necessities to communicate. Even then, I don't have to call a squad to kick the door open, I just kneel down before your throne of grace, and the doors of heaven swing wide open for me to access your provision. May the doors of heaven remain wide open throughout this year. In the name of Jesus, I pray."

****

Today's prayer: Lord you said, "For I will pour water on the thirsty land, and streams on the dry ground; I will pour out my Spirit on your offspring, and my blessing on your descendants" (Isaiah 44:3). Life without you is like a flower that fades away when there is no water. I stand in a desert where rain seems random. I am thirty yet pretending to be watered. Guide me to the well of the living water springing up to eternal life. Drill my well with your Word. And let the fountain of the river of life flow forth from my belly for others to partake of. In Jesus' name, I pray"

****

Today's prayer: "Lord, I want more of you. Intensify my passion for the truth. But at times, when I am hungry, I have the tendency of eating lies. Give me a discerning heart to partake only of the truth served on your menu. There can be no love without loyalty. Fix my eyes on your Word and guide my feet to follow my eyes. Without you I am crooked but in your hands I find value. You alone can draw a straight line when using a crooked stick. Mold me into your character. Turn this lower situation of mine into an upper situation of praising. In Jesus name, I pray".

****

Today's prayer: "Lord your Word says that "He that dwelleth in the secret place of the most High shall abide under the shadow of the Almighty" (Psalm 91:1). There is a secret dwelling place but no secret Christian life because our lives are open book for others to read. A secret place is a decision we make to fellowship with you. Every person can find that secret place wherever they are. When we perpetually choose to fellowship with you, we become the very reflection of your glory. That is when you become the shadow of our protection. To fellowship with you is to be in union with the Spirit of Christ. Abide in me as I abide in your Word. In Jesus' name. Amen."

****

Today's prayer: "Lord, you said that "As far as the east is from the west, so far hath he removed our transgressions from us" (Psalm 103:12). East will never meet with the west. East goes infinitely eastwards, and west goes infinitely westward. It means when you forgive, you will never bring the forgiven sins against me. You are Omniscient, and you have unlimited knowledge, awareness, understanding; perceiving all things. Yet you chose to forget my sins. Thank you, Lord, in Jesus' name I pray".

****

Today's Prayer: "Lord, the two most precious things in the course of the journey of life are our character and reputation. Yet they are our weakest points. Paul has an answer to the puzzle of life. He said that "But by the grace of God I am what I am: and his grace which was bestowed upon me was not in vain" (1 Corinthians 15:10). All of us are given the same measure of grace, yet we experience the required spiritual growth at different levels. Taking your grace in vain is working out holiness by my natural capabilities and also living in disobedience to your commandments and ignoring the assigned responsibilities. Help me to take advantage of the grace bestowed upon me by growing up.

****

Today's prayer: "Lord, it is never darkness to you because everything is in light before you. You saw me when I was weaved in the darkness of my mother's womb. And you see me through the darkness of this world. In every odd situation, there is a spark of the heavenly fire, which kindles up and beams and blazes in the dark hour of adversity. Indeed, you are actively involved in the affairs of your creations, and you make your presence noticeable and your will explicitly known. In my darkened minds, I am deficient of imagination. Quite often I make foolish, careless, and presumptuous choices but you never abandon me. You sustain and preserve me constantly through your common grace and providence. You ignite my faith so that I can illuminate this miserable world with hope. Real hope is in the unchanging character of the unchanging God. I just want to thank you, Lord.

****

Today's prayer: "Lord, thanks for 2016. They say that "In the end, it's not the years in your life that count. It's the life in your years." The year is ending but there are numerous testimonies of people with broken hearts everywhere. I am not an exceptional. At times bad happenings eat me all day long and some impulse triggers me up to testify about them. Teach me to testify only about your goodness. Give me a good testimony that will conceal all of the bad testimonies lingering around me. Your glory never fades away. Let it be the glory of my triumph rather than defeat. Navigate my circumstances and create opportunities that will deny my adversary an iota of glory. Lord, you came to heal the broken hearts. I would rather be the least in the kingdom of light than the best in the kingdom of darkness. In the name of Jesus, I pray."

****

Prophetic Prayer: "Forerunners, pioneers, destiny carriers, it is your time where the *Ruach* of God is breathing afresh over what you are incubating. I hear "completion" and "divine order" that you will release kingdom concepts and innovation that will advance the body of Christ into a time of increase and momentum through occupying your God given mental. The harvest has never been riper than it is now."

****

Somebody asked "The Bible says that we should pray in privacy. Why do some people post their photos on Facebook while praying in their private places? I am not allowed to judge anybody. However, the Bible says that, "But when you pray, go into your room, close the door and pray to your Father, who is unseen. Then your Father, who sees what is done in secret, will reward you" (Matthew 6:6). This is a caution to keep your prayer life away from the eye of the public and to let your transformed life demonstrate your prayer life. Neither is God impressed by our praying nor does he approve praying with intentions of impressing others. Avoid showing off when you pray because it takes the glory that belongs to God alone. Remember that you don't need public approval in order to secure answered prayers. Cooperative praying like getting together to pray or sharing prayer requests on the internet is biblical. God looks at the intents of the heart. When the intent is showing off instead of motivating others then it is bad.

****

The joy of the Lord is my strength! I can't retire from serving God because I can't give up the joy. Praying is 'joy'. Serving God is 'joy'.

****

The joy of praising guides us into worshiping. Praising is part of praying. Praising is bragging about the goodness of God. Prayer is not a ritualized mumbling of words but rather a song of thanksgiving or dancing of praise. It is exalting God by our melodies and anguished cries of our hearts over our sins. It is a plea from a yearning heart.

****

Worshiping is acknowledging who God is. The otherness of God is that He is holy, unlike me. He is awesome.

****

Why do we worship God? The prominence of God is His majesty. He is honesty and He is crowned with honest. God alone can be worshiped. Worship is an incredible privilege, not a religious duty.

****

Personal worship precedes & promotes public worship (Hebrews 10:19-25)

****

Revelation 4:10 – "The twenty-four elders fall down before him who sits on the throne and worship him who lives for ever and ever. They lay their crowns before the throne---" The Greek word translated here as "elders" is never used to refer to angels, only to men, particularly to men of a certain age who are mature and able to rule the Church. The word elder would be inappropriate to refer to angels, who do not age. The twenty-four elders in heaven represent the saints in heaven and on earth (Church). Like the angels, the elders in heaven do not do what they want but what God wants them to do. It is a requisite for us on earth to do like them: Let our praises be constant, not interrupted; united, not divided; thankful, not cold and formal; humble, not self-confident. The difference between heaven and earth is order. Order is having each thing in the right place, each subject at the right time and each word in the right style. Order finds its beauty in perfection. Whatever God does carries with it His fingerprint. And in the world around us, His fingerprint of orderliness is evident to anybody who is honest with the facts. Viable Order must be under the jurisdiction of God. Sin is the recipe for disorder. The corruption of the world is a display of the lunacy and the will of a corrupt man. The rejection of God is a rebuttal intended to obliterate the orderliness of God on the earth. The world groans in anticipation of orderliness from God.

****

There is a certain majesty in simplicity which is far above all the quaintness of wit. Everything we see is a reflection of the majesty of our Creator. The Lord is robed in majesty. We do not worship Jesus, the baby, in the manger. We do not worship Jesus nailed on the cross. We worship Jesus, the exalted King, seated on the highest throne of God. The train of His robe fills the heaven of the heavens (temple). Worshiping is to lift our eyes to the starry heavens above us, to pause, to wonder and stand rapt in awe of His presence. It is a moment when at times words may fail you, and you just weep when your eyes are washed with the tears of joy. Yet all of the trembling and the tears turn into words of adoration. He is exalted to lift us up. He is the King of kings. It means the King ruling over kings. We are kings because we are robbed in the majesty of His glory.

****

Somebody asked that, "What do you say about disco lights in churches during worshipping?" I am not in a position to judge others. However, I want to say that when we worship, God is the only audience we have. He is our object of worship. Worshiping is about God. Anything that takes away our attention from God should not be in our sanctuaries. Remember that in the Old Testament, the high priest entered the holy of holies with the altar of burning incense. The smoke rising from the incense represented our prayers rising up to heaven. The house of God is for prayers only: "… for my house will be called a house of prayer for all nations" (Isaiah 56:7). Also, the smoke covered inside the holy of holies to minimize obstruction. It is for the same reason in the past times, all people who served at the altars of our sanctuaries were required to wear uniforms or robes of the same color. It was intended to prevent the wandering minds. They didn't want the members of the congregation to focus on what the ministers and the choir are wearing. Therefore, I don't think that disco lights should be used in the worship services unless it is a show for entertaining.

****

End of November for Thanksgiving

Thanksgiving Day is a national holiday celebrated in Canada and the United States. It was originally celebrated as a day of giving thanks for the blessing of the harvest and of the preceding year. Thanksgiving is celebrated on the second Monday of October in Canada and on the fourth Thursday of November in the United States. If you don't have a plan for the day, please check out this one: We go to churches to fellowship with people who are like us (believers). But we are supposed to use our homes as places of hospitality to the strangers. On this Thanksgiving set up a table of reception and reconciliation in your house for the people who are not your friends and who are not like you (strangers). Strangers are disguised friends whom you have not yet met. Remember that you were also once a stranger to the people who call you a friend now.

****

Thanksgiving is here. I want to thank God for allowing me to continue to travel this voyage of life. It is simultaneously a smooth and rough voyage, yet pregnant of adventures. On this pilgrimage of life there is endless passion yet without a possibility of fulfillment; not until you are fulfilled by Christ. God positions people like you to help others to sprint to the finish line. Just want to thank God for my parents, family, brothers and sisters, relatives, and friends. Few people love truly like you do. There is one word I can use to describe all of you regardless of your status, and that word is "friend". According to history, the spirit of Thanksgiving is the spirit of sharing. It is a day when the White Settlers and the Native Americans discovered the common ground to share and celebrate their differences. If you are a Christian, the most precious item at your fingertips which you can share generously with others is your faith. Split your time for praying into two halves: Invest one-half in others by interceding for them. Be a viable witness of Christ to others. And don't forget to share your turkey with your neighbor. Have a great Thanksgiving Day, please.

****

John 11:41–44 - "Father, I thank you that you have heard me at this moment in time. Because of our intimate relationship, I know that you are always listening to me, but I have spoken these words for the benefit of the crowd who is standing here so that they may believe that you sent me". The Greek word used in this prayer is *eucharisteo* which, we recall from Chapter 3, means to express overflowing joy with thanksgiving and heartfelt gratitude. The verb that I translate as heard (you have heard) is known as an "aorist" verb. The aorist is used in the Greek to indicate something that has happened once. The word listening (you always listens), however, is a "progressive action" verb. A progressive verb indicates an action in progress. When Jesus prayed before raising Lazarus, He did not pray for the power to do the work but He prayed to honor and to acknowledge His Father: Jesus prayed with thanksgiving, in the same manner, we pray for our food before eating. We thank God for His provision as opposed to asking for food to put on our plate.

****

Philippians 4:6 - "Be careful for nothing; but in everything by prayer and supplication with thanksgiving let your requests be made known unto God." Praying and thanksgiving cannot be separated. The reason is because we move from victory to victory. When we recount the grace of God, then praising becomes our starting point.

****

Psalm 16:11 - "You will show me the way of life, granting me the joy of your presence and the pleasures of living with you forever". God wasn't with the psalmist some of the time but all of the time, without exception and on every occasion! The same is true for you and me. With God "right beside" us, we can stand firm rather than allow circumstances, fear, and trials to rob us of peace and cause us to experience distress. May we never forget what David said of God and His loving care: He's always there ~ Shiela Sunny Smith-Lowery.

****

Luke 6:35 – "But love your enemies, do good to them, and lend to them, expecting nothing in return." The people you help today are most likely to be your tomorrow's enemies. If you can't give it don't lend it. If you give it, don't expect returns.

****

Philippians 3:14 – "I press on toward the goal to win the prize for which God has called me heavenward in Christ Jesus." God is aware of everything we are going through because everything stands in the presence of God for accountability. We are called to bury our sufferings and past failures into our future blessed hope, which is the glory of Christ in us. Turn every negativity into an opportunity to press on towards the mark. The reality is that Jesus saved you at the cross and He assumes the responsibility to see you seated at His right hand on the highest throne in heaven.

****

To be thankful is not an obligation; it is a voluntary act out of a hilarious and cheerful heart. A thankful heart motivates the giver to give more whereas the unthankful attitude restrains your capacity to give and to receive. To be thankful is to appreciate what you are given, as opposed to what you would have been given. Never despise the small things given or done to you. Little is enough if the big God is in it. To think with deep gratitude of those who reach out to us is a great encourager. It keeps everything in perspective. "If the only prayer you ever say in your entire life is thank you, it will be enough."

****

Psalm 118:15 - "Shouts of joy and victory resound in the tents of the righteous: "The LORD's right hand has done mighty things!" At times to be quite is a tactical maneuver. But a thankful heart that is saturated with gratitude is never silent. Thankfulness is expressed gratitude. The climax is giving praises to the Lord. Praising is bragging about the goodness of the name of God. Make a joyful noise for what He has done in the past and in the present. If there is nothing worthy to sing about today, borrow from the future, and praise Him in anticipation for what He will do tomorrow. Praising is a joyful experience in response to the goodness of God. He is good because He is God, and He is ever faithful to His promises.

****

Paul said that "Five times I received from the Jews the forty lashes minus one. Three times I was beaten with rods, once I was pelted with stones, three times I was shipwrecked, I spent a night and a day in the open sea, I have been constantly on the move. I have been in danger from rivers, in danger from bandits, in danger from my fellow Jews, in danger from Gentiles; in danger in the city, in danger in the country, in danger at sea; and in danger from false believers" (2 Corinthians 11:24-26). Paul gives an account of his labors and sufferings; not out of pride or vain-glory, but to the honor of God, who enabled him to do and suffer so much for the cause of Christ. Thankfulness to God is not circumstantial but it is perennial. The Bible says that "Give thanks in every circumstance, for this is God's will for you in Christ Jesus" (1 Thessalonians 5:18). Do not extinguish the Spirit…give thanks in all circumstances; for this is God's will for you in Christ Jesus. For every single thing you are wronged in the physical there are several rights in the spiritual realm to be thankful for.

****

December – Birth of Christ

Isaiah 9:6 – "For to us a child is born, to us a son is given, and the government will be on his shoulders. And he will be called Wonderful Counselor, Mighty God, Everlasting Father, Prince of Peace". The Lord is known by numerous names because of the multiple blessings He brings to this universe. Every name appeals to His glorious character to increase the revelation of the grace in every heart of the redeemed upon the earth. He is called Mighty God because grace and power are in His hands. He alone can overcome the mighty evil of the world. He is the light that comes in the glory of God to expel the darkness that engulfed the earth from the deep and eclipsed the hearts of all men. I mean the darkness of Adamic sin and hence our separation from God. Light has no shadow likewise in Him there is no darkness (sin). Because of God's love for us, His righteousness was imputed to us, and God's wrath against all of our unrighteousness was poured on Him. Finally, the hope which eluded people since the fall of man is here for the people to embrace.

****

His name is Emmanuel meaning God is with us (Isaiah 7:14; Matthew 1:23). The little baby in the manger is God wrapped in human skin. He came with a glorious purpose to make God known and to reconcile us to God. Without the birth of Jesus, we would have been deprived of the proper understanding of God. For example, God appeared to Moses in a burning bush as described in Exodus 3:2. It is a theophany, the appearance of God in a form that is visible to man. The bush itself was most likely some kind of bramble or thorn bush, and the fire burning the bush was the visible presence of God. Fire is used as a picture of the purifying and refining quality of God's holiness. God's holiness means that He is set apart from everything He has made. Holiness is not simply His righteousness (although that is part of it), but also His otherness. But the burning bush was not something to relate to because it was not God. The Bible says concerning Jesus that, "In the beginning was the Word, and the Word was with God, and the Word was God" (John 1:1). Jesus (the Word) was with God (the divine) and the Word was God (divine). The birth of Jesus is the foundation truth of our knowledge of God. Now we can relate to Jesus and for the first time call His Father our Father. Jesus came in human form to bring to us the consciousness of the spiritual dimension. The very reason for our existence in human form is to bring the consciousness of the spiritual dimension into this world. Jesus came to replenish the earth with the glory of God. We are the image bearers reflecting God's purpose on the earth.

****

Matthew 1:23 - "Behold, a virgin shall be with child, and shall bring forth a son, and they shall call his name Emmanuel, which being interpreted is, God with us." God took on a thin skin of man and came to us as a baby. If He didn't, He could have been God for us but not God with us. The only way He can be God with us is by becoming like one of us. He came to us to become like us, but unlike us, He was without sin. His sinless humanity made it possible for Him to be the perfect sacrifice acceptable to God to atone for our sins. In His body, He paid the penalties for our sins.

****

Isaiah 9:6 – "For to us a child is born, to us a son is given, and the government will be on his shoulders. And he will be called Wonderful Counselor, Mighty God, Everlasting Father, Prince of Peace." The child is born is in reference to His beginning as a human being. The Son is given is in reference to His eternal existence.

****

Luke 1:30-33 - "And the angel said unto her, Fear not, Mary: for thou hast found favor with God." The angels are messengers of God. They carried with them the timely message of the coming of the King who was prophesied by Isaiah some seven hundred years ago to come as the redeemer. They heralded the message to Mary and the shepherds beginning with these words: "Do not be afraid" (Luke 1:30; Luke 2:10). Fear and shame are the characteristics of sin. After Adam sinned, the first thing he did is to hide from God. It is within the fallen nature of man to be afraid of God. Whenever Jesus revealed His divinity by His marvelous works (miracles), his disciples asked Him to depart from them (Luke 5:8). The angels came down singing with joy to expel fear. To Mary, they specifically said that "You have found favor with God". The word 'favor' means grace. You see, Mary like any other person needed the grace of God in order to host our Lord in her womb. We are all sinners desperate for the Savior. Why fear not? Because heaven has reconciled with the earth. The mandate of fear and shame on the universe has expired because the Prince of peace has come to usher in the eternal peace. "Glory to God in the highest heaven, and on earth peace to those on whom his favor rests" (Luke 2:14).

****

Luke 1:30-33 – "He shall be great, and shall be called the Son of the Highest: and the Lord God shall give unto him the throne of his father David: And he shall reign over the house of Jacob forever; and of his kingdom there shall be no end." In reality, there have been many great kings and kingdoms throughout history. History was shaped because of these kings, these rulers. Every one of these kings had their kingdom come to an end, if not for some political or military reason, at the least because for every one of them, their life has come to an end. A king cannot lead a kingdom when that king is no more. Nothing in this world lasts forever. Everything in this world is shakable (Hebrews 12:28). But the Lord God established Jesus to assume the throne of His father David, to rule over the house of Jacob, and of Jesus' kingdom, there will be no end. The promise of God to Israel was fulfilled in Christ. The kingdom of God will not be ultimately established until Jesus the King returns to the earth in person. And that is where history is heading to. The kingdom of God is what history is all about. It's the goal toward which everything else is moving. It's the last chapter in a story that started in the Garden of Eden. The risen Jesus will return as the ultimate King and will judge the world and save God's people, as He exercises God's rule on the earth. The choice is yours: either to meet Him as your Savior or judge.

****

"Then said Mary unto the angel, How shall this be, seeing I know not a man? And the angel answered and said unto her, The Holy Ghost shall come upon thee, and the power of the Highest shall overshadow thee: therefore also that holy thing which shall be born of thee shall be called the Son of God."

****

It was a silent night. Nature was silenced as heaven opened up to kiss the earth with the good news of the divine love. The angels descended down to the earth breaking the orchestrated silence with catchy praises to the newly born King. Nature bowed down worshipping the baby laying in a trough, in the manger, inside the cave, wrapped in swaddling clothes. This was not an ordinary baby, He was the glory of God veiled by humanity; the same glory which man cannot look at and live (Exodus 33:20). He was conceived by the Holy Spirit and born of the Virgin Mary (Luke 1:35). He is not just a holy man but the Holy Spirit in man (very God, very man). The value of something is determined by its price. The magnitude of the menace of our depravity is patently measured by the price paid by Jesus to save us. It would be a tremendous gain for man to become God but a deviation beyond imagination for God to become man. Yet, humiliation was the only means for joy and peace to invade the earth, and death and hell to be swallowed up in victory.

****

Luke 2:8-14 - "Suddenly a great company of the heavenly host appeared with the angel, praising God and saying, "Glory to God in the highest heaven, and on earth peace to those on whom his favor rests." The angelic annunciation of the birth of the Savior of the world came not to important dignitaries or kings, but to the shepherds tending their flocks in the middle of the night. The shepherds worked there, most probably taking care of the temple-flocks, the sheep meant for sacrifice. The shepherds were illiterate, outcasts and the lowest class of people whose information could not be carried with weight. This is the proof that the story of the birth of Jesus was not made up. This is only the second time in the whole Bible that a group of angels rather than one angel had appeared to people, so this proved that they had a very important message to give to them. The angels gave the message to the shepherds so that the good news should be carried to the world. The shepherds were the right people to deliver the mails because they were nomads, who never settled in one place but moved constantly to distant and uncharted places in search of green pastures. They proclaimed the news as they moved from place to place. The expectation of Jesus is that people know what you know. Jesus spent His whole life engaging people; most of us have spent our whole lives trying to disengage them and avoiding strangers. Witnessing is the greatest manifestation of the true disciples, which is probably the reason why so few engage in it.

****

1 John 4:2-3 - "By this you will know the Spirit of God: Every spirit that confesses that Jesus Christ has come in the flesh is from God, and every spirit that does not confess Jesus is not from God. This is the spirit of the antichrist, which you have heard is coming, and is already in the world at this time." Jesus is the Hebrew word yeshua or yehoshua, meaning "Jehovah saves". The word 'flesh' means human form. Clearly, the phrase "is come in the flesh" indicates that Jesus Christ existed prior to His incarnation as a babe in Bethlehem. The scripture tips us how to discern the spirit of the antichrist. Any person that does not believe that Jesus is Jehovah manifested to us in human form is the spirit of the Antichrist. The word 'Antichrist' means against or in place of Christ. John clearly saw a final individual Antichrist whose spirit "is already in the world" (1 John 4:3). The spirit of the Antichrist prepares the way for the coming of Antichrist figure, who wishfully hope to put Satan on the throne instead of Christ.

****

Just about everyone knows that the year 2000 A.D. (Anno Domini) was supposed to indicate the number of years since the birth of Jesus Christ. Why should the birth of a baby that took place thousands of years ago is still remembered today? This baby was the long awaited strength and consolation of God to God's people. He is the joy of all longing hearts. He is the deliverer for the entire human race from the slavery of sins.

****

The best gifts for Christmas are found in the hearts and not in the shopping malls. If you can't find a gift in the heart, you won't get it under the tree!

****

Uncle Jonathan Zake's posting on 25th December: God's true people never waited for Jesus Christ to be born in Bethlehem to start rejoicing! Abraham just saw Jesus' time and began to rejoice (John 8:56). Even the in-utero (womb) John leaped with Joy, not because of Jesus' Birthday, but because the Savior had indeed come! Luke (1:41-45). Mary started magnifying the Lord even when the baby was in her womb! (Luke 1:46-55). Yes, to God's true people, every day, they rejoice because they have the Savior all the time. It is not just on one day (Christmas), that they rejoice! (Matthew 28:20; 9:14-15). The greatest joy comes not from recognizing the day Jesus Christ was born, but from having your eyes opened to see all the truth (John 8:31, 32). The Blind man rejoiced and said "Whereas I was blind, now I see (John 9:25).

****

The spirit of Christmas begun way back with the promise of God in Genesis: "He will crush your head, and you will strike his heel." (Genesis 3:15). Then the promise was confirmed through Abraham to Isaac: "God himself will provide the lamb for the burnt offering" (Genesis 22:8). Therefore the little baby, Jesus, is not in the manger coincidently. All of the sheep in the sheepfold waiting to be sacrificed and those which were sacrificed before represented this baby. He is the perfect sacrifice of God, by God and for God to atone for our sins. This is God offering Himself as a sacrifice to save mankind. Whenever you say "Merry Christmas" you are basically acknowledging the virgin birth of Jesus Christ. It is useless to celebrate Christmas if you don't believe that Jesus is the begotten Son of God who existed eternally before He put on the human flesh. It is like saying 'happy birthday' to someone without believing that he was born. There can be no a birthday without a physical birth! Likewise, there cannot be Christmas without the virgin birth.

****

End of December – Return of our Lord

The First Coming of Jesus was intended to confront the corrupt system that held people into captivity. Apart from God, the sin of man cannot be fathomed. In the old covenant, God gave His Word (Law) to interpret sin, and to stimulate man's desire for the Savior. Then in the new covenant, because man couldn't save himself, God's Son—became guilty of the most despicable wickedness to save mankind from sin. It is important to understand the character of sin. The essence of man's sin is not outward but inward, for sin is a matter of the heart and the mind, which polluted the reasoning and thinking of all humanity. That is why repentance is the change of minds. There are outward manifestations of the root of evil and these manifestations are sins, but it is in the mind and the intents of the heart that the germination takes place. The First Coming confronted the root of sin. The Second Coming of Jesus is intended to confront the people that rejected God's ultimate solution to get rid of sin. These are the people who tried to overthrow the kingdom of God on the earth, by resisting His Spirit and defying His commandments. They refused to bow down saying, "It is better to die on your feet than to live on your knees." Their defiance will be finally suppressed. God will prove to these self-righteous rebels, who chose to live independent of God, that nothing can exist in the universe without His permission (Revelation 20:11-15).

****

Revelation 1:9-11 – "On the Lord's Day I was in the Spirit, and I heard behind me a loud voice like a trumpet, which said: "Write on a scroll what you see and send it to the seven churches: to Ephesus, Smyrna, Pergamum, Thyatira, Sardis, Philadelphia, and Laodicea." Unfortunately, nothing remains today from these seven churches. Most were probably not similar to our churches today, for the small Christian communities in these cities likely met in private homes, caves, or out of doors. But the Seven Churches of the Revelation still form the basis of an increasingly popular tour route in Turkey. All are located on or near the Aegean coast in western Turkey. One hundred years ago, one-third of the population of Istanbul, formerly known as Constantinople, was non-Muslim. It was home to hundreds of thousands of Jews and Christians. Today, Istanbul, the largest city of the modern state of Turkey, is less than one percent non-Muslim.

****

2 Peter 2:4-9 - "----but protected Noah, a preacher of righteousness, and seven others; if he condemned the cities of Sodom and Gomorrah by burning them to ashes, and made them an example of what is going to happen to the ungodly; and if he rescued Lot, a righteous man, who was distressed by the depraved conduct of the lawless (for that righteous man, living among them day after day, was tormented in his righteous soul by the lawless deeds he saw and heard)— if this is so, then the Lord knows how to rescue the godly from trials and to hold the unrighteous for punishment on the day of judgment." This scripture indicates that the rapture of the saints who are on earth will take place before the great tribulation.

****

Revelation 19:13 - "He is dressed in a robe dipped in blood, and his name is the Word of God". Jesus is coming when clothed with a vesture dipped in His own blood. The Word of God - The name of Christ, often used by John in his gospel, epistles, and in this book, John 1: 1. This being a name Which Principally belongs to Jesus as the Creator of all things, and as previous to His incarnation. All promises of God in His word are fulfilled in Him. This name, the Word of God, is used appropriately when He is going to judge the world. The Bible states the ultimate blessings of the saints who pursue after God and desire to be in His presence in the following way: "They shall see His face, and His name shall be on their Foreheads" (Revelation 22: 4). The metaphor is in reference to the brain because it is the major organ in the forehead. The Word (the name of our Lord) will be the distinguishing mark in their forehead, meaning inside the brains of the saints. These are the ones that hear and know His voice. They are the hearers and doers of His commandments (statutes). They shall see and know Him with intuitive knowledge of Him, even as they are known by Him (1Cor. 13:9-12).

****

Somebody asked me to explain 2 Peter 3:8. Peter said that, "But, beloved, be not ignorant of this one thing, that one day is with the Lord a thousand years, and a thousand years as one day". Reading in the context, Peter was explaining the promise of the return of our Lord. Peter did not intend to spiritualize one thousand years to be equivalent to one day. He was quoting Psalms 90:4, to show God's unlimited and timeless attributes. God's existence is outside time limitation. He is not limited by time and space. God sees the future promise of the return of our Lord as if it has already happened.

****

1 John 3:2 - "Dear friends, now we are children of God, and what we will be has not yet been made known. But we know that when Christ appears, we shall be like him, for we shall see him as he is." The First Coming of Christ is intended to transform your spirit to be conformed to His glory. The Second Coming of Christ is to transform the body to be conformed to His glory. Those who missed of being impacted by the First Coming will certainly not be impacted by the Second Coming.

****

Revelation 19:16 – "And He has a name written on His robe and on His thigh: King of kings and Lord of lords."

****

The Bible prophesized the coming of Jesus in two phases: "To proclaim the year of the Lord's favor and the day of vengeance of our God" (Isaiah 61:2). The First Coming of Jesus was intended to save His enemies (us) by His blood: "He is dressed in a robe dipped in blood, and his name is the Word of God" (Revelation 19:13). Also, "And He has a name written on His robe and on His thigh: King of kings and Lord of lords." (Revelation 19:16). The Second Coming is for vengeance against His enemies that rejected His offer of salvation: "I have trodden the winepress alone; from the nations, no one was with me. I trampled them in my anger and trod them down in my wrath; their blood spattered my garments, and I stained all my clothing (Isaiah 63:3).

****

"Joy to the world, the Lord is come! Let earth receive her King; Let every heart prepare him room, And heaven and nature sing." The hymn was composed by Isaac Watts for the Second Coming of Jesus Christ. However, it has turned out to be the most popular song for the First Coming of Jesus Christ (Christmas).

****

Somebody asked that, "Doesn't the book of Revelation say that God will judge us by His commandments?" True. God does not change and His Word does not change. The Ten Commandments is the standard revealing His holiness and the yardstick to measure our holiness. Unfortunately, none of us has kept all of them without a possibility of breaking one. That is why all of us need the Savior who was judged in our place. He saves us from judgment and teaches us to obey His commandments. Our judgment will be in form of rewarding (2 Corinthians 5:10).

****

The scariest words in all existence are, "Then I will tell them plainly, 'I never knew you; depart from Me, you workers of lawlessness" (Matthew 7:23).

****

Matthew 25:23 - "His master replied, 'Well done, good and faithful servant! You have been faithful with a few things; I will put you in charge of many things. Come and share your master's happiness!'" God will reward the faithful, "And I saw thrones, and they sat on them, and judgment was committed to them. Then I saw the souls of those who had been beheaded for their witness to Jesus and for the word of God, who had not worshiped the beast or his image, and had not received his mark on their foreheads or on their hands. And they lived and reigned with Christ for a thousand years."

****

Isaiah 11:6. – "The wolf will live with the lamb, the leopard will lie down with the goat, the calf and the lion and the yearling together; and a little child will lead them." The prophecy is speaking of a literal utopia on earth to come - a Golden Age - referred to as 'The Millennium'. Jesus will establish the theocracy (God's rule) on earth. In this fallen age, every living thing lives by eating another living thing, whether it be plants or animals. During the coming age of the Millennium, no living thing will live by taking another life.

****

Somebody asked that "According to science the dead body decays and it is reduced to a nonexistence status, how will we get our bodies back at the resurrection?" True, upon death our bodies are dismantled and cannot be replaced by any natural means. However, God who created all things out of nothing can bring back our bodies out of nothing. But these will not be our natural corruptible bodies but spiritual bodies.

****

Wisdom

Knowledge is knowing what to do. Wisdom is putting what you know in practice. Knowledge is knowing what to say. Wisdom is knowing whether or not to say it.

****

Knowing God begins by our relationship with Jesus Christ. The misconception is trying to study God. God is beyond our comprehension. The more we know Him the more we discover that we don't know Him, the more we seek to know Him.

****

"Let your faith roar so loud that you can't hear what doubt is saying".

****

Ignorance looks for excuses not to change. A stiff-necked person looks for mistakes in the scriptures instead of embracing the truth. Poignantly, the inerrancy of the scriptures projects that whenever you find a mistake in the Bible, it is because there is a mistake in your life.

****

Nothing in all the world is more dangerous than sincere ignorance and conscientious stupidity ~ Martin Luther King, Jr.

****

"A king without knowledge is no better than a slave" ~ Marylios Yvette Evans

****

Life has no remote, get up and change it yourself.

****

When you are confused and troubled, you can access the peace that surpasses natural understanding by sincerely confessing to the Lord that "Not my will but your will be done".

****

"Great dream or idea comes up when you are thinking of something other than yourself" ~ Ifeanyi Enoch Onuoha

****

"Some people will tell you lies to make you feel better about yourself. I will tell you the truth so that you can better yourself."

****

Truth demands scrutiny, and then tolerance without compromising.

****

"Common sense is a flower that doesn't grow in all gardens".

****

"Measure your mind's height by the shade it casts" ~ Robert Browning

****

You will lose a lot more trying to hold on a wrong person than you would just let them go!

****

Honesty is a very expensive gift. Don't expect it from cheap people!

****

Today's kids are so spoilt that they don't know that in our days you could be beaten for any of the following reasons: Crying after being beaten. Not crying after being beaten. Crying without being beaten.

****

"An idiot will never learn from his mistakes, a smart person will learn from his mistake, but a genius will learn from other people's mistakes".

****

"The truth is a snare: you cannot have it, without being caught. You cannot have the truth in such a way that you catch it, but only in such a way that it catches you" ~ Soren Kierkegaard

****

"No one is rich enough to buy yesterday but if you hustle hard tomorrow could be yours" ~ Prof. Wole Sonyinka

****

You are not a real survivor until you lose it all and get it back!

****

Don't trouble trouble before trouble troubles you!

****

You can never run away from yourself; the only choice you have is to accept who you are or to take on a new version of you by being born again.

****

Words spoken can be forgotten but history can never be erased!

****

If you love life, don't waste time, for time is what life is made of.

****

"Destiny is not written for us but by us" ~ Annet Nanteza

****

Life is like a mountain, hard to climb but when you get on the top, the view is beautiful!

****

There is nothing wrong with objective desires but there is everything wrong when you let such desires to control you.

****

"I am not secretive I am just selective".

****

"Hypocrites people cannot be trusted because they're the real parasites that can destroy your life in silent" ~ Angelina Justine

****

Every opportunity that presents itself to you is an ultimate choice for you to make. Every choice you make has some consequences whether it be suddenly or later on.

****

What we value, we honor. What we shun we lose. Honor what you value.

****

Some people are ignorantly arrogant!

****

I don't care about likes, I just want you to think! "A mind is a terrible thing to waste." Yet this fact has not settled into the minds of the young ones. "Emotions always follow decisions - Think."

****

"We are all failures- at least the best of us are."

****

Life is full of up's and down; when you don't know which way to go - Go up to God... The Bible says that "He cuts out rivers among rocks; and his eye sees every precious thing" (Job 28:10).

****

Happiness consists in activity. It is running steam, not a stagnant pool - John Mason Good

****

Sometimes God will put a Goliath in your life, for you to find the David within you!

****

"There's no better way in the world to aggravate somebody who's trying to make it hard for you than by acting like you're not bothered."

****

One who conquers others is strong but one who conquers himself is mighty.

****

Your world is determined by the limits of your minds.

****

People lie to make themselves look better, steal the credit, cover up poor performance, conceal mistakes, deflect the blame, protect their reputations, and deceive and manipulate people. Regardless of the motive, the ultimate results are the same. As someone once said, "The worst thing about being lied to is knowing you're not worth the truth."

****

"Great lives are not curved out of the comfort brought about by the multitude of friends and possessions at hand. Contrary, they are molded out of discomfort that compels them to spend nights on edges of stiff rocks bordering fierce waters" ~ Godfrey E N Nsubuga

****

I'm a good enough person to forgive, but I am not stupid enough to trust you again.

****

"No horse gets anywhere until he is harnessed. No steam or gas drives anything until it is confined. No Niagara is ever turned into light and power until it is tunneled. No life ever grows great until it is focused, dedicated, disciplined." ~ Harry Emerson Fosdick

****

"It's probably my job to tell you life isn't fair, but I figure you already know that. So instead, I'll tell you that hope is precious, and you're right not to give up" ~ C.J. Redwine, Defiance

****

At times the long arm of the law is slow & clumsy but it never fails.

****

When people spread rumors or tell lies about you, and you find out, just take it as a compliment. It means your light is shining bright enough to talk about. And God will reverse the cloud of darkness into light to repel the falsehood.

****

Strength is when you have so much to cry for but you smile instead!

****

"A friend who understands your tears is much more valuable than a lot of friends who only know your smile" ~ Sam Kyeyune

****

"Sometimes we move miles to look for love yet the ones who love us are next door" ~ Marthur Oma

****

Courage is being yourself every day in the world that expects you to be someone else.

****

"No problem can be solved from the same level of consciousness that created it" ~ Albert Einstein

****

"Skeptical scrutiny is the means, in both science and religion, by which deep insights can be winnowed from deep nonsense" ~ Dr. Carl Sagan

****

"A cynic is a man who knows the price of everything, and the value of nothing." ~ Oscar Wilde

****

"The oldest and strongest emotion of mankind is fear, and the oldest and strongest kind of fear is fear of the unknown" ~ H. P. Lovecraft

****

"Close scrutiny will show that most "crisis situations" are opportunities to either advance, or stay where you are." ~ Maxwell Maltz quotes

****

"When you're up in life, your friends get to know who you are. When you're down in life, you get to know who your friends are."

****

False humility will not take you to your destiny but true humility will.

****

"Respect fools to avoid noise." ~ Hussein Lumumba Amin

****

It is the idle mind that wanders into other people's businesses. Tending to your own soul is enough to keep you busy.

****

"Do not think that love, in order to be genuine, has to be extraordinary. What we need is to love without getting tired" ~ Mother Teresa

****

"We are not called by God to do extraordinary things, but to do ordinary things with extraordinary love" ~ Jean Vanier

****

To err is human to blame someone else is politics!

****

By others faults, the wise correct their own.

****

If a flower doesn't bloom, you fix the environment in which it grows, not the flower.

****

A man who does not think for himself does not think at all!

****

A willing helper does not wait to be called.

****

What you say tells other people what you are.

****

To know when you have enough is to be rich!

****

"You only live once ... work it right and once is enough" ~ Kareena Maria Cox

****

Be loyal but don't let your loyalty become slavery.

****

Light comes but not without shadows. Of course, the greatest shadow is your own shadow. Your greatest troubles are the troubles of you own making. The best way to stay out of trouble is for you to deal with the trouble in you.

****

You can either trust people until they fail you, or distrust people until they're proven trustworthy.

****

There is no cosmetic for beauty like happiness

****

"Laughter is the shortest distance between two people" ~Vicor Borge

****

"If you want to make life easy, make it hard." Johann Wolfgang

****

A mistake repeated is a deliberate decision.

****

"The only thing that stands between a man and what he wants from life is often merely the will to try and the faith to believe that it is possible." ~Richard M. DeVos

****

"Real knowledge is to know the extent of one's ignorance." Confucius.

****

"You pile up enough tomorrows, and you'll find you've collected a lot of empty yesterdays ~ "Harold Hill

****

"He, who fears he will suffer, already suffers from his fears." Michel Eyquen.

****

"The bad news is time flies. The good news is you're the pilot" ~ Michael Althsuler.

****

They say that black hairs work for gray hairs – Young folks work for the aged.

****

Strangers are just friends waiting to happen ~ Menton Kronno

****

"Never try to make a mountain out of a molehill."

****

The only way of getting to the top is by getting to it from the bottom.

****

"It's better to climb out of your pit than to fall down from the sky. Keep your feet on the ground".

****

You will never understand the value of a moment until it becomes a memory.

****

Everyone thinks of changing the world but no one thinks of changing himself.

****

No more retrogression, slow motion, delay and backwardness in Jesus' name.

****

"Words fitly spoken are like apples of gold in silver pitchers"

****

Anger is like acid. It damages the container and the surrounding as well!

****

"Forgetting is something time alone takes care of, but forgiveness is an act of volition, and only the sufferer is qualified to make the decision" ~ Simon Wiesenthal

****

When someone doesn't like you, they will work hard to make sure others don't like you as well, even if it means making up lies. That's why you need to judge people for yourself and not listen to what others say about them.

****

"If sin becomes an abomination to you, you will have a hundred percent victory over it" ~ Sunday Adelaja

****

Complaining about a silent God while your Bible is closed, is like complaining about not getting texts when your phone is turned off.

****

Don't tell people more than what they need to know but just enough for them to know.

****

"A promise made is a debt unpaid."

****

An open world begins with an open mind. You can learn what you don't know, and you can unlearn what you learned.

****

Most times in mathematics the answer is in the question. So, when a problem is given, also the answer is presented to you ~ Bishop Tudar Bismark

****

Take a flower out of dirt and it will die. Take a fish out of the water and it will die. Take God out of the Church and it will die. Take God out of man and he will die, for without God there is no life ~ Paul Gaultiny

****

"Times of suffering do reveal our level of dependence on and trust in God (Job 1:21-22, 2:9-10). But the journey through deep waters also becomes an opportunity for the revelation and growth for ourselves and for others."
~ Sheila Sunny Smith-Lowery

****

Normally, the very people that deserve help are the least likely to give it. Decide to be the love you received!

****

"A person can be educated and still be stupid, and a wise man can have no education at all." ~ Jennifer A. Nielsen

****

There comes a time when you have to stop crossing oceans for people who wouldn't even jump puddles for you.

****

I have changed because I have realized that I'm only the person I can depend on.

****

People will notice the change in your attitude towards them, but won't notice their behavior that made you change.

****

Warning: Looking directly toward the Son may reverse blindness.

****

Grass is always greener on the other side, until you reach there.

****

10 Beautiful life tips:

1. Everyone have two Eyes ... But no one has the same View...
2. The most important quality of successful people is their willingness to change.
3. Human beings are very strange. They have the ego of their knowledge but, they don't have knowledge of their ego.
4. People who judge do not matter. People who matter do not judge.
5. Alphabet "O" stands for Opportunity which is absent in Yesterday" Available only once in "Today", and thrice in "Tomorrow".
6. "Pain is unavoidable but, suffering is optional"
7. Never ignore a person who loves and cares for you, because one day you may realize that you've lost the moon while counting the stars.
8. Sometimes life doesn't give you something you want, not because you don't deserve it, but because you deserve more.
9. If the road is beautiful then, worry about the destination, but if the destination is beautiful, then don't worry about the road!
10. Only messages are not life, but.... our life should be a message to others. (Kasoma J)

The Proverbs

A "proverb" is a wise saying. It is similar to a parable, in fact, it bears a hidden message. Most of the writings of Proverbs have been credited to the pen of Solomon. The purpose of the book is for moral instructions on everyday living. The main topic is the fear of the Lord. In fact, the "Fear of the Lord" is mentioned fourteen times. Solomon's instructions were very good. He would have been better off if he had heeded his own instructions. Solomon, in his later life, strayed from his own teaching.

****

Proverbs 16:31 – "The Grey hair (hoary head) is a crown of glory, if it be found in the way of righteousness."

Old age is wisdom in a righteous person but a disgrace in the unrighteous person. There is nothing as ugly as meeting an old creepy godless person.

****

Proverbs 25:28 - "He that hath no rule over his own spirit is like a city that is broken down, and without walls".

It is easier to conquer a city than to conquer your spirit. It is not easy to tame and control your inner self. Better to be patient than powerful; better to have self-control than to conquer a city. "Two things define you: The patience when you have nothing and the attitude when you have everything"

****

Proverbs 10:3 - "The LORD will not suffer the soul of the righteous to famish: but he casteth away the substance of the wicked."

God takes care of His own. You may have a few problems but they are intended to strengthen you, you will not go hungry, and you will inherit eternal life. The wicked may seem to prosper temporarily, but in the end, they will lose their souls.

****

Proverbs 11:27 – "Whoever seeks good finds favor, but evil comes to one who searches for it."

Seek peace and it will follow you!

****

Proverbs 3:25-26 – "Have no fear of sudden disaster or of the ruin that overtakes the wicked, for the Lord will be at your side and will keep your foot from being snared."

\# Without the guidance of the Holy Spirit, the human heart is wicked and inclines towards evil.

****

Proverbs 22:1 – "A good name is more desirable than great riches; to be esteemed is better than silver or gold".

\# I might lose everything including my fortune but my name is not for sale.

****

Proverbs 22:10 - "Throw out the mocker (baiter, harasser, heckler, tormentor, persecutor, quiz, quizzer, ridiculer, taunter, torturer, trouble-maker, attacker) and fighting goes, too. Quarrels and insults will disappear."

\# "When you are full of pride on the inside, it makes you stiff, stubborn, and it creates strife with others".

****

Proverbs 16:27- "Idle hands are the devil's workshop".

\# Lazy people sleep soundly and exercise less. They find themselves in the wrong place doing what they are not supposed to do.

****

Proverbs 12:18 –"There is that speaketh like the piercings of a sword: but the tongue of the wise is health."

"Kind words can be short and easy to speak, but their echoes are truly endless".

****

Proverbs 28:2 - "A rebellious nation is thrown into chaos, but leaders anointed with wisdom will restore law and order."

The fish rots from the head. When leaders are corrupt, the people they lead will be corrupted.

****

Proverbs 13:3 –"He that keepeth his mouth keepeth his life: but he that openeth wide his lips shall have destruction."

God has given us two ears, but one tongue, to show that we should be swift to hear, but slow to speak. God has set a double fence before the tongue, the teeth and the lips, to teach us to be wary that we offend not with our tongue.

****

Proverbs 16:3 – "Commit to the Lord whatever you do, and he will establish your plans."

A building's strength depends on its foundation. Allow God to be the solid rock on which you stand.

****

Proverbs 13:10 – "Where there is strife, there is pride, but wisdom is found in those who take advice. Hunger affects the peasant, noble and the king indiscriminately"

Pride is the spark that sets on fire the hearts of all men. "It was pride that changed angels into devils; it is humility that makes men as angels." A pride person decides to die of hunger instead of asking for help!

****

Proverbs 18:10 – "The name of the Lord is a strong tower; the righteous run to it and are safe."

God protects those who fear Him. He is your secret place and shelter.

****

Proverbs 27:9 – "Oil and perfume make the heart glad, So a man's counsel is sweet to his friend".

It is good to take counsel but choose wisely whom you lend your ear to. Better to be alone standing on the truth than to be in the company of people who are in error!

****

Proverbs 27:5-6 – "Better is open rebuke than love that is concealed. Faithful are the wounds of a friend, but deceitful are the kisses of an enemy."

I've come to realize that most people don't want the truth, most prefer telling them lies that go along with their feelings to make them momentarily happy, rather than being told the truth... since the truth offends them.

****

Proverbs 24:25 - "But to those who rebuke the wicked will be delight, And a good blessing will come upon them".

"The people who would like to manipulate and use you won't tell you your blind spots. They may plan to continue using them to their advantage." Comfort evil and repulse it. Being honest may not get you many friends but, but it will always get you the right ones

****

Proverbs 18:24 – "One who has unreliable friends soon comes to ruin, but there is a friend who sticks closer than a brother."

Love many but trust a few. Look for quality in the quantity.

****

Proverbs 6:34 - "For jealousy makes a man furious, and he will not spare when he takes revenge".

A jealous person overreacts because he is suspicious of everything and everybody whom you interact with.

* *
***** ***

Proverbs 14:27 - "The fear of the Lord is a fountain of Life, to turn one away from the snares of death."

We respect God when we obey God. Showing respect for God means learning what He wants us to do and then obeying Him completely. To please the Lord we must do His work His way. Receiving Jesus Christ is eternal life; rejecting Jesus is eternal condemnation.

****

Proverbs 1:5 –"A wise [man] will hear, and will increase learning; and a man of understanding shall attain unto wise counsel".

The Bible is the whole counsel of God where we go for wisdom.

****

Proverbs 18:15 –"The heart of the prudent gets knowledge; and the ear of the wise seeks knowledge."

Finding knowledge from the right source and place makes a difference.

****

Proverbs 27:2 – "Let someone else praise you, and not your own mouth; an outsider, and not your own lips---"

"Don't highlight and brag on self" ~ Joy Marie

****

Proverbs 11:22 - "Beauty in a woman without good judgment is like a gold ring in a pig's snout"

Your beauty will attract many men to you but be discerning. Everyone likes to pick a good fruit but not for the sake of the fruit but for the sake of their stomach! Men will keep coming to you regardless, be discerning because they do it at your expense.

****

Proverbs 10:17 –"He [is in] the way of life that keepeth instruction: but he that refuseth reproof erreth."

Righteousness is the path to life.

****

Proverbs 1:7 –"The fear of the LORD [is] the beginning of knowledge: [but] fools despise wisdom and instruction."

Wisdom begins with God. He must be the foundation of every structure built on earth.

****

Proverbs 9:9 –"Give [instruction] to a wise [man], and he will be yet wiser: teach a just [man], and he will increase in learning."

Learning is a process that continues as long as you are breathing.

****

Proverbs 4:5-6 - "Get wisdom, get understanding: forget [it] not; neither decline from the words of my mouth."

David instructed Solomon never to depart from the instructions handed to him because they are from God.

****

Proverbs 12:13-14 - "Evildoers are trapped by their sinful talk, and so the innocent escape trouble. From the fruit of their lips, people are filled with good things, and the work of their hands brings them the reward."

Those who engage in slander and gossip attempt to set traps for others to bring them down will eventually be trapped in their utterances. Edify others by your words of encouragement instead of cutting them down by your words. Whoever seeks good finds favor, but evil comes to one who searches for it.

****

Proverbs 10:19 – "When words are many, transgression is not lacking, but whoever restrains his lips is prudent."

Stop verbal diarrhea. Know all you tell…. Don't tell all you know.

****

Proverbs 24:16 - "For though the righteous fall seven times, they rise again…"

The grace of God is greater than our sins. In case of sin, we should repent and run to the throne of grace to be restored.

****

Proverbs 14:9 – "Fools make a mock at sin but among the righteous there is favor."

Sin is the root cause of all the problems we have. People who underestimate the power of sin are mocked by sin. For example, a drunkard who brags about his drinking capability when his health is badly deteriorating due to the toxin of alcohol.

****

Proverbs 12:22 – "Lying lips are abomination to the Lord: but they that deal truly are his delight."

Lying is not just a bad habit, it is a sin. You do to yourself a greater injury by lying than you do to him of whom you tell a lie.

****

Proverbs 13:20 - "Whoever walks with the wise becomes wise, but the companion of fools will suffer harm."

Misery seeks associates. Take a look at your friends, that's what you're going to be like in a few years. Hang around people who influence you to do better than them. Success depends on being picky in particular when choosing your close companions. Like dieting, you win when you lose, in this case, it is losing bad friends and gaining impetus.

****

Proverbs 8:32-35 – "Blessed is the man that heareth me, watching daily at my gates, waiting at the posts of my doors. For whoso findeth me findeth life, and shall obtain favor of the Lord."

When you embrace the full counsel of God, you discover your manhood!

****

Proverbs 6:23 – "For the commandment is a lamp; and the law is light; and reproofs of instruction are the way of life".

Jesus is the light. He is the Word (Torah or Law) that became flesh for demonstration purpose. When we are led by the Holy Spirit, we allow Jesus Christ to manifest His life in and through us.

****

Proverbs 3:3 - "Let not mercy and truth forsake thee: bind them about thy neck; write them upon the table of thine heart"

Meditate on the Word of God all of the times.

****

Proverbs 22:7 – "The rich rule over the poor, and the borrower is a slave to the lender."

Cut your coat by your own piece of cloth. If necessary, avoid borrowing.

****

Proverbs 12:11 - "A hard worker has plenty of food, but a person who chases fantasies has no sense."

Common sense says that "No pain, no gain." Yet common sense is not cheap!

****

Proverbs 31:30 – "Charm is deceptive and beauty is fleeting; but a woman who fears the Lord is to be praised."

External looks are deceptive. Don't let the beauty of the wrapper of something take all your attention and forget what's inside. Remember the wrapping is usually thrown out. Never brag about your beauty because that treasure you are flaunting is just nothing on the scale of others!

****

Proverbs 27:19 – "As water reflects the face, so one's life reflects the heart."

the kingdom of God is like a glass; everything is transparent, and there is no place to hide a dark heart.

****

Proverbs 26:4 - "Do not answer a fool according to his folly, or you will be like him yourself."

Never argue with a fool, people may not tell the difference.

****

Proverbs 20:14 - "The buyer haggles over the price, saying, "It's worthless," then brags about getting a bargain!"

Anyone can find the dirty in someone. Be the one that finds gold. "If you live by people's praise you will die by their criticism".

****

Proverbs 21:2 – "A person may think their own ways are right, but the LORD weighs the heart."

The heart of the problem is the problem of the heart. "Truth never damages a cause that is just."

****

"For the Lord detests the perverse, but takes the upright into His confidence." – Proverbs 3:32

All human beings without Christ are immoral by virtue of their conscience and intents.. Our confidence is in Christ alone. "Some people are exposed by pride, running around spiritually naked. Let us pick up humility and wear it as clothing. Let it be as close as the skin upon our bones."

****

Proverbs 13:7 – "There is that maketh himself rich, yet hath nothing: there is that maketh himself poor, yet hath great riches."

Lay for yourself treasures in heaven. All of the riches of the earth are vanity. When a man dies the earthly glory dies with him.

****

Proverbs 29:2 – "When the righteous are in authority, the people rejoice: but when the wicked beareth rule, the people mourn."

A fish rots from its head!

****

Proverbs 21:16 – "The man that wandereth out of the way of understanding shall remain in the congregation of the dead.

Dead people are the living people who are without Jesus Christ. The departed ones who died in Christ are living.

****

Proverbs 27:1 - "Do not boast about tomorrow, For you do not know what a day may bring forth.

In order to brag about tomorrow, trust in the God of tomorrow.

****

Proverbs 27:20 – "Hell and destruction are never full; So the eyes of man are never satisfied."

Keeping on making a mockery of God is not a smart move. There's room at the cross now for you and room in hell which are never full. Choose wisely.

African **Proverbs**

"A roaring lion kills no game." ~ African proverb

You won't achieve anything by just sitting around and talking about it.

****

"Never call a forest that shelters you a jungle." ~ African proverb

Never insult somebody that takes on the responsibility of taking care of you.

****

"Stormy rain never stop early, and never spares the wobbly roof" ~ Baganda's proverb

Trouble comes in a bundle, one after another, and will not spare your house just because you just come out of it.

****

The Baganda proverb goes "If you squeeze your nose so hard, never be surprised at what comes out of the nose".

Constant oppression may cause unrepressed response from the oppressed.

362

****

The Baganda proverb in Luganda says that: *"Agamyuka akasolo gegamyuka n'omutezi"*. The meaning is that the hunter suffers the same way as the prey.

Nothing is achieved on a silver plate without pain.

****

It is an insult to flinch your fingers before a fingerless leper. He might mistake your act as mimicking him. - Baganda's proverb

Jokes and humor can at times be interpreted as teasing and can be offensive.

****

"Be careful when a naked person offers you a shirt."

Can't give what you don't have. I don't trust people who don't love themselves and tell me, 'I love you.'

****

"What we know of houses are only roofs. Only those who live in them know the dust and smoke-soot underneath...."

Prejudgment is inappropriate. Never judge somebody without having all of the details at your fingertips. Even beauty cannot be judged by mere external appearances.

****

Marriage is like a groundnut; you have to crack it to see what is inside - Ghanaian proverb

There is more to know about marriage than what you were told. Much of it cannot be explained but it can only be experienced practically. No wonder while many people are seeking to get married, many married people are looking for an exit to get out of it.

****

A carpenter opts to build his workshop on the highway primarily to seek advice as opposed to selling his furniture. (Proverb of Baganda).

Seek advice whenever it is necessary; it is better to look a fool once than to be a fool all times!

****

The axe cannot trim the nails. *"Amaanyi tegalya..... kubanga embazzi tesala njala"* ~ (Baganda proverb).

At times, good performance does not depend on strength.

****

The gourd that is regularly used for brewing is most likely to develop wrinkles and cracks

A leader that does not want to live power faults his characters and eventually destroys himself.

****

Until the lions learns how to write. Every story will glorify the hunter ~ African proverb

Be the first to tell your side of the story because when you let others tell it they will distort from it.

****

Keep your meals far from poison in order to avoid fatality.

Keep the evil people far away from your company.

****

Burying the dead bodies in shallow graves brings the stench to the surface. (Baganda's proverb).

Keep evil far from you in order to avoid being vulnerable.

****

"The beautiful ones are not yet born".

It means that even though we have the beautiful people around us, we are yet to see budding ones and the unborn.... hence the beautiful ones are not yet born. Never be swayed by the beauty of the person because many more beautiful people are still coming.

****

Beautiful ladies are compared to fresh banana leaves, whenever you need a fresh one, you are likely to get it. Because whenever a tree loses a leaf, another one grows in its place

Never be desperate when a woman you love does not love you; there is always someone out there that will value your value.

****

Where you find a lion, there is most likely to be a hyena.

A hyena is a skillful hunter that follows a lion in case of the leftovers. When you are rich, many people will volunteer to be your close companion.

****

The tighter the string is drawn (stretched) on the bow the more powerful the arrow.

We are the shaft being rubbed with Holy Spirit oil causing us to be straight and to hit the mark.

****

"An elephant which kills a rat is not a hero" (African proverb).

Greatness is not merely measured by the size of your challenges you overcome. Greatness is a ratio of our accomplishments to our abilities.

****

A group of bees is called a 'swarm of bees'

A group of cattle is called a 'herd of cattle'

A group of sheep is called a 'flock of sheep'

A group of gorillas is called a 'band of gorillas'

****

Humor

Everybody loves to be liked but I think it is fine when the devil doesn't like you!

****

"...but the Lord laughs at the wicked" (Psalm 37:13).

****

He says that, "Satan deceived me!" But you know that he is Satan and he is a lair. Why did you let him do that to you? Never let Satan gamble on your conscience.

****

According to the national survey, the majority of the people who have never heard the gospel are the ones who attend churches regularly.

****

Don't worry if people don't like you. Most people are struggling to like themselves.

****

I downsized the circle of trusted friends. My circle is so small, I started talking to myself because it is better than talking to somebody.

****

Don't fight with the pig. Both of you will get dirty and muddy but the pig will enjoy it!

****

My mother told me that when I eat fish, I will be very smart. Then I asked her how many presidents were fishermen? ~ Lester Sumrall

****

A man told a woman whom he wanted to marry that his dog is his best friend but he wants two friends. The woman replied that "Then go buy for yourself a second dog".

****

Some girls are like computer viruses, they enter your life, scan your pockets, transfer your money, download problems and later delete your happiness.

****

If you want to change the world, do it when you are still single. Once you get married you can't even change a T.V channel.

****

Girls that bleach, if on the Judgment Day, your face does not match the one on Angel Gabriel's laptop; don't argue. Just go to hell.

****

Love is when your husband catches you naked with another man and still says *baibe* dress up let us go home... Death is when you follow him...

****

If your Birthday is in September-we all know what your parents did during Christmas - Ssonyonjo Enock

****

When nails grow long, we cut nails, not fingers. Similarly, when misunderstandings grow up, cut your ego, not the relationship!

****

Women are like iPhones; you have to touch them all over before they respond.

****

A woman said that all men are goats. I asked her "Have you fed your dad with grass?"

****

Respect that woman who values your attention more than your money.

****

Some girls have seen more boxers than Muhammad Ali ~ June Kezia

****

The popular slang for women is that "Little things matter". But it is not so when it comes to bedroom affairs!

****

"Silence may be golden, but can you think of a better way to entertain someone than to listen to him?"

****

I guess even farting around creepy guys isn't enough to get them to leave you alone!

****

When a woman is crazy about you, pray she doesn't get well because getting well means another man other than you is giving her medication.

****

Ladies, if your primary objective is to be sexy. Then you will attract men whose primary objective is to have sex!

****

"When I die, I want a man who would kill himself to make sure I am not talking to other men in heaven" ~ Ethel Nabulime

****

Respect pregnant women because it's not easy walking around with evidence that you've had sex ~ June Kezia

****

It's hard to bewitch African girls these days. Every time You take a piece of her hair to the witch Doctor, either a Brazilian innocent woman gets mad or a factory in China catches fire ~ Robert Mugabe

****

"People assume that because I'm peaceful, I must also be a pushover. I'm not. People assume that because I'm new to Facebook, that I'm new to the internet. I'm not. Please don't make assumptions or demands of me" ~ Charlotte Black

****

Marriage is just a fancy word for adopting an overgrown male child who cannot be handled by his parents anymore.

****

Ironically, the wedding day is basically a funeral day whereby each of the two people involved in the marriage agrees to die to 'self' so that they might live for the other.

****

"Women are Angels. When someone breaks our wings we simply continue to fly on a broomstick. We are flexible like that!"

****

The most dangerous animal in the world is a silent and smiling woman.

****

God made a woman out of a man. My wife is my rib. But why is it that my wife is more beautiful than the man she came from?

****

Being rude to a man will only earn you more days in your father's place.

****

"Silence is ever speaking; it is the perennial flow of language" ~ Ramana Maharshi

****

Everyone else can cook…. I'm a beast with the microwave!

****

Recently, I discovered that the monster wasn't under the bed------The monster was sleeping next to me!

****

Men blame menopause for women's attitude about things. What is the cause when men have some issues?

****

"The worst words to express what a lot of people feel about Love relationships: Lost, broken, empty, alone, heavy… it's not Love!"

****

I don't know if I'm a hermit or I'm hiding from the world. I feel like a misfit.

****

"I'm told I'm very charming when people do what I want" ~ Steven Brust,

****

I don't care what people think of me. At least mosquitoes find me attractive.

****

I never feel alone because loneliness is always with me.

****

Don't trouble trouble before trouble troubles you!

****

Sometimes you have to play the role of a fool to fool the fool who thinks they are fooling you.

****

If you don't find the way to make money while asleep, you will die while working.

****

It is called 'breakthrough' because something must break so that you can go through ~ Sam Kyeyune

****

There are too many people and too few humans!

****

"Trust but with caution because sometimes even your own teeth bite your tongue!"

****

Accountability is created, and it comes from character.

****

"Now please pull out a sheet of white paper and put it next to your skin... Are you both the same color? The paper is white and your skin is not white. The so-called black is not black but a chocolate dark brown".

****

The mirror is my best friend because when I cry it doesn't laugh! ~ Alex Niwagaba

****

Loyalty is more than words it is packaged with actions. If not then it is empty.

****

Love is not sex. Sex is not love. Love is love!

****

"Sex is not love... it is only the sealant, the bonus to love because being in love is to be with that one person who makes you happy and comfortably content in a way no other can" ~ Kereena Miria Cox

****

To all men. "When you build a house let your wife decorate the ceiling, she has seen more ceiling designs than you" ~ June Keziah

****

The best way for a wife to be romantic in the house is to show up from the bedroom naked!

****

Guys mistaken every girl's dream to be to get a good guy. My dream is to eat all I can without getting fat!

****

It's a man responsibility to feed the wife coz the last time a woman fed the man they were all chased out of the Garden of Eden ~ June Kezia

****

When you are dead, you won't even know that you are dead. It is a pain only felt by others. Same thing when you are stupid.

****

When I was young, I used to eat all kinds of junk food but at my age, now, I eat to live as opposed live to eat!

****

Most of our goals in life are like a needle in haystack, you shall search all day and when you find it, you realize they're not worth it ~ William Shakespeare.

****

People say nothing is impossible, but I do nothing every day".

****

Going back to your ex-lover it's like watching the Titanic Movie the second time and expect the ship won't sink.

****

It is only when a mosquito lands on your testicles that you realize there is always a way to solve problems without using violence.

****

Why can't the morning news ever say: "Today has been canceled.... go back to sleep."

****

Sleeping is good for the resting of the body but it does not help when it's your soul that is tired.

****

"Chasing the dollar trenches wherever Dollar can." ~ Tim Key

****

Dating a broke guy will only revive a more broken heart.

****

Now I know from experience that men are the problem I hate solving.

****

When I was foolish, I detested sagacity. I ate the fruits of my foolishness and ignorance.

****

The difference between a dead person and a person who is alive but who is not born again is a coffin!

****

When you are dead, you don't know that you are dead. It is difficult and a problem for others. It is the same when you are stupid.

****

"Laugh not at the dead, for the corpse at your feet is prophetic of your own destiny."

****

Everybody wants to go to heaven but nobody wants to die. "Even those who want to go to heaven would rather kill than be killed"

****

"Some people dream of success while others wake up and work for it."

****

They are called cell phones because people are prisoners to their phones.

****

A cell phone has replaced your house phone, computer, and camera. Don't let it replace your family.

****

Cell phones bring you closer to a person far from you. But it takes away from you the ones sitting next to you.

****

The best way to avoid disappointment is not to expect anything from anyone.

****

Sometimes I feel like throwing in a towel but they would only make more laundry for me!

****

I can live without you because you are not my phone charger.

****

"The only reason why some guys bath with their women is to prevent them from going through their phones. But those women think it's romantic!"
~ June Keziah

****

If they act like they 'can' live without you. Help them do it.

****

Never confuse people who are always around you with people who are always there for you.

****

Don't get mad when you hear that people are talking about you. It's your fan's job to keep you relevant.

****

If you decide to go, just don't stand in the way to block the traffic.

****

One good thing about music is that when it hits you, you feel no pain - Kaitesh Presh

****

We do ridiculous things like praying to God to bless the meals we are about to eat, to nurture our bodies, even when the food on the plate is junk food.

****

"I am not interested in listening to what God told you because I have already read everything He told you in the Bible".

****

Don't confuse my personality with my attitude, my personality is who I am, my attitude depends on who you are.

****

That knife you stuck in my back became useful to me when it came time for me to cut my ties with you.

****

I speak my mind because it hurts to bite my tongue.

****

The hardest thing is for people to reveal their real nature. When people show you who they are, thank them and thank God.

****

"Man is the only animal, "that laughs and weeps; for he is the only animal that is struck with the difference between what things are, and what they ought to be" - William Hazlitt

****

The pastor said: "Raise a holy hand to Heaven". So I placed my hand on my chest because there's no location of heaven better than inside of us.

****

Because Facebook does not require a minimal I. Q. score before a person can post something, you can post anything.

****

If loving Jesus is a mistake I have committed then I am sorry, I am going to continue committing this crime, I am afraid.

****

The reason the marriage ring is placed on the fourth finger from the thumb of your left hand is because it is the only finger that has a vein which is directly connected to the heart.

****

"Wearing a turtleneck feels like being strangled by a really weak man all day long" ~ Mitch Hedberg

****

When it comes to love, age is just a number!

****

"There is no half loving when it comes to the way God loves you. So why do you expect it from others?" ~ Amber Ashley

****

Whenever you are tempted to question how God could bless or use another just remind yourself that someone just may be wondering the same thing about you ~ David Hyles

****

The greatest distance between two people is a misunderstanding.

****

According to scientific studies, unfaithful people have lower IQs.

****

Do not be fooled by the three thousand friends you have on Facebook, Jesus had only twelve and was still betrayed!

****

"How many women have a Saul before they see a Paul? Two men, one of you has to go..... I pick Paul! Grace is always the best choice" ~ Sharn Grace Ceasor

****

President Mugabe orders the release of the gay couple languishing in jail when one gets pregnant.

****

He said it: Robert Mugabe

Robert Mugabe is one of Africa's longest-serving presidents. At ninety two, Uncle Bob still has the energy of a teenager. He has made us cry and laugh at the same time. Here are some of the funniest quotes from President Robert Mugabe:

1. Virginity is the best wedding gift any man would receive from his newlywed wife but lately, there's nothing as such any longer because it'll have already been given out as a Birthday gift, token of Appreciation, Job assurance, Church collection, Examination marking schemes & for Lorry fares!"

2. Treat every part of your towel nicely because the part that wipes your buttocks today will wipe your face tomorrow.

3. We are living in a generation where people "in love" are free to touch each other's private parts but cannot touch each other's phones because they're private"

4. Sometimes you look back at girls you spent money on rather than send it to your mum and you realize witchcraft is real.

5. If you are a married man, and you find yourself attracted to school girls, just buy your wife a school uniform.

6. If President Barack Obama wants me to allow marriage for same-sex couples in my country (Zimbabwe), he must come here so that I marry him first.

7. South Africans will kick down a statue of a dead white man but won't even attempt to slap a live one. Yet they can stone to death a black man simply because he's a foreigner.

8. What is the problem? We now have airplanes which can take them back quicker than the ships used by their ancestors.

9. Mr. Bush, Mr. Blair and now Mr. Brown's sense of human rights precludes our people's right to their God-given resources, which in their view must be controlled by their kith and kin. I am termed dictator because I have rejected this supremacist view and frustrated the neo-colonialists.

10. Cigarette is a pinch of tobacco rolled in a piece of paper with fire on one end and a fool on the other end.

11. Even Satan wasn't gay. He approached naked Eva instead of naked Adam.

12. Girls need to start looking for guys who have goals, ambition and education. Because ten years from now 'swag' isn't going to pay the bills.

Printed in the United States
By Bookmasters